THE GAZA C<

GILBERT ACHCAR is Emeritus Professor of Development Studies and International Relations at SOAS, University of London. His many books, published in more than twenty languages, include *The Clash of Barbarisms: The Making of the New World Disorder*; *Perilous Power: The Middle East and US Foreign Policy*, with Noam Chomsky; *The Arabs and the Holocaust: The Arab-Israeli War of Narratives*; *The People Want: A Radical Exploration of the Arab Uprising* and *The New Cold War: The United States, Russia and China, from Kosovo to Ukraine*.

GILBERT ACHCAR

THE GAZA CATASTROPHE

The Genocide in
World-Historical Perspective

SAQI

SAQI BOOKS
Gable House, 18–24 Turnham Green Terrace
London W4 1QP
www.saqibooks.com

First published in Great Britain 2025 by Saqi Books

ISBN 978-1-84925-091-7
eISBN 978-1-84925-092-4

A full CIP record for this book is available from the British Library.

The EU GPSR authorised representative is Logos Europe,
9 rue Nicolas Poussin, 17000 La Rochelle, France.
E-mail: contact@logoseurope.eu

Printed and bound in Great Britain by Clays Ltd, Elcograf S.p.A

FSC
www.fsc.org
MIX
Paper | Supporting
responsible forestry
FSC® C018072

Contents

Preface

ON 24 FEBRUARY 2025, the United States and Israel stunned the world by voting alongside Russia, North Korea, Belarus, Nicaragua, and twelve other states – mostly Russia-linked African states – against the United Nations General Assembly's Resolution ES-11/7, titled "Advancing a comprehensive, just and lasting peace in Ukraine". That resolution merely emphasized the relevance of basic principles of the UN Charter to "the full-scale invasion of Ukraine by the Russian Federation" and called for "a peaceful resolution of the war" in line with international law. It was supported by most countries that are traditionally part of the geopolitical West, or Western-friendly, while sixty-five countries of what may be described as the non-aligned bloc of the Global South, including China, India, Brazil and South Africa, abstained.

Four days later, the world was further shocked, and to a much greater degree, by the way in which Ukrainian president Volodymyr Zelensky was treated by US president Donald Trump and his very arrogant vice-president, JD Vance, at a media gathering in the Oval Office. These two events – along with a few others, such as Vance's outrageous performance at the Munich Security Conference in mid-February – unmistakably signaled the collapse of what I called in the summer of 2024, a few months before it became common wisdom, "the fall of Atlanticist liberalism" (a.k.a. "the liberal international order").[1] This observation was made at a time when it was not at all certain that Donald Trump would win a second presidential term, thus inaugurating what I have called "the age of neofascism", leading to a convergence between neofascists on the backs of oppressed peoples.[2]

It is since its inception at the end of World War II that Atlanticist liberalism has been gradually undermined by the countless inconsistencies manifested by its key upholders, chief among them being the United States. This historical process culminated with the administration of Joe Biden, due chiefly to its full complicity in the perpetration of the Gaza genocide. The way was thus paved for a further surge in neofascism – a surge that is the direct consequence of the abysmal wreckage of the traditional upholders of liberalism and their own relentless shift to the right ever since neoliberalism prevailed globally. Gaza was a key landmark in that regard.

The Gaza catastrophe that has unfolded since 7 October 2023 is indisputably the worst episode in the Palestinian people's long ordeal – worse even than the 1948 Nakba, an Arabic term that means "catastrophe". Whereas the key feature of the Nakba was what has come since then to be called "ethnic cleansing", "genocide" is the keyword of the present catastrophe, which deserves the stronger Arabic name for catastrophe: *Karitha*.

This book sets itself three objectives: a) a long-term analysis of the tragic history that predates the Gaza genocide, from Zionism's origins to Hamas's takeover of Gaza and the beginning of Israel's repeated onslaughts on the Strip; b) a close observation of the events that began on 7 October 2023, placing them in historical context and perspective; and c) a reflection, from a more detached and all-encompassing viewpoint, on various aspects of the tragedy, including a critique of Hamas and considerations on the far-right drift of Israel's society and polity, as well as on the global context of a surging far right and the decadence of Western liberalism, against which the Gaza genocide constitutes a watershed in world history.

The book has four components. Part I – "Reflections on the Gaza Genocide and Its World-Historical Significance" – was written as the introductory chapter to this book, and completed in December 2024. Part II – "Background to the Catastrophe" – is a selection of articles providing a contextualization that is necessary in order to understand the tragedy that has unfolded since 7 October 2023. It includes articles written over three decades, from 1994 to 2024. Part III – "Gaza, Nakba, Genocide" – gathers articles written since 7 October 2023, during the first year of the ensuing war. It starts with immediate reactions to the Hamas-led attack from Gaza and the beginning of the Israeli onslaught on the Strip, and continues with analyses of the 7 October operation, Israel's genocidal war, its aims, and its outcomes. The book's epilogue was completed in February 2025.

The events that have been unfolding since 7 October 2023 have understandably led to a plethora of books reflecting upon them. Many came out just as the first year of war was ending, some of them by authors who had never previously written on Palestine and Israel but felt prompted to comment on the immensity of the tragedy that unfolded before the world's eyes. I have deliberately not engaged with this prolific literature, although it includes some excellent contributions. The reason for this is that I did not want to engage in a metadiscourse – a discourse on other discourses – not only because this would have delayed the completion of this book, but also because I believed that readers would be primarily interested in my own first-hand analysis as an Arab internationalist writer with a long familiarity with the topic.

I very much hope that this book will be perceived as a useful contribution to the understanding of the Gaza genocide and the world-historical period into which it has emerged.

London, 1 March 2025

NOTES

1   Gilbert Achcar, "Anti-Fascism and the Fall of Atlanticist Liberalism", translated from my weekly column in Arabic in the London-based daily *Al-Quds al-Arabi*, 13 August 2024, on my blog at gilbert-achcar.net/anti-fascism-and-atlanticist-liberalism.

2   Likewise in my weekly Arabic column, translated on my blog: "The Age of Neofascism and Its Distinctive Features", 4 February 2025, at gilbert-achcar. net/age-of-neofascism, and "Peace Between Neofascists and War on Oppressed Peoples", 18 February 2025, at gilbert-achcar.net/peace-between-neofascists.

Part I

Reflections on the Gaza
Genocide and its World-Historical
Significance

TWO PRELIMINARY QUESTIONS

In what sense is Israel's genocidal onslaught on the Gaza Strip a consequence of the Hamas-led attack on 7 October 2023? The best way to answer this question is to resort to an allegory. Imagine a Native American who, having intended to set a few houses on fire in a nearby white settler colony, inadvertently sets off the gigantic blast of a huge buildup of explosive material, purposely amassed with the intention of inflicting death and mayhem on the native reservation to which the arsonist belongs. The same type of causality pertains in both the deadly attack of 7 October and the Gaza genocide.

How is the Hamas-led attack related to the antisemitic pogroms of the Pale of Settlement in the Russian Empire of the nineteenth and early twentieth centuries, and/or to the Nazi genocide of the Jews in 1941–45? The only indisputable relation between the 7 October attack and the dreadful history of European antisemitism lies in the fact that the atrocious fate of the European Jews was the main factor that led to the creation in Palestine, on the flank of the Arab Middle East, of the settler-colonial state of the Jews that Theodor Herzl, the founder of political Zionism, had called for.

That state has very sadly confirmed Herzl's cynical assertion-cum-prophecy that antisemitism is "a movement useful to the Jewish character. It represents the education of a group by the masses, and will perhaps lead to its being absorbed. Education is accomplished only through hard knocks. A Darwinian mimicry will set in. The Jews will adapt themselves."[1]

The Darwinian mimicry has indeed set in, to the point that Israel has become a state ruled by a coalition of neofascists (Benjamin Netanyahu's Likud) and neo-Nazis (the likes of ultraright ministers Itamar Ben-Gvir and Bezalel Smotrich) that has perpetrated *the first genocide – including the intentionality entailed in the concept – executed by a technologically advanced state since the final defeat in 1945 of the far-right Axis powers' coalition of World War II.* What is more, it is history's first genocide to be broadcast live on television.

GENOCIDE AND DENIAL

There is no need here to provide yet another account of the astounding extent of Israel's almost total physical destruction of the Gaza Strip, and its extermination of a huge number of Palestinians, a majority of whom have been children and women (who are certainly non-combatants). A few such provisional accounts can be found in Part III below; and, most importantly, three thorough examinations of the record were released in December 2024: Amnesty International's *"You Feel Like You Are Subhuman": Israel's Genocide Against Palestinians in Gaza*, Médecins Sans Frontières' *Gaza: Life in a Death Trap*, and Lee Mordechai's *Bearing Witness to the Israel–Gaza War* – this last one a database compiled by a former officer in the Israeli armed forces, presently teaching history at the Hebrew University of Jerusalem.[2] It is sufficient to recall here that the number of deaths identified by the Gazan health services well exceeds 45,000 at the time of writing. To these must be added the 10,000 unidentified dead believed to lie under the rubble – an estimate that is very probably conservative, if only because this figure has not been revised for several months.

Consider now the letter by three public health experts who, in July 2024, sounded the alarm in the venerable medical journal *The Lancet*, reminding the world that

> Armed conflicts have indirect health implications beyond the direct harm from violence. Even if the conflict ends immediately, there will continue to be many indirect deaths in the coming months and years from causes such as reproductive, communicable, and non-communicable diseases. The total

death toll is expected to be large given the intensity of this conflict; destroyed health-care infrastructure; severe shortages of food, water, and shelter; the population's inability to flee to safe places; and the loss of funding to UNRWA, one of the very few humanitarian organisations still active in the Gaza Strip. In recent conflicts, such indirect deaths range from three to 15 times the number of direct deaths.[3]

If we follow the three experts in applying to the war on Gaza a conservative estimate of four indirect deaths per one direct death, we could now say, after them, that it is not implausible to estimate that up to 220,000 or even more deaths have occurred or are about to occur as a consequence of the ongoing onslaught on the Strip. We are thus getting close to *one-tenth of the total population* of Gaza, which was estimated at close to 2.4 million before the war. This is regardless of the variety of neologisms made with the suffix "cide" (killing) that went along with the Gaza genocide: ecocide, domicide, culturicide, educide or scholasticide, etc.

Even if we set aside the undeniable intentionality of the destruction of 66 per cent of the total structures in the Gaza Strip until early September 2024, including an estimated total of 227,591 damaged housing units,[4] the intentionality of the human carnage that went along with this destruction can be denied only by those who wish to keep their eyes wide shut. For, if anything, the intentionality is made even more obvious by the multiplicity of means of mass murder, a combination of extremely intensive bombing and other uses of lethal firepower against densely populated urban zones, with the starvation of a whole population by deprivation of food and the finishing off of its sick and wounded by deprivation of healthcare necessities – all three means plainly documented by international organizations. The same combination of killing, starvation and deprivation of healthcare was at work in the Nazi extermination camps, albeit to an even more atrocious and murderous degree.

Let us now compare the foregoing with the well-known definition of genocide in Article II of the "Convention on the Prevention and Punishment of the Crime of Genocide", adopted by the United Nations General Assembly (UNGA) on 9 December 1948, which stipulates that genocide means any of the following acts committed with intent to destroy, in whole or in part, a national, ethnical, racial or religious group, as such:

a)   Killing members of the group;
a)   Causing serious bodily or mental harm to members of the group;
a)   Deliberately inflicting on the group conditions of life calculated to bring about its physical destruction in whole or in part ...[5]

No intellectually honest and righteous person can fail to see the reality of genocide in the case of Gaza. Omer Bartov is professor of holocaust and genocide studies at Brown University. Born Israeli, he served in Israel's armed forces, and was severely wounded in 1976. His testimony is important:

> On 10 November 2023, I wrote in the *New York Times*: "As a historian of genocide, I believe that there is no proof that genocide is now taking place in Gaza, although it is very likely that war crimes, and even crimes against humanity, are happening ... We know from history that it is crucial to warn of the potential for genocide before it occurs, rather than belatedly condemn it after it has taken place. I think we still have that time."
>
> I no longer believe that. By the time I travelled to Israel, I had become convinced that at least since the attack by the IDF on Rafah on 6 May 2024, it was no longer possible to deny that Israel was engaged in systematic war crimes, crimes against humanity and genocidal actions. It was not just that this attack against the last concentration of Gazans – most of them displaced already several times by the IDF, which now once again pushed them to a so-called safe zone – demonstrated a total disregard of any humanitarian standards. It also clearly indicated that the ultimate goal of this entire undertaking from the very beginning had been to make the entire Gaza Strip uninhabitable, and to debilitate its population to such a degree that it would either die out or seek all possible options to flee the territory.[6]

The recognition that Israel has perpetrated a genocide in Gaza is hence not a token of some "new antisemitism" – a phrase used by the neoconservative historian and Armenian genocide denier Bernard Lewis to designate anti-Israel stances among Arabs and Muslims.[7] Rather, it is the refusal to recognize this plain fact that constitutes a new variant of genocide denial. And like all genocide denial, this one is upheld by the perpetrators and their supporters, whose number in the West is all the more significant, since the perpetrators of the Gaza genocide have the particularity of claiming the moral inheritance of the main victims of the Nazi genocide, carried out in Europe with the active or passive complicity (the latter, that of bystanders) of all countries of the present geopolitical transatlantic West.

GAZA BEFORE 7 OCTOBER 2023

This tragedy did not begin on 7 October 2023 – far from it.[8] The Hamas-led attack crossed the Iron Wall, which is the name commonly given to the fence that Israel built around Gaza, turning the Strip into a huge open-air internment camp. That confinement was achieved with the complicity of Egypt's dictatorial government, which allowed only intermittent and restricted passage through the single crossing from the Strip into its territory. Israel started constructing the barrier around Gaza in 1971, completing it twenty-five years later. After Israel's unilateral withdrawal from the Strip in 2005, it was enhanced with a sophisticated surveillance and deterrence system, including remote-controlled machine guns.

The Gazan population has been suffering an unendurable ordeal at the hands of Israel ever since it occupied the Strip in 1967 – and more than ever after Hamas's takeover in 2007. Since 7 October, several authors have drawn attention to Benjamin Netanyahu's peculiar relationship with Hamas. Adam Raz, a historian working at the Akevot Institute for Israeli-Palestinian Conflict Research in Haifa and the author of *How Israel Stole Palestinian Property*,[9] wrote a long piece on this relationship for *Haaretz* two weeks into the conflagration.[10] Although he indulged in a lax use of concepts like "terrorism" and "pogrom", Raz convincingly explained:

For over a decade, Netanyahu has lent a hand, in various ways, to the growing military and political power of Hamas ... Releasing Palestinian prisoners, allowing cash transfers, as the Qatari envoy comes and goes to Gaza as he pleases, agreeing to the import of a broad array of goods, construction materials in particular, with the knowledge that much of the material will be designated for terrorism and not for building civilian infrastructure ...

Take note: It would be a mistake to assume that Netanyahu thought about the well-being of the poor and oppressed Gazans – who are also victims of Hamas – when allowing the transfer of funds ... His goal was to hurt Abbas and prevent division of the Land of Israel into two states ...

The prime minister himself spoke briefly at times about his position regarding Hamas. In March 2019, he said during a meeting of Likud MKs, at which the subject of transfer of funds to Hamas was under discussion, that, "Whoever opposes a Palestinian state must support delivery of funds to Gaza because maintaining separation between the PA [Palestinian Authority] in the West Bank and Hamas in Gaza will prevent the establishment of a Palestinian state."[11]

Netanyahu's cynical attitude was indeed not motivated by "the well-being of the poor and oppressed Gazans". In a 2019 report on socioeconomic conditions in the Strip, Ghazi Sourani, a Gaza-based intellectual well known in the Arab world and a founding member of the Popular Front for the Liberation of Palestine (PFLP), emphasized that half of the labor force in the Strip had become unemployed, while the poverty rate had increased to 53 per cent measured by consumption patterns, and 67.6 per cent by income, with close to 38 and 53.9 per cent of the Gazans, respectively, living in abject poverty.[12] Begging was on the rise among women and children. Electricity and drinking water were provided only a few hours per day, while pollution of both sea and aquifers was worsening due to the dumping of untreated waste.

This dire background sharply contrasted with "the ostentatious privileges of layers of the upper bourgeoisie (historically linked to the Muslim Brotherhood and presently Hamas) consisting of rich wholesale traders, real estate and money exchange speculators, and a few industrial and touristic businesses, whose commerce has increased since Hamas achieved a monopoly on the rule of Gaza".[13] It contrasted as well with the "millionaires" who took advantage of the tunnels into Egypt to organize large-scale smuggling with Hamas's complicity.[14] Sourani also denounced Hamas's "imposition of an occult fundamentalist logic on education curricula in the Gaza Strip",[15] its promulgation of "legislations limiting freedoms in general and freedom of opinion and belief in particular, its prohibition of all political or cultural meetings without prior authorization by the security services", and its "imposition of the hijab on female students in all universities and secondary schools" and "of the 'Islamic shorts' (covering the knees) on all males on the seaside".[16]

Hamas's increasingly repressive government of Gaza naturally led to anger and protests, culminating in a mass uprising against its rule of the Strip in the summer of 2023. Since this story is hardly known, it is useful to quote at length from a report published by *Al-Monitor* in early August:

> Thousands of Palestinians took to the streets last Sunday [30 July 2023] and again this Friday [5 August] in various areas of the Gaza Strip in rare public protests against Hamas, which has ruled the enclave since 2006. Masses gathered in Gaza City, Nuseirat, Khan Yunis, the Jabaliya refugee camp, Rafah, Bani Suheila and Shujaiya. The protesters chanted, "Hamas leave us be", "We want to live", and "The people want the end of the division [between Gaza and the West Bank]" ...
>
> The protests came in response to calls by activists on social media, which grew stronger as the electricity crisis worsened in the past month, with Gazans barely getting five hours of power daily amid a scorching heat wave. Hamas' security forces cracked down on the peaceful protesters and assaulted several people with batons. Dozens of protesters were injured and many had to be hospitalized ...
>
> Among the protesters' demands is also for Hamas to allow municipal elections in the Gaza Strip. Since Hamas' rise to power in 2007, the Islamist movement has banned all forms of elections, including general, municipal, chambers of commerce, and even university students' council elections. Hamas fills those positions from its own ranks and allies without any electoral process.

Hamas has launched an arrest campaign against citizens who took part in the protest. Last Sunday, Hamas' security forces stormed Abu Youssef Al-Najjar Hospital in Rafah governorate, and took three patients who were being treated for injuries sustained during the protests. They were eventually released ...

Although rare, these are not the first anti-Hamas protests in Gaza. In March of 2019, similar demonstrations under the same slogan, "We Want to Live", lasted for four days ... One of the groups advocating for the "We Want to Live" movement released a statement following the protests on Sunday, that read, "The time of silence over injustice and the exploitation of religion for oppression is over." Despite the crackdown, activists on social media continue to call for new protests.[17]

It was against this background of rising anger at Hamas's rule of Gaza that the 7 October attack took place. This is not to insinuate that it was launched in order to distract from the popular wrath and nip the uprising in the bud before it gathered further momentum. Indeed, it is clear that Hamas had been preparing its operation since much earlier than the summer of 2023. But what is equally obvious is that radicalism in the (very legitimate) detestation of Israeli oppression of the Palestinian people had all along been Hamas's official raison d'être, and was therefore a convenient cover for the socially, politically, and culturally reactionary character of its religious fundamentalist perspective. In that sense, there has been a functional complementarity between Hamas and the Israeli far right, which has translated into interplay between them.

Ariel Sharon – who, during his rule (2001–06) was then the most right-wing prime minister Israel had seen – mastered this game, every now and then assassinating a senior member of Hamas in order to provoke new indiscriminate suicide attacks by the movement in retaliation, and hence rekindle his own popularity. Benjamin Netanyahu sought instead a modus vivendi with the Islamic Resistance Movement (whose Arabic acronym is Hamas), taking advantage of it for the reasons explained above by Adam Raz. However, Netanyahu too surfed on Israeli society's animosity toward Hamas, exploiting in particular the episodic launching of rockets from Gaza into Israeli territory. He regained the prime ministership after winning the Israeli legislative election of 10 February 2009, in the wake of the first major Israeli onslaught on Hamas-ruled

Gaza, which had ended on 18 January of the same year. His Likud party increased its number of seats in the Knesset, the Israeli parliament, at the March 2015 election, after the second major Israeli onslaught on Gaza, led by Netanyahu himself in the summer of 2014.

ON HAMAS'S STRATEGY

This permanent tension with the Israeli warden of Gaza's open-air prison was used by Hamas to justify its repressive behavior inside the Strip. At the same time, it genuinely adhered to a messianic vision of its struggle against Israel – a vision shaped by Islamic fundamentalism, along with a mixture of European-imported antisemitism and anti-Jewish pronouncements found in Islamic scriptures.[18]

The secular Palestine Liberation Organization (PLO), which presided over the Palestinian struggle after Israel's defeat of Arab armies in the 1967 Six-Day War, soon reached the conclusion that it was vain to try to achieve the liberation of Palestine from the Jordan River to the Mediterranean Sea by violent means, which Israel possesses in much greater abundance. It thus pursued the more limited goal of a Palestinian state in the 1967-occupied Palestinian territories (OPT) of Gaza and the West Bank by means of diplomatic pressure, exerted by the rich Arab oil producers whose revenues had increased suddenly and sharply after the 1973 oil shock. These efforts, too, ultimately proved fruitless. But the PLO managed to ride the wave of the First Intifada (Arabic for "uprising") that started in December 1987 and peaked the following year, constituting the most important and impactful episode in the long history of the Palestinian struggle. The PLO leadership used the Intifada's impact to obtain recognition from the United States – though not without its chief, Yasser Arafat, publicly and shamefully declaring, "We totally and absolutely renounce all forms of terrorism" in order to meet Washington's condition for that purpose.[19]

Five years later, in September 1993, Arafat was on the White House lawn, signing the famous Oslo Accords between the PLO and the Israeli government of Yitzhak Rabin and Shimon Peres. Prompted by a flare-up in Hamas's activities to recognize the PLO in their turn, the Laborite Zionist pair concluded a deal with Arafat inspired by an updated version of the 1967 Allon Plan – a plan that sought to annex to Israel key strategic parts of the 1967-OPT, and hand direct control over their densely populated parts initially to the Jordanian monarchy.[20]

Hamas would thereafter expand in direct proportion to the increasing failure of this grand scheme, predicated on a fool's bargain that allowed Israel not only to pursue its colonization of the West Bank, but to accelerate it tremendously. The Islamic movement would resort extensively to suicide attacks during the initial post-Oslo years. The entire "peace process" irreversibly collapsed after, in September 2000 – seven years after the signing of the Oslo deal in Washington – Sharon deliberately provoked a second uprising, known as Second Intifada, or Al-Aqsa Intifada, in the 1967-OPT. Unfortunately, the Arafat leadership fell into the trap of using the light weapons that Israel had authorized the PA (set up under the Oslo Accords) to hold for the purpose of policing the enclaves that it was tasked to tame. Israel would seize the opportunity of what then took the shape of an armed confrontation in order to escalate its violence in the 1967-OPT to an unprecedented level, making use of the full spectrum of its military force.

Arafat's death in 2004, and his succession by Mahmoud Abbas, created the conditions for the 2006 electoral victory of Hamas. Sensing the opportunity, the Islamic movement had decided to suspend its commitment to armed struggle and enter the electoral arena.[21] This was nevertheless intolerable for Washington, though it had insistently demanded that these elections be held in the hope that they would bestow legitimacy on Abbas. The coup jointly orchestrated by Abbas's PA and Washington failed to subdue Hamas, but resulted in the political partition of the 1967-OPT into two rival "authorities" ruling Gaza and the West Bank, respectively.[22]

Although Hamas took charge of the government of the Gaza Strip from then on, it nevertheless continued to cultivate a mystical belief in the liberation of Palestine by armed means. This perspective had become its ideological trademark in the face of the approach of the West Bank's PA, which it denounced as a traitor to the Palestinian cause and a subcontractor of Israel's subjugation of the Palestinian people. One patently counterproductive manifestation of Hamas's "armed struggle" strategy is its intermittent resort to launching rockets across the fence surrounding the Strip, despite the obvious fact that Israel's retaliation would be incomparably more brutal and murderous on each occasion.

This strategy is irrational: it makes little sense to assault one's enemies on the very terrain upon which they hold insurmountable superiority. Zionist settler-colonial domination of historical Palestine is not comparable to the settler-colonial domination of Algeria and South Africa. In both these countries, the settler-colonial population was a minority exerting domination over the indigenous majority. In Palestine, as is well known, Zionist settler-colonialism uprooted the indigenous population, thus cancelling the natives' overwhelming majority. Even with the present demographic quasi-parity between Palestinians and Israeli Jews in the entire area between the river and the sea, the balance of armed forces is overwhelmingly to Israel's advantage, thus perpetuating the subjugation of one population by the other.

Under such circumstances, to take the initiative of violence in confronting the Israeli state (in contrast to the reasonable resort to armed defense in the face of attacks by Zionist settlers adopted in the West Bank) is plainly irrational. "Who really wants to confront a nuclear superpower with four slingshots?" Unless you already knew it, you would never guess who made that statement. It was Yahya Sinwar himself, Hamas's leader in Gaza, and the man who took the fateful decision to prepare and launch the 7 October attack. That was in a 2018 interview with an Italian journalist published in Israel's *Yedioth Ahronoth* and Italy's *La Repubblica*.[23] Indeed, against an enemy with such overwhelming military superiority, the only rational strategy is to wage the struggle on the terrain upon which it holds no superiority, but is rather in a position of moral inferiority. This is principally mass nonviolent struggle against the occupier, best epitomized by the First Intifada that peaked in 1988, provoking a deep ethical and political crisis among the Israeli population – including its armed forces, and up to the highest echelons.

Whatever cost such nonviolent struggle entails for the Palestinians (1,600 were killed by the Israelis during the First Intifada between the end of 1987 and 1993; and 223 Palestinians were later killed by Israel during the eighteen months of the 2018–19 Great March of Return in Gaza), it remains significantly less than that of armed engagements between Palestinians and Israelis (over 3,000 Palestinians were killed by Israeli forces during the Second Intifada, from September 2000 until the end of 2004; and over 2,300 were killed in Gaza in less than two months in July–August 2014). On the other hand, the political impact of nonviolent struggle by Palestinians is incomparably more positive for their cause.[24]

Only through this kind of struggle – along with its natural complement abroad, which is the solidarity movement spearheaded by the Boycott, Divestment, and Sanctions (BDS) campaign – can the Palestinian movement hope to achieve its goal of obtaining equal rights, self-determination on its historical land, and recognition of the right of Palestinian refugees to return to it. For only thus can it hope to achieve the indispensable condition for the attainment of this goal, which is to split Israeli Jewish society, thus offsetting its military superiority. Launching rockets instead – or, worse, irresponsibly launching such a dreadful attack as that of 7 October – will lead only to the further unification of Israeli society around hatred of the Palestinians, reinforcing its rightward drift and tolerance for killing sprees.

EXCURSUS I: FIFTEEN YEARS AGO

The above considerations have long been obvious. In the spring of 2009, Ghazi Sourani, quoted above, acting for the Central Cultural Department of the PFLP's Gaza branch,[25] invited me, along with a few other authors, to contribute to a special issue of their publication *Al-Hayat Al-Jadida* ("The New Life") commemorating the sixty-first anniversary of the 1948 Nakba. Below are excerpts from my contribution, entitled "The Imminent Nakba and How to Confront It":

> Just as the failure of Oslo led to the downfall of its Israeli protagonists, the leaders of the Zionist Labor Party, whom Sharon replaced in heading the government, the failure of his own project led to the downfall of the party that he founded, Kadima [Sharon split from Likud in 2005], which was replaced by the right-wing Likud in coalition with open advocates of ethnic cleansing. No doubt that their shared conviction is that coexistence is not possible with the Palestinians, and that Israel's security will not be established without "cleansing" most Palestinians of all areas close to where Israelis live, including Israeli settlers on the West Bank. This would be achieved by deporting the majority of Palestinians across the Jordan River and into the Sinai Desert after

exterminating part of them to terrorize the rest in order to achieve that purpose. In other words, what is looming on the horizon and threatening the Palestinians remaining on the land of Palestine is a new Nakba that, if it happens, will inevitably be much worse in terms of killing and destruction than the first, the 1948 Nakba.

In the face of this impending catastrophe, a radical review of the Palestinian liberation strategy is necessary by returning to the axioms that were self-evident in the past, in the era of political hegemony of the Arab nationalist movement in general and Nasserism in particular throughout the Arab nation. The self-evident truth forgotten since then is that the Palestinian struggle cannot achieve victory in isolation from the Arab hinterland and that it has no prospects unless it acts as the spearhead of the entire Arab liberation struggle ...

The most accurate expression of this awareness was perhaps the idea expressed by Dr George Habash during the struggle in Jordan, that the Palestinian revolution must have a Hanoi, like what was available to the Vietnamese revolution in its heroic struggle to liberate the occupied southern part of the Vietnamese homeland ... Dr Habash saw that it was necessary to start by transforming Amman into an Arab Hanoi so that the struggle to liberate western Palestine could find its necessary rear base ...

Of the Arab-Israeli pincer imposed on the Palestinian people, the Jordanian regime constitutes the weakest jaw due to the demographic composition of the Hashemite Kingdom, where there is a majority of Palestinians, not to mention that the majority of "East Jordanians" hold anti-Zionist and anti-imperialist nationalist sentiments that prevail over the narrow provincialist sentiments promoted by the monarchy. Transforming Amman into an Arab Hanoi is an indispensable condition for the effectiveness of the struggle to turn the largest possible part of the 1967-occupied Palestinian territories into liberated zones. For as long as those territories remain caught between the jaws of a pincer as they are now, any thought of turning them into liberated zones is nothing more than a naïve dream, as naïve as Arafat's dream.

The second long-term part of the liberation strategy, the part related to the first Nakba of 1948 and its dire consequences, is dependent on what Abdel Nasser himself realized after the June 1967 defeat, the last war before it was confirmed that the Zionist state had become a nuclear power. Betting on eliminating the Zionist state by military force applied from outside is a naïve dream too, or rather suicidal madness, as there is no doubt that it will not hesitate to resort to its nuclear weapons if it faces a threat of military defeat ...

This means that no rational strategy in confronting the Zionist state is possible without relying on the combination of the Palestinian and Arab struggle with the effort to split Israeli Jewish society from within. This last goal requires Palestinian and Arab liberation forces to be able to address the Israeli Jews and detach a significant portion of them from the Zionist mindset. Here the degree to which the very nature of the religious fundamentalist movement conflicts with the requirements of liberation becomes evident. The rise of that movement in the Palestinian and Arab spheres has led to the rallying of Israeli Jews behind their most reactionary leaders in a way that exceeded any previous stage in our region's history.[26]

7 OCTOBER 2023: A CATASTROPHIC MISCALCULATION

Before 7 October, the clearest illustration of the counterproductive character of Hamas's violent strategy is what happened in May 2021, when the movement's action aborted the Unity Intifada that had started in Jerusalem on the sixth day of that month, and over the following days rapidly spread to the West Bank, and even to Palestinian citizens of Israel. This was commonly perceived as the beginning of a new Intifada, reconnecting with the first, which peaked in 1988. On 10 May, Hamas jumped into the fray by delivering a swaggering "ultimatum" to Israel to withdraw, by early evening on the same day, all its security forces from the Temple Mount and Sheikh Jarrah in Jerusalem – the sites where the new uprising had been ignited – as if anyone could conceive in their wildest imagination that Israel would yield to such a threat. On that same evening, Hamas, along with Islamic Jihad, started launching rockets into Israeli territory, dubbing their bombing campaign the Sword of Jerusalem Battle. Israel's response was predictably swift and brutal, leading to the usual disproportionate number of Palestinian casualties (256 killed in Gaza alone over ten days). More pertinently, though, this action aborted the budding Intifada, demobilizing the Palestinian youngsters who had set it in motion.

How Sinwar, who had stated with much perspicacity in 2018 that it made no sense to "confront a nuclear superpower with four slingshots", could succumb to a state of such delusion as to believe, in 2021, that Hamas was able to intimidate the Israeli state into backtracking – or, later, that the attack his movement launched on 7 October 2023 would be the opening salvo in the liberation of Palestine – is unfathomable from the standpoint of practical rationality, or what Max Weber would call the "ethic of responsibility". It only makes sense from the standpoint of mystical belief – Weber's "ethic of conviction" in which practical rationality is usurped by faith. In the decision to launch the Al-Aqsa Flood operation on the morning of 7 October 2023, a religious mystical dimension was unmistakably involved. Any dismissal of this blatant reality against the evidence of Hamas's own pronouncements, under the pretext that it would constitute an Orientalist interpretation in the sense of the term popularized by Edward Said, is simply an instance of Orientalism in reverse: a view predicated on the belief that "Islamism" is merely a "language" of Muslims devoid of specific consequences.[27] Religious beliefs, however, are not just the specific form of expression of a rational-practical kernel – and this is no less true in the case of Hamas than that of any other Islamic fundamentalist organization, from the moderate Muslim Brotherhood to the extremist Islamic State, to consider Islam alone. They are sincere beliefs, and it is insulting and condescending to those who profess them to claim the contrary.

This fervent belief in a forthcoming liberation of Palestine thanks to divine intervention was most patently translated prior to the Al-Aqsa Flood in the convening in Gaza on 30 September 2021, under the auspices of Hamas, of a so-called Foresight Conference, entitled "Promise of the Hereafter – Palestine after Liberation", officially held "Under the Patronage of the Leader Yahya Sinwar, 'Abou Ibrahim'". The conference discussed and adopted a detailed blueprint for the administration of a hypothetically liberated Palestine, down to settling issues such as the future state's provisional legal system, its land and sea border arrangements with neighboring states, the issuing of a new

Palestinian currency, and the fate of the Israeli Jews. Among the last, those who surrendered would be allowed to remain or given time to leave, whereas the conference decided "to keep for a while the Jews that are scholars and experts in medicine, engineering, technology and both civil and military industry".[28] The conference's resolution concluded by stating that "we have a date with victory, which God promised to His worshipers". In his message to the conference, Sinwar assured the participants that the battle for liberation had become closer than ever, explaining that "the Sword of Jerusalem Battle was a model of preparation and development" for this goal. Thus, "liberation has become close in time and our patronage of this conference conforms to our vision of victory's imminence".[29]

This same mystical vision – which a rational mind can only perceive as a rather pitiful instance of taking one's dreams for realities – presided over Hamas's launch of the 7 October attack. As it started to unfold, the operation was announced by an audio message recorded by Muhammad al-Deif, the commander-in-chief of the Al-Qassam Brigades, Hamas's armed wing. Here are some excerpts of what he said, after summarizing the crimes committed by the Zionist oppressors:

> We decided to put an end to all of this, with God's help, so that the enemy understands that the time for them to revel without being held accountable has ended ... Our righteous Mujahideen, this is your day for you to let this criminal enemy understand that their time has ended ... Fight, and the angels will fight with you as your vanguard, God will reinforce you with the horse-riding angels and will fulfil His promise to you ... Our young people in the West Bank, all our people regardless of your organizations, today is your day to sweep this occupier and its settlements from all our land in the West Bank and to make them pay for the crimes they perpetrated throughout those long, difficult years ... Our people in Jerusalem, rise up to support your Al-Aqsa Mosque, expel the occupation forces and the settlers from your Jerusalem, and demolish the dividing walls. Our people in the occupied interior, in the Negev, Galilee, and the Triangle, in Jaffa, Haifa, Acre, Lydda, and Ramla, ignite the soil with fire under the feet of the usurping occupiers, by killing, burning, destroying, and closing roads ...

Our brothers in the Islamic resistance, in Lebanon, Iran, Yemen, Iraq, and Syria, this is the day on which your resistance merges with your people in Palestine so that this terrible occupier understands that the time of rampaging and assassinating religious scholars and leaders has ended, the time of plundering your wealth has ended, the almost daily bombing in Syria and Iraq has ended, the time of dividing the nation and scattering its forces in internal conflicts has ended. Now is the time for all Arab and Islamic forces to unite to sweep this occupation away from our sanctities and our land.

Today, today, everyone who has a gun should take it out, for the time has come, and whoever does not have a gun should use their knife, hatchet, axe, Molotov cocktail, truck, bulldozer, or car ... This is the day of the great revolt to end the last occupation and the last apartheid regime in the world. O righteous men and women, the finest memorizers of the Book of God, O worshipers who fast and stand, kneel and prostrate themselves – gather in your mosques and places of worship and return to God and urge Him to send down their death upon us, to provide us with His trusted angels, and to fulfil through us your hopes of praying at Al-Aqsa, liberated ...[30]

Countless attempts have been made to justify the 7 October operation and demonstrate its rationality. One argument was that it was judiciously launched at a time when Israeli society was deeply divided, with weekly demonstrations against Benjamin Netanyahu. The problem is that it only succeeded in superseding this division and unifying the Israelis behind full support for the genocidal war launched by their government – whatever resentment a portion of them would maintain toward Netanyahu. Another argument was that 7 October served to draw the world's attention back to the Palestinian cause at a time when it had been descending into oblivion. Since the price of temporarily drawing attention in this way was tens of thousands, if not hundreds of thousands, of people massacred, a whole territory erased, and Israel's permanent reoccupation of this territory, this would be the worst bargain ever made. Such a defense of the attack betrays a deplorable lack of human empathy with the terrible fate that befell the Gazan population, let alone what happened during the attack itself.

There is no possible vindication for what has been the most catastrophic miscalculation ever in the history of anticolonial struggle. To be sure, the resentment of the Gazans against Israel was fully understandable and legitimate. This is why I commented on 16 October 2023 that "The most crucial issue with Hamas's conception of the fight against Israeli occupation and oppression is not moral, but political and practical."[31] One of the worst flaws in Hamas's miscalculation is that it disregarded the fact that Israel was led by the most far-right government in its history, including people who openly advocate the expulsion of the Palestinians from their historical land – a gang of anti-Palestinian racists who would not hesitate to seize any suitable opportunity to launch a genocidal war on the Strip and reoccupy it permanently. All of them are known to have bitterly opposed the unilateral Israeli withdrawal from Gaza implemented by Ariel Sharon in 2005.

ISRAEL'S ROAD TO THE GAZA GENOCIDE: I. THE DRIFT TO THE FAR RIGHT

"The most right-wing government in Israel's history." This same appraisal of a newly formed Israeli government has been made countless times since 1977, the year when the Likud, that heir to Mussolini-admirer Ze'ev Jabotinsky's far-right Zionist Revisionism, won the legislative election for the first time. Ever since, the Israeli polity has been subject to a rightward trend, interrupted only by the divisive impact of Israel's invasion of Lebanon in 1982 – the Zionist state's first obvious "war of choice" – and later by that of the First Intifada at its peak in 1988, as well as by the widening opposition at the end of the last century to the continuation of Israel's costly occupation of South Lebanon. These events contributed to the restoration of the Laborite wing of Zionism into power, first in 1984–86, then in 1992–96 (leading to the Oslo Accords), and finally in 1999–2001 (the withdrawal from Lebanon in 2000).

Overall, however, of the forty-seven years from the moment Likud first came to power up to 2024, the party has governed Israel for thirty-four years, half of them under Netanyahu's leadership. The continuous drift of Israel's society and polity to the far right has culminated in the present cabinet, formed by Netanyahu at the very end of 2022 – a coalition of the neofascist Likud with a collection of far-right groups of such a nature that it led Holocaust historian Daniel Blatman, of the Hebrew University of Jerusalem, to make a very alarming statement to *Haaretz*, used as title of the interview that the newspaper published with him: "Israel's Government Has neo-Nazi Ministers. It Really Does Recall Germany in 1933."[32]

How to explain this drift, whose sinister character is significantly amplified by the fact that it has occurred in a state founded by people most of whom had escaped from Nazism or survived the genocide that it perpetrated, a state that justifies its existence by the need to anticipate the possible recurrence of something like Nazism? The truth is that the Darwinian mimicry evoked by Theodor Herzl cannot work as an explanatory factor in isolation from the context in which the founder of statist Zionism sought to insert his project – namely, the colonial undertaking and its inherently genocidal tendency – common to all colonial endeavors – to dehumanize the "barbarians" whose land it seizes.

The paradox, however, is that the colonial means by which Herzl dreamt of realizing his project came to fruition at the very onset of decolonization. In that sense, as Maxime Rodinson – a French Marxist scholar of the Middle East, of Jewish descent – put it in the aftermath of the 1967 Six-Day war, "the Zionists were unlucky":

> The conscience of the world had developed, and no longer accepted right of conquest, or accepted it more reluctantly ... Zionism began as a living force in the era of nationalism, of which it was itself a manifestation, and it pursued its career during the era of decolonization ...
>
> Arab opposition [to Jewish settlement] manifested itself the moment that the Zionist intention to establish a Jewish state by detaching Palestine's territory from the Arab world became clear. This opposition mounted as the true nature of the Zionist project became obvious, and grew more irreconcilable as the Zionists came nearer to success. Therefore the Arabs were not rejecting the foreigners as such; they were rejecting foreign occupation of their territory – whether we choose to classify this phenomenon as colonialism or not. The conflict therefore appears essentially as the struggle of an indigenous population against the occupation of part of its national territory by foreigners.[33]

By a historical paradox, this new settler-colonial state was created in the very same year that the largest of all colonial empires was losing its "jewel in the crown". It was in 1947, the year of India's independence, that the UNGA adopted the resolution providing for the establishment of a "Jewish State" in Palestine. In this antithetical symmetry, there was nonetheless a common element: that of partition – except that the partition of Palestine was a colonial decision, whereas that of India was a legacy of decolonization. The United Nations that voted for the partition of Palestine against the will of its native population was composed of only fifty-six states, dominated by the Global North, including the USSR, with a very preponderant role played by the United States at a time when most of the rest of the world needed its economic benevolence. Thirteen out of the thirty-three countries that voted in favor of partition were Latin American countries under Washington's spell, far away from the Middle East.

In flagrant violation of the "principle of equal rights and self-determination of peoples" enshrined in the UN Charter, then recently adopted, the thirty-three-state majority of the UNGA granted the "Jewish State" over 56 per cent of the territory of Palestine between the River Jordan and the Mediterranean Sea in full knowledge that the Jewish population constituted barely one-third of its total population – to say nothing of the fact that this population was overwhelmingly composed of migrants who had arrived during the previous fifteen years. Resolution 181, enacting this decision, was adopted on 29 November 1947, and is well known. Much less known, though just as strikingly skewed in Israel's favor, is UNGA Resolution 273, adopted on 11 May 1949. This admitted to UN membership the new state of Israel, within borders that it had vastly expanded (by 40 per cent – from 56 per cent to 78 per cent of Palestinian territory) through its 1948 war with its Arab neighbors and the Palestinians. This was again a flagrant violation of international law, of which the prohibition of the acquisition of territory by force is a cornerstone. The wording of the 1949 resolution is stunning. The UNGA majority decided that "Israel is a peace-loving State which accepts the obligations contained in the Charter and is able and willing to carry out those obligations." Rarely has a resolution adopted by the United Nations been so clearly shown, over time, to express the exact contrary of the truth.

Whereas Israel was backed during those initial years by both major victors of World War II, the United States and the USSR – in practical terms, even more by the latter than the former – it would soon join the Western camp in the Cold War. Along with its specific type of militarization, the new state could display the kind of liberal democracy (albeit based on a racial discrimination that was then a feature shared by some Western states, starting with the United States itself) by which the geopolitical West distinguished itself from "communist totalitarianism". As Rodinson has explained,

> Militarization did not exclude democracy, and in a sense was one aspect of it. Hence the contrast between Israel as seen by the Arabs and the vision of her cherished by Europeans. To the former, Israel was a colonial offshoot of the Western world, imposed on the Oriental world by force and therefore the very epitome of injustice and oppression. The word "Zionism" has acquired in Arabic a meaning sinister in itself, evocative of evil, like the words "imperialism", "colonialism" and, for many people nowadays, "capitalism". For them, seen on the world scale, Israel is an armed camp peopled by aggressive conquerors. Indeed, Israel is an armed camp set in the midst of hostile territory, like the makeshift forts surrounded by palisades which European pioneers erected feverishly, Western-style, in every alien territory into which they penetrated, posting lookouts to scan the prairie anxiously for the movements of unfriendly tribes. But the West had solemnly endorsed the legitimacy of this island transplanted from the Western world, and no longer questioned it; what interested Westerners was the internal structure of the state. To admit and even exalt its virtues helped to eradicate, retrospectively, all the wrongs which had been done to the European Jews.[34]

No state could take better advantage of this last way of claiming to be assuaging its guilt toward European Jews than West Germany – a state whose institutions were riddled with former Nazis, and whose crucial role in funding and arming Israel during the latter's years of consolidation served to whitewash its Nazi legacy and secure its official entrance ticket to the Western club.[35] This same combination of narcissistic identification with Israel as a Western state, on the one hand, with the guilt complex that most Western states are still grappling with because of their active or passive complicity in the Nazi genocide of

European Jews, on the other hand, has been at work continuously over the years, and has now reached a peak in the face of the Gazan genocide.

Israel's aggression against its Arab neighbors in 1967, and its seizure of the 22 per cent of Palestinian territory that it had been unable to conquer in 1948, along with vast swathes of territory taken from Egypt (the Sinai peninsula) and Syria (the Golan Heights), were hence framed as a victory of David against Goliath, despite the fact that, in 1967 as in 1948, Israel's military power was in fact superior to that of its Arab neighbors. What restrained Israel from annexing the remnant of British Mandate Palestine that it had then conquered (it formally annexed East Jerusalem alone) was not any fear of unlikely Western castigation, however, but merely the fact that the 1948 Nakba scenario was not repeated in 1967. Having witnessed the fate of the 80 per cent of Palestinians who had fled the territory seized by the Zionist state in 1948 and were never allowed to return – their dwellings, lands, and belongings were seized by the conquerors, and close to 400 of their towns and villages were erased, like the Gaza Strip has now been – most Palestinians of the West Bank and Gaza had learned the lesson, and clung accordingly to their towns and villages.

In December 2024, *Haaretz* published the explosive findings of an examination of the minutes of Israeli cabinet meetings in the aftermath of the 1967 Six-Day War and succeeding years. They focused on the deliberations over the future of the Palestinians in the Gaza Strip. Held in Israel State Archives, the minutes revealed, in the words of the article's author, Ofer Aderet, that

> the present aspiration of the far right to "encourage emigration" of Palestinians from the Gaza Strip only echoes ideas and proposals that came up for discussion in the past – by prime ministers, ministers and leaders in left-wing governments, who were among the country's founding fathers.
>
> The ministers had no shortage of ideas for solving the problem that was laid on their doorstep with the occupation of the Gaza Strip and the West Bank in the Six-Day War. At the time there were about one million Palestinians in the territories, about 400,000 of them in the Gaza Strip. There were proposals to send them out of the Gaza Strip to the West Bank, Jordan, Sinai, Arab countries or any other place in the world that could

receive them – by force, by consent, by subterfuge and with all kinds of incentives.[36]

But the crucial difference between then and now is twofold: Laborite Zionism was more sensitive to its "democratic" image abroad than is the far right that presently rules Israel, while other countries were certainly less supportive, even where they were tolerant, of potential Israeli far-right behavior than they are today. Thus, none of these plans could be implemented, and Israel therefore had to confront a dilemma: it could not forcefully expel the Palestinians without exhausting the limit of the West's benevolence, especially given that such an expulsion would have inflamed anti-Western sentiments in the Arab- and Muslim-majority worlds. By the same token, however, Israel could not annex these remaining parts of Palestinian land due to the size of the population that clung to them.

Annexing the 1967-OPT while refraining from granting citizenship to their Palestinian inhabitants would create a situation of official apartheid that would ruin the image of Israel as a beacon of Western democracy. Granting Israeli citizenship to the OPT's Palestinian inhabitants would potentially jeopardize the Zionist state's Jewish majority. Thus, either of these two moves would imperil one of the two terms of the contradictory equation with which Israel defined itself, encapsulated in the oxymoron of the "Jewish and democratic state".

The foremost critic of this oxymoron was none other than Meir Kahane, the neo-Nazi ultra-right Zionist, and the most extreme politician Israel had ever had. Kahane was a member of the Knesset from 1984 to 1988, and was thereafter barred from election for racism by Israel's Central Elections Committee – a decision approved by the country's Supreme Court on the basis of an amendment to the Basic Law of Israel barring political parties that openly incited racism, adopted by the Knesset in 1985 for the very purpose of barring the man and his group of followers. In that same year, during his stint at the Knesset, "Kahane maintained that there is a basic 'contradiction' between the State of Israel being both a democracy and a Jewish State":

Two years later, in 1987, Kahane became preoccupied with the "demographic threat" posed by the Arabs, which he called incredibly dangerous – while the solution "lies within us, in our souls, in our wish to admit to the truth". What is that truth? That there is an "insurmountable contradiction" between the concept of Zionism and a Jewish state, and the concept of western democracy. Anybody who doesn't grasp that is obtuse, he said.

According to Kahane, the Jewish state by definition cannot be democratic. In his vision, Israel should be a "state with Jewish sovereignty ... in which the Jew determines his own future and fate, and the Jew is the captain of the ship." Non-Jews have no say in national decisions that determine the fate of the state and the nation, Kahane averred.

Why couldn't Israel be Jewish and democratic? Because, Kahane said, "Western democracy rejects the concept of a Jewish state with disgust" because it requires a state ruled by the majority, whoever the majority might be. If the Arabs were the majority, Kahane said, then it would be their right to set up a state as they please, and they would eliminate the Jewish state.

His solution, presented to the Knesset, was to move them out of Israel, willing or not.[37]

To measure the extent of the far-right drift of Israel's polity, it is enough to note that Kahane's discourse was regarded as anathema by mainstream Zionism in his time, while his views are now openly upheld by his disciples – not only in the Knesset, but even in the Israeli cabinet. Needless to say, the ban on racist political parties has sunk into oblivion. But in 1967, what Kahane would vehemently denounce as a hypocritical oxymoron was very much the Zionist state's official language, in tune with the conditions of the international support that it enjoyed.

There was hence a need to resolve the open contradiction between Israel's wish to annex the newly occupied territories and its unwillingness to take on board their population and grant them citizenship, as it had done for the minority of Palestinians who remained on the territory conquered in 1948. A compromise solution was designed during the weeks that followed the 1967 war to circumvent the dilemma. Under the Allon Plan, Israel was to work toward turning over the densely populated Palestinian areas to Jordanian control while keeping the rest of the land – including all strategic locations, such as the Jordan Valley.[38]

This proved illusory, as the Jordanian monarchy could not possibly accept such a deal lest it appear to be in collusion with the Zionist state – even more blatantly than in 1948.[39] Thus, a situation developed over the years of protracted occupation of densely populated territories – combined with de facto apartheid toward Palestinian citizens of Israel within its pre-1967 borders, who are treated as second-class citizens. Quite naturally, this situation considerably exacerbated a trend that was intrinsic to the very constitution of the Zionist state, and built into its political DNA. This trend was emphasized by Rodinson in 1967 with reference to Israel's genesis:

> Wanting to create a purely Jewish, or predominantly Jewish, state in an Arab Palestine in the twentieth century could not help but lead to a colonial-type situation and to the development (completely normal sociologically speaking) of a racist state of mind, and in the final analysis to a military confrontation between the two ethnic groups.[40]

Quite a few liberal Zionists warned early on against the potential consequences for Israel's society and polity of the prolongation of Israel's occupation of the 1967 territories. One of them is Saul Friedländer, who wrote in 1969:

> Faced with the presence of a vast Arab population inside Israel, one can conceive the reinforcement of Jewish extremist tendencies inspired as much by economic as by religious or national motives, to demand the expulsion of all the Arabs or the application of an "apartheid" regime. If these elements succeeded in imposing themselves, the Jewish state would be cut off from the world and the Jews of the Diaspora themselves.[41]

Israel's congenital tendency to drift to the far right was indeed considerably boosted by the 1967 occupation. Ten years later, the Likud came to power, and has held it for most of the time since then. The drift continued after the Oslo parenthesis: it was even further boosted by the increasingly violent turn of Israel's occupation of the West Bank and Gaza, as well as by the resort of Palestinian factions to violence in facing it; the Second Intifada provoked what Dahlia Scheindlin called "seismic shifts" to the right in Israeli society.[42] However, as Tel Aviv University's Nir Evron emphasized in a remarkable article written before Netanyahu returned to the prime ministership in December 2022, when he took on board with him those furthest to Israel's right,

> A casual observer would be forgiven for thinking that Israel's Jewish majority is divided by profound ideological disagreements. In truth, when it comes to the issues that matter most for the country's future – the control of the West Bank, the blockade of Gaza, and the status of non-Jewish citizens – Israeli Jews have never been more united. Unfortunately, that consensus places Israel's Jewish majority far to the right of any recognizably liberal worldview ...
>
> Some would argue that it is misguided to ask why Israel is becoming increasingly illiberal. Israel, they would say, is not, never has been, and cannot by its very nature become a liberal democracy. True, Israel has never regarded the members of its Arab minority as equal citizens, let alone treated them as such. This is not a bug but a feature of Israel's self-definition as a Jewish state – a project devoted to the welfare and future of an ethnically defined majority ... Israel inside the Green Line [the pre-1967 border] is not merely a "flawed democracy", as its liberal-Zionist advocates like to put it. All democracies are flawed. Israel is a country whose operating system is fundamentally at odds with the values that define the Western democracies with which it so energetically affiliates itself.[43]

But Evron did not dispute the fact that "Israel's Jewish majority has, indeed, become more emphatically and unapologetically illiberal since 2000", and asserted that a major factor in this shift had been the "backlash against the increasingly vocal demands for recognition and equality on the part of Israel's Arab citizens".[44] Another major factor in Israel's rightward drift has been migration – both emigration and immigration, as more and more of Israel's left-wing and moderate citizens, as well as its Arab citizens, have been leaving the country, disgusted at its political drift, while ever more right-wing and religious Jews have been flocking in.[45]

Eventually, groups that belong to what used to be the extreme far-right fringe of Zionism, and were regarded as eccentric by Likud itself, would enter the mainstream and access government one after another – most prominently Rehavam Ze'evi's Moledet, Avigdor Lieberman's Yisrael Beiteinu, Bezalel Smotrich's Religious Zionist Party, and, last but not least, Itamar Ben-Gvir's Otzma Yehudit, which is heir to Meir Kahane's Kach party, a group that was designated as terrorist by several Western countries, including not only the United States, but Israel itself. Netanyahu played a key role in mainstreaming these parties: in 2019, he brokered a deal between three far-right groups – Smotrich's, Ben-Gvir's, and a group called Jewish Home – whose short-lived alliance managed to secure five Knesset seats in that year's election.[46]

However, as the Jewish commentator and Israel critic Peter Beinart rightly remarked, confirming Evron's above observation,

> Israel is not deeply ideologically polarized. It's already an ethnocracy and no major political party wants to change that. That's what sets Ben-Gvir apart from figures like Trump and Le Pen: His rivalry with his centrist foes may be politically fierce, but it's not a contest over the basic definition of the state. In the global struggle between group supremacy and equality under the law, Ben-Gvir and his centrist rivals are on the same side.[47]

ISRAEL'S ROAD TO THE GAZA GENOCIDE:
2. THE "MOST MORAL ARMY"

Israel's rightward drift went along very naturally with increasingly unrestrained violence in Israel's dealings with its enemies. The first to suffer the systematic deterioration in Israel's "rules of engagement" – hitherto supposed to enable it to claim the title of the world's "most moral army", a boast it continues to recycle – were the Lebanese. This was a result of Israel's huge frustration at having incurred what had been widely perceived as its first defeat: its forced decision to withdraw from Lebanon's south in 2000, to cut short its troops' harassment in guerrilla mode by the Lebanese resistance dominated by Hezbollah. It was in the aftermath of this resentful setback that the Israeli military conceived what would become known as the Dahiya doctrine – a reference to Beirut's southern suburb, a Hezbollah stronghold, which was largely destroyed during Israel's next onslaught on Lebanon, in 2006.

Starting from 1994, Israel's armed forces – misnamed the Israel Defense Forces (IDF, Hebrew acronym: Tsahal), although they have engaged in a long series of aggressions since their very foundation – elaborated a code of ethics, pompously titled "Spirit of the Israel Defense Forces", which was revised in 2000. A prominent feature at the heart of this code is the principle of "purity of arms", set out as follows: "An IDF soldier will ... maintain their humanity during combat and routine times. The soldier will not use their weapon or power to harm uninvolved civilians and prisoners and will do everything in their power to prevent harm to their lives, bodies, dignity and property."[48]

Israel's armed forces were thus keen to cultivate the reputation that they had forged since inception, as part of the Zionist state's ideological argument and its aspiration to be perceived as part of the Western world. To be sure, the pretense of purity was always factitious – ever since the countless so-called abuses committed by the troops of the newborn Israeli state in 1948.[49] At best, the Israeli armed forces would pretend to resent being compelled to commit crimes – a posture that is described by the expression "shooting and crying", well illustrated in Ari Folman's 2008 animated cartoon *Waltz with Bashir* on Israel's 1982 invasion of Lebanon. In other words, "I hate you for making me do this".

But the Dahiya doctrine no longer pretended to pull punches. Its shortest statement, under the more revealing title of Disproportionate Force, was penned in 2008 by reserve colonel Gabi Siboni, who led a division in the 2006 war on Lebanon and is director of the Military and Strategic Affairs Program at the Tel Aviv University's Institute for National Security Studies (INSS). His statement is edifying indeed:

The current predicament facing Israel involves two major challenges. The first is how to prevent being dragged into an ongoing dynamic of attrition on the northern border similar to what in recent years developed along the border with the Gaza Strip. The second is determining the IDF's response to a large-scale conflict both in the north and in the Gaza Strip. These two challenges can be overcome by adopting the principle of *a disproportionate strike against the enemy's weak points as a primary war effort*, and *operations to disable the enemy's missile launching capabilities as a secondary war effort.*

With an outbreak of hostilities, the IDF will need to act immediately, decisively, and with force that is disproportionate to the enemy's actions and the threat it poses. Such a response aims at *inflicting damage and meting out punishment to an extent that will demand long and expensive reconstruction processes.* The strike must be carried out as quickly as possible, and must *prioritize damaging assets over seeking out each and every launcher* ... In Lebanon, attacks should both aim at Hezbollah's military capabilities and should *target economic interests and the centers of civilian power that support the organization.* Moreover, the closer the relationship between Hezbollah and the Lebanese government, the more the elements of *the Lebanese state infrastructure should be targeted.* Such a response will create a lasting memory among Syrian and Lebanese decision makers, thereby increasing Israeli deterrence and reducing the likelihood of hostilities against Israel for an extended period. At the same time, it will force Syria, Hezbollah, and Lebanon to *commit to lengthy and resource-intensive reconstruction programs.*[50]

This doctrine is in blatant violation of basic war ethics and international humanitarian law (IHL), including the Geneva Conventions. Two essential principles of IHL are those of proportionality and prohibition of direct attacks against civilians. The Dahiya doctrine openly advocates the use of disproportionate force, and calls for it to be primarily applied to "economic interests and the centers of civilian power" that support the enemy, inflicting upon its civilian environment a level of damage "that will demand long and expensive reconstruction processes". After Lebanon 2006, the Dahiya doctrine was applied to Gaza in 2008–09 and 2014, and again to Lebanon during the Israeli onslaught on Hezbollah from 17 September to 27 November 2024.

The war on Gaza belonged, however, to a qualitatively different register, that of genocidal wars. There is hardly any article or principle of IHL that Israel's armed forces have not very deliberately violated since October 2023 – including attacks on hospitals, and depriving non-combatants of food, water, and basic life necessities. All this was done under the pretext of "eradicating Hamas", while accusing it of using civilians as "human shields" by hiding among them – an absurd accusation that implies that the Palestinian fighters should have gathered in open-air terrain, as used to occur in eighteenth-century wars.

Given the Gaza Strip's heavy urbanization and dense population, the goal of "eradicating Hamas" was in itself potentially genocidal. In the first place, it made no distinction between the political movement and its armed wing (the Al-Qassam Brigades), even though Hamas was a mass political organization in Gaza, with tens of thousands of members, perhaps over a hundred thousand if both wings are combined – that had developed a whole network of civil and social services during the sixteen years it had ruled the Strip. Hamas members were part of the staff of the various apparatuses and services of the statelet that the Islamic movement established in the Strip, and they were naturally inseparable from the rest of the population. Moreover, even if Israel had only targeted the Al-Qassam Brigades, the goal of eradicating them, as opposed to defeating them, would have required a large-scale massacre.

Aside from eradicating Hamas, the goal of reoccupying the entire Strip, which the Israeli government and armed forces clearly assigned to themselves in reaction to the 7 October attack, also entailed a genocidal logic. In that respect, it was the indirect consequence of the post-Lebanon shift of the Israeli military to those "'post-heroic' conditions, in which the invariable limiting factor [is] low tolerance of casualties", as Edward Luttwak remarked early in the post-Cold War era.[51] As I explained in an article published on 23 October 2023,

> the only way for Israel's army to invade any part of so dense and vast an urban landscape as the Gaza Strip with minimal Israeli losses is to flatten the areas that it strives to occupy by way of intensive bombing before launching the ground offensive. This is indeed what started in the immediate aftermath of 7 October, with a level of damage that, in both extent and intensity, goes way beyond prior Israeli bombing campaigns, from Lebanon in 2006 to the successive wars on Gaza. Flattening vast swaths of urban territory was not possible for the Israeli military in any of the previous wars – not for lack of destructive power, of course, but for the absence of the necessary political conditions.[52]

That is exactly what Yagil Levy, a professor at the Open University of Israel, summarized in *Haaretz*, on 12 December 2024, in one sentence:

"The approach that strives for 'zero risk' to our soldiers encourages unrestrained fire with no concern for civilians." Levy elaborated:

> Israel would have refrained, as in the past, from launching a ground operation in Gaza had it not secured international legitimacy for harming Gazan civilians, thereby reducing the risk to IDF soldiers ... "Transferring the risk" to Gazan civilians means that Israel broke the chains that once restrained it in the past. It allowed itself to execute massive bombings of residential buildings to kill Hamas combatants. It also created "zones of destruction" where virtually any male, including civilians, immediately became a legitimate target.
>
> This significantly reduced the risks faced by Israeli soldiers in ground combat. That is the gist. The argument is based on the concept of a trade-off between exposing your soldiers to risk and transferring the risk to enemy civilians – an issue that raises ethical dilemmas. The result is reflected in the death ratio of your soldiers versus that of enemy civilians.[53]

Add to this the fact that the Israeli society's drift to the far right, combined with the maddening impact of the atrocities committed during the 7 October attack, made of most Israeli soldiers "willing executioners" – to borrow here the title of a controversial book about the responsibility of ordinary Germans in the Holocaust[54] – as manifested in the countless and shameless videos circulated by Israeli soldiers displaying a sadistic inebriety at the atrocities they were contributing to. This pattern has been emphasized by many reports, like this poignant testimony published by *Haaretz* in December 2024, depicting the indiscriminate shooting of people in the so-called Netzarim corridor inside Gaza:

> A recently discharged Division 252 officer describes the arbitrary nature of this boundary: "For the division, the kill zone extends as far as a sniper can see." But the issue goes beyond geography. "We're killing civilians there who are then counted as terrorists", he says. "The IDF spokesperson's announcements about casualty numbers have turned this into a competition between units. If Division 99 kills 150 [people], the next unit aims for 200."

These accounts of indiscriminate killing and the routine classification of civilian casualties as terrorists emerged repeatedly in *Haaretz*'s conversations with recent Gaza veterans.

"Calling ourselves the world's most moral army absolves soldiers who know exactly what we're doing", says a senior reserve commander who has recently returned from the Netzarim corridor. "It means ignoring that for over a year, we've operated in a lawless space where human life holds no value. Yes, we commanders and combatants are participating in the atrocity unfolding in Gaza. Now everyone must face this reality."[55]

We find here again an instance of what the famous former Nazi political theorist Carl Schmitt described, in lectures delivered in 1962 in Francoist Spain, as "absolute enmity" toward the "absolute enemy". Schmitt concluded with a reflection on the weapons of mass destruction, pointing to what was in his opinion more dangerous than the weapons themselves, or a general human disposition to kill:

> [T]he ultimate danger exists not even in the present weapons of mass destruction and in a premeditated evil of men, but rather in the inescapability of a moral compulsion. Men who use these weapons against other men feel compelled morally to destroy these other men ... They must declare their opponents to be totally criminal and inhuman, to be a total non-value. Otherwise, they [themselves] are nothing more than criminals and brutes.[56]

The dehumanization of the enemy is indeed the indispensable condition without which the perpetrators of massacres would feel that they themselves were inhuman brutes (hence, the typical labeling as "brutes" by Conrad's Kurtz of those Africans whose extermination he famously demanded)[57] – that is, of course, if those perpetrators pretend or believe that they are morally sound. Schmitt was well placed to know this, as he had had his share in that prominent instance of dehumanization – indeed, a prelude to genocide – that was the Nazi classification of several categories of people, especially the Jews, as *Untermenschen* (subhumans). Israel's soldiers were even incited to dehumanize the population they attacked at the very onset of their offensive by none other than their own "minister of defense" Yoav Gallant, when he infamously proclaimed: "We are fighting human animals and we are acting accordingly."[58]

The Gaza genocide was thus ushered in by a combination of all the above factors: the Israeli "zero risk" approach, itself predicated on an evaluation of the other side's civilian lives as dispensable compared to one side's soldiers' lives; the post-7 October determination to reoccupy the entirety of the Gaza Strip; the deliberate intent to inflict maximum damage on Hamas as well as on its civilian environment; the fact that all this happened under the supervision of a coalition of neofascists and neo-Nazis, intent on achieving a second Nakba by means of an "ethnic cleansing" of Gaza or at least parts of it; and the Israeli military's murderous fury, combined with the dehumanization of Palestinians.

WESTERN SUPPORT FOR ISRAEL'S ONSLAUGHT ON GAZA

Another crucial consideration was that all of this took place in the almost total absence of restraining influences. "Israel would have refrained, as in the past, from launching a ground operation in Gaza had it not secured international legitimacy for harming Gazan civilians", as Yagil Levy, quoted above rightly observed. This, of course, related to those states that might have effectively exerted such an influence on Israel, which means above all the United States – the main financial and military backer of Israel since the late 1960s. Yet, far from exerting any restraint on its Israeli ally, Washington enthusiastically (for several months at least, before toning its enthusiasm down a little) participated in what was arguably the first joint US–Israeli war, though falling short of the direct participation of US troops in the bombing of Gaza itself.[59]

Why did this happen? There is no plausible "materialist" or "realist" explanation for Joe Biden's zealous support for Israel. It is a simple matter to demonstrate that his stance went against hegemonic US interests in the strategically and economically crucial Middle East. Nor was it the outcome of the pressure of the pro-Israel lobby, by which John Mearsheimer and Stephen Walt attempted to explain the 2003 invasion of Iraq in their 2007 bestseller.[60] The only plausible explanation was ideological – more straightforwardly so than in the case of Donald Trump's support for Israel, which, during his first term, went way beyond the limits set by what had hitherto been a matter of bipartisan consensus in US foreign policy.

Whereas Biden was expected to reverse Trump's wildly pro-Israel measures, as he had promised to do during his electoral campaign, he in fact continued his predecessor's policy toward Israel and even surpassed it in qualitative terms by lending Israel's protracted onslaught on Gaza his full and unconditional support. So much was this the case that Doug Rossinow, a professor of history, could assert in *Time* magazine, as early as on 29 November 2023: "President Biden is proving himself, by some measures, the most pro-Israel president in American history."[61]

But this should not have come as a surprise. Arguing against Biden's candidacy ahead of the 2020 Democratic Party's presidential primaries, Peter Beinart warned of "Joe Biden's alarming record on Israel". In a lengthy and well-informed article published in *Jewish Currents*, he explained that "during a critical period early in the Obama administration, when the White House contemplated exerting real pressure on Benjamin Netanyahu to keep the possibility of a Palestinian state alive, Biden did more than any other cabinet-level official to shield Netanyahu from that pressure."[62]

Just as Richard Nixon privately told the Jewish-American businessman Leonard Garment in the midst of the 1973 Arab-Israeli War, "I am a Zionist. You don't have to be a Jew to be a Zionist",[63] Joe Biden has made the same claim in public during his presidency, not once but repeatedly. The record of his statements on the White House website shows that, during his first presidential visit to Israel on 13 July 2022, Biden asserted on arrival: "You need not be a Jew to be a Zionist." He added:

> I'm proud to say that our relationship with the State of Israel is deeper and stronger, in my view, than it's ever been. And with this visit, we are strengthening our connections even further. We've reaffirmed the unshakable commitment of the United States to Israel's security, including partnering with Israel on the most cutting-edge defense systems in the world.[64]

Then, during his second presidential visit, on 18 October 2023 – ten days into Israel's onslaught on Gaza – Biden remarked, "If there weren't an Israel, we'd have to invent one ... You don't have to be a Jew to be a Zionist", repeating this last sentence.[65] He reiterated the same assertion on 5 December 2023 during a campaign reception: "I got in trouble many times for saying you don't have to be a Jew to be a Zionist, and I am a Zionist. I make no apologies for that. That's a reality."[66] And again, on 11 December 2023, at a Hanukkah Holiday Reception held at the White House: "I got in trouble – got criticized very badly by the southern part of my state and some of the southern parts of the country when, 35 years ago, I said, 'You don't have to be a Jew to be a Zionist, and I'm a Zionist' ... And, by the way, you don't have to be a Jew to be a Zionist."[67]

A year after the 7 October attack, at a time when the genocidal character of Israel's onslaught on Gaza had become plainly evident and had been pointed out by both the International Court of Justice and the International Criminal Court as well as by prominent human rights organizations, Joe Biden boasted: "No administration has helped Israel more than I have. None. None. None."[68] A few days later, he told American Jewish faith leaders during a call:

> You know, at my direction, last week, the United States military took unprecedented action again to actively assist the successful defense of Israel. You've – you've heard me say before that I got very badly criticized as a young senator for saying, "I'm a Zionist." You don't have to be a Jew to be a Zionist. It's not necessary.[69]

Biden's quasi-obsessive insistence on portraying himself as a Zionist won him Netanyahu's warm praise during the latter's visit to Washington in July 2024 to deliver his fourth speech to a joint session of Congress, thereby beating the previous historical record – which he shared with Winston Churchill – of delivering three speeches to that audience. "From a proud Israeli Zionist to a proud Irish American Zionist, I want to thank you for 50 years of public service and 50 years of support for the state of Israel", Netanyahu told Biden.[70] The remarkable constancy in Joe Biden's unshakable support for the Zionist state is evidently idiosyncratic, rooted in his own personal history (in the speeches from where the above statements are excerpted, Biden has more than once attributed to his father's influence his commitment to Israel, which he likes to describe as "ironclad").

Biden's self-definition as a Zionist was, moreover, considerably sharpened by the traumatic character of the Hamas-led 7 October 2023 operation. The awful images of the attack on the Nova music festival, in particular, aroused in the West a very strong reaction of what I have termed "narcissistic compassion" – "a form of compassion evoked much more by calamities striking 'people like us', much less by calamities affecting people unlike us" – in describing the striking disproportion between, on the one hand, the empathy aroused in Western countries toward the Americans in reaction to the 11 September 2001 attacks, particularly with regard to the staggering destruction of the World Trade Center's twin towers in New York, and, on the other hand, the lack of interest expressed toward much greater tragedies in the Global South, especially in Sub-Saharan Africa.[71]

The effect of 7 October in whipping up Western narcissistic compassion for the Israelis, along with the guilt complex in those Western European countries that had been perpetrators or enablers of the Nazi genocide of the Jews – Germany, Austria, France, and Italy, in particular – led to an unprecedented degree of unconditional solidarity with the Zionist state, at the very moment when it was ruled by people who certainly had more in common with the Nazis than with their victims, be they victims of racist hatred or members of the left that the Nazis targeted for annihilation. This also happened at the very moment when Israel was launching a massive onslaught on a tiny and densely populated territory, accompanied by statements that left no possible doubt about the fact that a massacre of enormous scale had been set in motion. The key to this apparent paradox is to be found in an ethnocentric, particularist interpretation of the lessons of the Holocaust, as opposed to a humanistic, universalist one.

EXCURSUS 2: NEVER AGAIN

When, in April 2012, the great German writer and Nobel Prize recipient Günter Grass published a poem titled "What Must Be Said" (*Was gesagt werden muss*) denouncing his country's delivery to Israel of submarines that could be equipped with nuclear missiles, all hell broke loose in Germany. I was asked by the Frankfurt-based magazine *Hintergrund*, along with other authors, to comment on the brawl.[72] Below is an excerpt from the original text of my contribution, written in English:

[F]or a descendant of a Nazi parent, or for any German or Austrian – since popular majorities in the two countries subscribed to the Nazi perspective until its defeat – there are two ways of drawing lessons from the Nazi genocide of the European Jews: one leads to saying "Never again to them, the Jews" and the other "Never again" tout court.

The former conclusion stems from a sense of guilt toward the specific victims of the Nazis, without a clear repudiation of the generic dimension of their crime and ideology. Thus, it reverses the Nazi perspective in taking the side of "the Jews" against their enemies, whoever and wherever they may be. Antisemitism is thus replaced with "philosemitism". As the historian of antisemitism, Eleonore Sterling, whose parents were murdered in a concentration camp during World War II, put it very aptly in *Die Zeit* twenty years after the end of the war: "Antisemitism and the more recent idolization of the Jews have a good deal in common. Both are symptomatic of a sort of hypothermia of complex human relationships and derive from a mental incapacity truly to respect the 'other.' Jews remain foreigners for antisemites and philosemites alike."[73]

Whereas the Nazis saw "the Jews" as the embodiment of evil, the German holders of the philosemitic perspective believe that the defense of "the Jews" – whom they see represented in the State of Israel, notwithstanding the fact that this representation is highly contested by a vast number of people of Jewish descent – is a duty superseding all others. In the name of this duty, they end up supporting the oppressive acts committed by Israel's government against the Palestinian people, and applaud the provision of the Israeli state with means of mass annihilation. They do so moreover at a time when Israel's government is dominated by forces which the founders of the State of Israel themselves did not hesitate to label as fascists, nay to compare to Nazis – however outrageous such comparisons may be.[74]

On the latter conclusion – "Never again" tout court – Germans join persons of Jewish descent and indeed any human being who regards this principle as superseding all national, ethnic or "racial" groups, in a common fight for universal humanistic values. Upholders of such values, on the other hand, whether Germans or Jews or to whatever ethnicity they belong (or are seen to belong), believe that their supreme moral duty is to fight against the core exclusivist and nationalistic set of views that characterized Nazism, and to warn against any project of inflicting a collective punishment on any people in the name of defending another – be it "the Jewish people" or any other.[75]

A WORLD-HISTORICAL WATERSHED

I described the Gaza genocide at the beginning of this text as *the first genocide – including the intentionality entailed in the concept – executed by a technologically advanced state since the final defeat in 1945 of the far-right Axis powers' coalition of World War II.* This observation suggests an issue of world-historical significance.

The global far right's defeat in 1945 at the hands of a global coalition dominated by the United States – at a time when Franklin Delano Roosevelt and Eleanor Roosevelt were still in the White House – was supposed to usher in a new historical era characterized by the global prevalence of a liberal international rules-based order, of which the Charter of the newborn United Nations was meant to constitute the cornerstone and the organization itself the central edifice. The Charter was an outgrowth of what came to be known as the Atlantic Charter, issued on 14 August 1941 by the leaders of the two empires that sustained the aspiration to a new world order: the old decaying British Empire and the still young and burgeoning US empire. It is worth recalling here some of the principles enunciated in this famous document by US President Franklin Roosevelt and the UK's Prime Minister Winston Churchill, "on which they base their hopes for a better future for the world":

[T]hey desire to see no territorial changes that do not accord with the freely expressed wishes of the peoples concerned; ... they respect the right of all peoples to choose the form of government under which they will live; and they wish to see sovereign rights and self-government restored to those who have been forcibly deprived of them ... [T]hey hope to see established a peace which will afford to all nations the means of dwelling in safety within their own boundaries, and which will afford assurance that all the men in all lands may live out their lives in freedom from fear and want; ... they believe that all of the nations of the world, for realistic as well as spiritual reasons must come to the abandonment of the use of force ... They will likewise aid and encourage all other practicable measures which will lighten for peace-loving peoples the crushing burden of armaments.[76]

Major steps were later to be taken in that direction, most importantly the 1945 founding of the United Nations, the 1945 establishment of the International Court of Justice (ICJ) to arbitrate disputes between states, the 1948 UNGA adoption of the Universal Declaration of Human Rights (eight countries abstained: six Communist-ruled countries headed by the USSR, along with the Saudi kingdom and South Africa), the 1949 adoption of further Geneva Conventions and Protocols as a cornerstone of enhanced international humanitarian law regulating the conduct of war, and the elaboration and adoption of rules of engagement in conformity with IHL by the militaries of various countries.

The death of Roosevelt in April 1945 and replacement by his right-wing anti-communist vice-president, Harry Truman, constituted the key event that caused the end of World War II to dissolve rapidly into the Cold War. The August 1945 nuclear bombings of Hiroshima and Nagasaki represented the first major act largely inspired by the looming rivalry with the USSR. They were also the gravest violation ever of all civilized rules of engagement and humanitarian principles in the conduct of war. French colonialism, overseen by a member of the US-led Western bloc, perpetrated two major massacres, killing tens of thousands of natives in Algeria in 1945 and Madagascar in 1947–49. As we have seen, both the 1947 UNGA endorsement of the Zionist project of a "Jewish state" in Palestine and the 1949 UNGA endorsement of the acquisition of further territory by force by the new state were blatant violations of key principles inscribed in the UN Charter. Very quickly, little would remain of the "liberal international rules-based order" on either side of the Iron Curtain and in the relations between the two rival global empires, the US-led Western bloc and the USSR-led Eastern bloc.

The Cold War – in the name of countering Soviet totalitarianism for some, US imperialism for others – became the pretext for a wide-ranging disregard of the UN Charter, as well as of the Universal Declaration of Human Rights, by many of its signatories, starting with the United States itself. The same Atlantic Charter that had inspired the UN Charter would come to be construed as the building block of the North Atlantic Treaty Organization (NATO), founded in 1949 by twelve states that included António de Oliveira Salazar's quasi-fascist Estado Novo in Portugal. The liberal aspirations expressed during World War II were reduced to an ideological weapon in the Cold War. Atlanticist liberalism replaced liberalism tout court, and came to be used as the foundational cement of the Free World in the face of Communist totalitarianism, while basic liberal principles were negated by features common to leading states of the purportedly free world: colonialism; imperialism; racial and gender discrimination and oppression; authoritarianism; alliances with major violators of human rights, including very basic women's rights – and so on.

The end of the Cold War, which saw the meltdown of the Soviet bloc, was seen by the opposite side as a major ideological victory, bolstering the radical alteration of the global balance of power. Predictably, it was seized by the United States, at a time when Reaganite triumphalism was in full spate, as a new historical opportunity to reclaim and revamp the "liberal international rules-based order" under Washington's firm leadership. Against the backdrop of a brewing US-led war on Iraq, George H. W. Bush, addressing a Joint Session of Congress in 1990, announced a "new world order":

> We stand today at a unique and extraordinary moment. The crisis in the Persian Gulf [Kuwait's invasion by Saddam Hussein's troops], as grave as it is, also offers a rare opportunity to move toward an historic period of cooperation. Out of these troubled times ... a new world order can emerge: a new era – freer from the threat of terror, stronger in the pursuit of justice, and more secure in the quest for peace. An era in which the nations of the world, East and West, North and South, can prosper and live in harmony.
>
> A hundred generations have searched for this elusive path to peace, while a thousand wars raged across the span of human endeavor. Today that new world is struggling to be born. A world quite different from the one we've known. A world where the rule of law supplants the rule of the jungle. A world in which nations

recognize the shared responsibility for freedom and justice. A world where the strong respect the rights of the weak.[77]

Today it is difficult not to smile ironically at these lines, which sound more parodic than historic – even though, in the same speech, George H. W. Bush eulogized America's military power, urging Congress to maintain military spending at a high level, lest some might be tempted to believe that disarmament was back on the agenda:

Recent events have surely proven that there is no substitute for American leadership. In the face of tyranny, let no one doubt American credibility and reliability. ... American interests are far reaching. Interdependence has increased. The consequences of regional instability can be global. This is no time to risk America's capacity to protect her vital interests.[78]

Bush's grandiloquence was even followed, during the "unipolar moment" opened by the implosion of the Soviet sphere, by "idealist" efforts – in the sense of international relations theory – to turn the "new world order" into a "cosmopolitan democracy" by way of upgrading the "liberal international rules-based order".[79] These efforts translated into the creation of a second international judicial body, the International Criminal Court (ICC), with jurisdiction to prosecute individuals for four types of crimes: genocide, crimes against humanity, war crimes and aggression. The statute of the ICC was adopted in 1998, and the court itself was established in 2002.

Another fruit of the "cosmopolitan" drive to transcend the sovereignty of states, that pillar of the UN Charter, was the UNGA's adoption in 2005 of the Responsibility to Protect (R2P) principle, authorizing

collective action, in a timely and decisive manner, through the Security Council, in accordance with the Charter, including Chapter VII, on a case-by-case basis and in cooperation with relevant regional organizations as appropriate, should peaceful means be inadequate and national authorities manifestly fail to protect their populations from genocide, war crimes, ethnic cleansing and crimes against humanity.[80]

Adapting to this zeitgeist, Washington inaugurated a series of "humanitarian interventions" in the Horn of Africa, followed by the Balkans. In the latter region, it attached great importance to labeling as genocide the massacre of Bosnians perpetrated by Serbian forces, which was much lesser in its scale and intensity of violence than the Gaza hecatomb whose genocidal character it now obstinately refuses to recognize.

At the same time, in contrast with its displays of liberal good intention, Washington embarked in the 1990s on a course in international relations that would soon provoke a New Cold War.[81] Instead of dissolving itself, NATO for the first time entered a phase of collective military interventionism, and expanded its membership to include an increasing number of states that had formerly been under Moscow's thumb, including former Soviet Republics. Before the end of that transitional decade, the United States had led its NATO allies into the first major breach of international legality since 1990: the 1999 Kosovo War, launched by circumventing the UN Security Council (UNSC) to avoid Russian and Chinese vetoes. The "new world order" had proved short-lived indeed.

Although the United States and Israel had both voted against the ICC's Rome Statute in 1998, they both signed it two years later – but never ratified it, thus confirming that their signatures were purely a political tactic. They both officially withdrew from it soon after: the United States in 2002, prior to its invasion of Iraq – its second major breach of international legality, and the most serious such breach between the end of the Cold War and Russia's 2022 invasion of Ukraine (Russia withdrew from the ICC in 2016); and Israel at the same time as Washington, as it started multiplying its violations of IHL from 2001 onward, launching a full-spectrum war against the Palestinians to quell the Second Intifada. The "war on terror" – the common banner under which George W. Bush's administration and Ariel Sharon's government waged their wars – thus replaced anticommunism as the central pretext for ignoring the rules of the international "rules-based order".

As for the Responsibility to Protect, its most prominent use was to provide cover for the US-led intervention in Libya in 2011, which quickly overstepped what the UNSC resolution had greenlit, with abstentions from Moscow and Beijing. This precedent led to legitimate distrust of the West's instrumentalization of R2P, and therefore a blockage of its use in subsequent major cases of large-scale massacre, most prominently Syria. Most importantly, R2P was blocked by Western powers in consideration of the present Gaza genocide. As Jeremy Moses aptly put it in an article on the "political and moral failure" of R2P, in which he discussed why attempts at invoking it for Gaza have remained limited and unheeded,

> In the end, the true test of the value of any norm is not whether it is useful in situations where it aligns with the interests of the powerful; rather, it is when it runs against those interests. By this measure, it is not only the R2P that has been proven to be of at best marginal value in relation to Gaza. We could also say that the entire edifice of international humanitarian law, human rights law and humanitarianism in general is in question.[82]

The entire legal edifice of the international rules-based order is indeed crumbling. The novelty of the use against Israel, the West's spoiled child, of this edifice's two key pillars, represented by the ICJ and ICC, and the negative reaction of most Western powers to their use – thus displaying a flagrant double standard highlighted by the contemporaneity of the Russian invasion of Ukraine and the Israeli invasion of Gaza, and by the Western powers' contrasting reactions to the ICC's arrest warrants against Vladimir Putin and Benjamin Netanyahu – have conspired to finally discredit the Western liberal pretense. As the *Financial Times*, a major organ of Western liberalism, complained:

> The elaboration of international humanitarian law was a pillar of the postwar rules-based framework. The creation in the 1990s of tribunals for the former Yugoslavia and Rwanda, and later the ICC, as mechanisms to prosecute those accused of war crimes, helped to top out that framework – even if Russia, China and India, plus the US and Israel, stayed out of the ICC ...
>
> [M]any developing-world leaders will see the western divisions over [the ICC's] warrants [against Netanyahu and Gallant] as a sign of hypocrisy and a readiness to pick and choose how to apply international law. The US was already considered complicit by many in the global south for unyielding support for Netanyahu's far-right government.

> This will be all the more damaging as it follows a broader erosion of the courts and domestic rule of law by populist leaders in a series of western democracies – which has now spread to the US. A convicted felon who sought to use the law to overturn the result of the last presidential election has been voted back into the White House.[83]

This venerable economic journal is absolutely right to connect the erosion of the domestic rule of law with the unravelling of the international rule of law. The world is indeed going through a twenty-first-century version of the past century's interwar years, which saw the global rise of the far right in the guise of Italian Fascism, German Nazism, and related movements. By endorsing the criminal deeds of a coalition of neofascists and neo-Nazis ruling Israel, Western liberal governments, political parties and intellectuals have largely contributed to the banalization of the far right. At the same time, they have condoned the whitewashing of the European and American far right's antisemitism that Benjamin Netanyahu embarked upon several years ago[84] – to the point of trying to absolve Adolf Hitler of the intent to perpetrate a genocide of the Jews, so as to accuse Amin al-Husseini (the Mufti of Palestine, who took refuge in Berlin and Rome between 1941 and 1945) of having suggested it to the Nazi Führer.[85]

The "new antisemitism" attributed en bloc to Muslims, as well as to left-wing defenders of Muslim immigrants' rights and critics of Israel, has thus come to serve as ideological cover to absolve the European and American far right of their past and present antisemitism, in order to collude with them on the ground of Islamophobia, nowadays the main feature of their racism and xenophobia. In the name of countering this purported antisemitism, a racial double standard is applied, fostering indifference to Palestinian suffering and leading to partake in a new instance of genocide denial. Those Western liberals who have indulged in such cowardly behavior have further discredited their own ideological standing in the face of the global surge of the far right. Thus, they have been digging their own grave.

Atlanticist liberalism is now definitively discredited.[86] Far-right forces are on the rise within the Atlantic Alliance, including the two Atlantic strongholds of resistance to the Axis powers in World War II: the United States, where the far right has now prevailed, and Britain, where it may well prevail in the face of a very pale and uninspiring alternative. The second attempt to revitalize the "liberal international rules-based order" in the post-Cold War era has failed miserably, not because of the far-right surge that in fact came later, but due to the inconsistency, hypocrisy, and hegemonic hubris of the upholders of Atlanticist liberalism themselves. Western condoning of the Gaza genocide has indeed been the final nail in the coffin of that purported rules-based order. The Western promise of rule of law made in 1945 and renewed in 1990 is now dead. The law of the jungle reigns supreme. May this relapse of international relations into barbarism be reversed before it leads to a new global catastrophe.

NOTES

1 Raphael Patai, ed., *The Complete Diaries of Theodor Herzl*, trans. Harry Zohn, New York: Herzl Press/Thomas Yoseloff, 1960, p. 10. See also Chapter 2, below.

2 Amnesty International, *"You Feel Like You Are Subhuman": Israel's Genocide Against Palestinians in Gaza*, London: Amnesty International, 2024; Médecins Sans Frontières, *Gaza: Life in a Death Trap*, Geneva: MSF, 2024; and Lee Mordechai, *Bearing Witness to the Israel–Gaza War*, 5 December 2024, all available online.

3 Rasha Khatib, Martin McKee, and Salim Yusuf, "Counting the Dead in Gaza: Difficult but Essential", *Lancet*, 20 July 2024, p. 237.

4 "UNOSAT Gaza Strip Comprehensive Damage Assessment", at unosat.org/products/3984.

5 "Convention on the Prevention and Punishment of the Crime of Genocide", adopted on 9 December 1948 as General Assembly resolution 260 A (III), OHCHR website. Acts (d) "Imposing measures intended to prevent births within the group" and (e) "Forcibly transferring children of the group to another group" do not apply to the Gaza case.

6 Omer Bartov, "As a former IDF soldier and historian of genocide, I was deeply disturbed by my recent visit to Israel", *Guardian*, 13 August 2024. See also Isaac Chotiner, "A Holocaust Scholar Meets with Israeli Reservists", *New Yorker*, 2 July 2024.

7 See Gilbert Achcar, *The Arabs and the Holocaust: The Arab-Israeli War of Narratives*, trans. G. M. Goshgarian, 2nd edn, London: Saqi, 2025, esp. pp. 260–70.

8 The most comprehensive presentation of the background to the Gaza tragedy is the remarkable historiography devoted to the enclave by Jean-Pierre Filiu, *Gaza: A History*, trans. John King, London: Hurst, 2014 (a second, updated edition was published in 2024). Filiu's work offers a detailed account of the episodes from Gaza's recent past discussed in this book. The author concluded the

original edition by emphasizing the centrality of Gaza for the future of Israeli–Palestinian relations at a time when the Strip was relegated to the margins by most observers.

9   Adam Raz, *How Israel Stole Palestinian Property*, trans. Philip Hollande, London: Verso, 2024.

10   Adam Raz, "A Brief History of the Netanyahu–Hamas Alliance", *Haaretz*, 20 October 2023.

11   Ibid.

12   Ghazi al-Surani, "Qita' Ghaza: Al-Taghayyurat al-Ijtima'iyya wal-Iqtisadiyya", 10 March 2019, available at ahewar.org/debat/files/630600.pdf.

13   Ibid., p. 15.

14   Ibid., p. 16.

15   Ibid.

16   Ibid., p. 22.

17   Ali Adam, "Despite Hamas' Crackdown, Gaza Protests Continue in Rare Defiance", *Al-Monitor*, 6 August 2023. One of the slogans chanted was apparently mistaken for "The people want the fall of the regime", which sounds quite similar, and is corrected here. The latest poll conducted in Gaza before 7 October 2023 indicated that 73 per cent of those polled believed that "there is corruption" in "the institutions controlled by Hamas in the Gaza Strip" and that 59 per cent believed that people there could not "criticize the authority without fear" (Palestinian Center for Policy and Survey Research, "Public Opinion Poll No. 89", 13 September 2023, pp. 12–13).

18   See Achcar, *Arabs and the Holocaust*, pp. 236–43.

19   "Press Conference Statement of Yasir Arafat Clarifying His Speech Before the UN General Assembly", 14 December 1988, at palquest.org/en/historictext/9679/press-conference-statement-yasir-arafat-clarifying-his-speech-un-general-assembly. On the PLO's evolution, see Gilbert Achcar, *Eastern Cauldron: Islam, Afghanistan, Palestine and Iraq in a Marxist Mirror*, New York: Monthly Review/London: Pluto, 2004, pp. 115–232.

20   See Chapter 3, below.

21   See Chapter 4, below.

22   See the preamble to Chapter 5, below.

23   Francesca Borri, "Hamas Leader Sinwar: 'I Don't Want Any More Wars'", *Ynet News*, 4 October 2018, and the longer version, Francesca Borri, "Sinwar: 'It's Time for a Change, End the Siege'", *Ynet News*, 5 October 2018 (Italian version: Francesca Borri, "Palestina, il leader di Hamas Sinwar: 'Non voglio più guerre'", *La Repubblica*, 4 October 2018). This interview is one of the smartest ever given by a Hamas leader. Assuming that it was simply a ploy to assuage Israel would credit Sinwar with a formidable ability to consistently embody a radically different rationale. Sinwar was later criticized for having granted an interview to an Israeli newspaper, and declared that he was not aware of this – whereas the Italian journalist maintained that he had given her the interview in plain knowledge that it would be for *Yedioth Ahronoth* as well as for *La*

Repubblica. See Ruth Eglash and Hazem Balousha, "Hamas Leader Gave Rare Interview to Israeli Newspaper, then Said He Was Duped", *Washington Post*, 4 October 2018.

24   On the 2018 march in Gaza, see Haidar Eid, "Back to the Future: The Great March of Return", *Al-Shabaka*, 24 July 2018; and for an assessment of the march from a regional perspective, see Ahmed Abu Artema, "From the Arab Spring to the Great March of Return", *Al-Jazeera*, 6 March 2021.

25   Unlike the rest of the organization, which allied with Hamas and would later support Syria's Assad regime, the main characteristic of the PFLP's Gaza branch was to confront Hamas's oppressive rule as one of the rare, tolerated opposition voices in the Strip.

26   Gilbert al-Ashqar, "Al-Nakba al-Muhdiqa wa Kayfiyat Muwajahatiha", in PFLP–Central Cultural Department–Gaza, *Al-Hayat al-Jadida*, special issue on the occasion of the 61st commemoration of the Nakba, May 2009, pp. 31–5. The text of the Arabic original was still available at the time of writing at redeagle. ahlamontada.com/t13298-topic.

27   See Gilbert Achcar, "Orientalism in Reverse: Post-1979 Trends in French Orientalism", in Achcar, *Marxism, Orientalism, Cosmopolitanism*, London: Saqi/ Chicago: Haymarket, 2013, pp. 40–67.

28   "Tawsiyat Mu'tamar Wa'd al-Akhira – Filastin ba'd al-Tahrir", 30 September 2021, at palinfo.com/news/2021/09/30/60902. An English translation is available on the Zionist website MEMRI, which specializes in monitoring the Arabic media to spot statements and events of this kind that can be used to discredit Israel's enemies: "Hamas-Sponsored 'Promise of the Hereafter' Conference for the Phase Following the Liberation of Palestine and Israel's 'Disappearance': We Must Differentiate between Jews Who Should and Should Not Be Killed, and Prevent a Jewish 'Brain Drain' from Palestine", MEMRI, 4 October 2021, at memri. org/reports/hamas-sponsored-promise-hereafter-conference-phase-following-liberation-palestine-and. The conference provoked a wave of mockery among Palestinians on social media. See Rania al-Lawh, "Awham Mu'tamar 'Wa'd al-Akhira'", Palestine Daily News, 4 October 2021, at pdn.ps/p/18544.

29   "Wa'd al-Akhira. Al-Sinwar: Tahrir Filastin Huwa Markaz al-Ru'ya al-Istratijiyya li-Hamas", 30 September 2021, at palinfo.com/news/2021/09/30/266464.

30   I searched in vain for a transcript of this audio message to quote it in my weekly column in Arabic in the London-based daily *Al-Quds al-Arabi*, in a piece reflecting on the already dreadful balance-sheet two months into the war triggered by the 7 October attack. I ended up transcribing part of it, which I published in my article titled "Al-Aqsa Flood and Miscalculation" (5 December 2023), of which an English translation, posted on the same day, is available on my blog (gilbert-achcar.net/aqsa-flood-miscalculation). A week later, on 13 December 2023, a website called *Oasis* published an English translation of the whole message under the title "We Announce the Start of the Al-Aqsa Flood" (oasiscenter.eu/en/we-announce-the-start-of-the-al-aqsa-flood).

31   See Chapter 7, below.

32   Ayelett Shani, "'Israel's Government Has Neo-Nazi Ministers. It Really Does Recall Germany in 1933'", *Haaretz*, 10 February 2023.

33   Maxime Rodinson, *Israel and the Arabs* [1968], trans. Michael Perl and Brian Pearce, 2nd edn, Harmondsworth: Penguin, 1985, pp. 320–1.

34   Ibid., p. 41.

35   See Daniel Marwecki, *Germany and Israel: Whitewashing and Statebuilding*, London: Hurst, 2020.

36   Ofer Aderet, "'We Give Them 48 Hours to Leave': Israel's Plans to Transfer Gazans Go Back 60 Years", *Haaretz*, 5 December 2024.

37   Ofer Aderet, "Kahane's Knesset Legacy: If There's No Torah, the Pigs Will Take Over the Country", *Haaretz*, 27 February 2019.

38   See Chapter 3, below.

39   See Avi Shlaim, *Collusion Across the Jordan: King Abdullah, the Zionist Movement, and the Partition of Palestine*, New York: Columbia University Press, 1988.

40   Maxime Rodinson, *Israel: A Colonial-Settler State?*, New York: Monad, 1973, p. 77.

41   Saul Friedländer, *Réflexions sur l'avenir d'Israël*, Paris: Seuil, 1969, p. 146.

42   Dahlia Scheindlin, "The Right Keeps Winning in Israel Because Israelis Are Right Wing", *Haaretz*, 19 November 2018.

43   Nir Evron, "Israel's Rightward Turn", *Dissent*, Fall 2022.

44   Ibid.

45   See, for example, Hilo Glazer, "Are Israel's New Immigrants Keeping Netanyahu in Power?", *Haaretz*, 6 April 2019; Shany Littman, "After Losing Hope for Change, Top Left-wing Activists and Scholars Leave Israel Behind", *Haaretz*, 23 May 2020; Lee Yaron, "The October 7 Effect: The Israelis Leaving Israel, and the Diaspora Jews Replacing Them", *Haaretz*, 6 September 2024.

46   Marcy Oster, "Why Netanyahu Brokered a Deal with Kahane's Political Heirs, and Why It Matters", *Times of Israel*, 21 February 2019.

47   Peter Beinart, "Israel's Ascendant Far Right Can't Be Understood by Analogy", *Jewish Currents*, 7 November 2022. On the most recent developments in this regard at the time of writing, see Mairav Zonszein, "The Mainstreaming of Israeli Extremism", *Middle East Institute*, 18 December 2024.

48   Israel Defense Forces, "The Spirit of the IDF", at idf.il/en/mini-sites/our-mission-our-values.

49   Even someone like Benny Morris – a once critical Israeli historian turned rabid Zionist in the present century – did expose many of these abuses in his *1948: The First Arab-Israeli War*, New Haven: Yale University Press, 2008.

50   Gabi Siboni, "Disproportionate Force: Israel's Concept of Response in Light of the Second Lebanon War", *INSS Insight* 74, 2 October 2008. My emphases.

51   Edward N. Luttwak, "A Post-Heroic Military Policy", *Foreign Affairs* 75: 4 (July–August 1996), p. 42.

52   See Chapter 9, below. To be sure, the network of underground tunnels that Hamas had built for its combatants in the Strip increased the Israeli army's fear of invading it without their prior demolition.

53   Yagil Levy, "An Army's Morality Is Measured by a Single Factor. The IDF Has Failed This Test", *Haaretz*, 12 December 2024.

54   Daniel Goldhagen, *Hitler's Willing Executioners: Ordinary Germans and the Holocaust*, New York: Alfred A. Knopf, 1996.

55   Yaniv Kubovich, "'No Civilians. Everyone's a Terrorist': IDF Soldiers Expose Arbitrary Killings and Rampant Lawlessness in Gaza's Netzarim Corridor", *Haaretz*, 18 December 2024. See also Dahlia Scheindlin, "'They Only Understand Force': The Deadly Racism behind Israel's Policy toward the Palestinians", *Haaretz*, 22 October 2024.

56   Carl Schmitt, *Theory of the Partisan: Intermediate Commentary on the Concept of the Political*, trans. G. L. Ulmen, New York: Telos, 2007, p. 94.

57   See Chapter 7, below.

58   Emanuel Fabian, "Defense Minister Announces 'Complete Siege' of Gaza: No Power, Food or Fuel", *Times of Israel*, 9 October 2023.

59   See Chapter 11, below.

60   John Mearsheimer and Stephen Walt, *The Israel Lobby and US Foreign Policy*, New York: Farrar, Straus & Giroux, 2007. In that specific case, I have always believed that the "materialist" explanation in terms of US imperialist interests and designs is more convincing than the explanation in terms of the role of the pro-Israel lobby, as I explained in 2003, in the introductory chapter, "US Imperial Strategy in the Middle East", of my collection *Eastern Cauldron*, pp. 9–45, esp. pp. 17–20. See also Noam Chomsky's brief but powerful discussion of Mearsheimer and Walt's thesis in Noam Chomsky and Gilbert Achcar, *Perilous Power: The Middle East and US Foreign Policy*, ed. Stephen R. Shalom, 3rd edn, Abingdon: Routledge, 2024, pp. 229–30.

61   Doug Rossinow, "Joe Biden Is Turning Out to Be America's Most Pro-Israel President Ever", *Time*, 29 November 2023.

62   Peter Beinart, "Joe Biden's Alarming Record on Israel", *Jewish Currents*, 27 January 2020.

63   Recorded on 18 October 1973, in the *White House Tapes*, held at the Richard Nixon Presidential Library in Yorba Linda, California.

64   "Remarks by President Biden at Arrival Ceremony", Ben Gurion Airport, Tel Aviv, Israel, 13 July 2022, at whitehouse.gov.

65   "Remarks by President Biden at Community Engagement to Meet with Israelis Impacted or Involved in the Response to the October 7th Terrorist Attacks | Tel Aviv, Israel", 18 October 2023, at whitehouse.gov.

66   "Remarks by President Biden at a Campaign Reception | Weston, MA", 5 December 2023, at whitehouse.gov.

67   "Remarks by President Biden at a Hanukkah Holiday Reception", 11 December 2023, at whitehouse.gov.

68   Colleen Long, "Biden Says He Doesn't Know Whether Israel Is Holding Up Peace Deal to Influence 2024 US Election", Associated Press, 4 October 2024. For the context of this quote, see Chapter 13, below.

69   "Remarks by President Biden During a Call with Jewish Faith Leaders for High

Holidays", 9 October 2024, at whitehouse.gov.

70   Tovah Lazaroff, "Netanyahu to Biden: 'From One Zionist to Another, Thank You for 50 Years of Friendship'", *Jerusalem Post*, 25 July 2024 (also quoted in Chapter 13, below).

71   Gilbert Achcar, *The Clash of Barbarisms: The Making of the New World Disorder* [2002], trans. Peter Drucker, 2nd edn, London: Saqi/Routledge, 2006, p. 34 (see Chapter 1, below).

72   Hintergrund.de, "Was auch noch gesagt werden muss!", 6 April 2012, at hintergrund.de/feuilleton/zeitfragen/was-auch-noch-gesagt-werden-muss.

73   Eleonore Sterling, "Judenfreunde – Judenfeinde. Fragwürdiger Philosemitismus in der Bundesrepublik", *Die Zeit* 50, 10 December 1965 (note from the original article).

74   See, for example, David Ben-Gurion's opinion of Menachem Begin, the founder of Likud, presently the ruling party in Israel, as related in Tom Segev's *The Seventh Million: The Israelis and the Holocaust*, trans. Haim Watzman, New York: Owl, 2000 (note from the original article).

75   From the English original, Gilbert Achcar, "Never Again (On the Günter Grass Poem Affair)", posted on ZNet, 2 May 2012, at znetwork.org/znetarticle/never-again-on-the-g-nter-grass-poem-affair-by-gilbert-achcar.

76   "The Atlantic Charter", 14 August 1941, at www.nato.int/cps/en/natohq/official_texts_16912.htm.

77   George Bush, "Address Before a Joint Session of the Congress on the Persian Gulf Crisis and the Federal Budget Deficit", 11 September 1990, at presidency.ucsb.edu/documents/address-before-joint-session-the-congress-the-persian-gulf-crisis-and-the-federal-budget. I first commented on this speech in the introduction to my book *The Clash of Barbarisms*.

78   Ibid.

79   See Daniele Archibugi and David Held, eds, *Cosmopolitan Democracy: An Agenda for a New World Order*, Cambridge, UK: Polity, 1995.

80   United Nations, Office on Genocide Prevention and the Responsibility to Protect, "About the Responsibility to Protect", at un.org/en/genocide-prevention/responsibility-protect/about.

81   For a detailed discussion of this issue, see Gilbert Achcar, *The New Cold War: The United States, Russia and China, from Kosovo to Ukraine*, London: Saqi Books and Chicago: Haymarket Books, 2023.

82   Jeremy Moses, "Gaza and the Political and Moral Failure of the Responsibility to Protect", *Journal of Intervention and Statebuilding* 18: 2 (2024), pp. 211–15.

83   The editorial board, "The Unravelling of the International Legal Order", *Financial Times*, 22 November 2024.

84   See my blog entry, "When the Accusation of Antisemitism Becomes a Weapon in the Hands of Neofascism", 2 July 2024, at gilbert-achcar.net/accusation-of-antisemitism.

85   See Peter Beaumont, "Anger at Netanyahu Claim Palestinian Grand Mufti Inspired Holocaust", *Guardian*, 21 October 2015 (including a video of Netanyahu's outrageous distortion of the historical facts). On the role of Amin al-Husseini, see

Achcar, *Arabs and the Holocaust*, Chapter 4.

86　See my blog entry, "Anti-Fascism and the Fall of Atlanticist Liberalism", 13 August 2024, at gilbert-achcar.net/anti-fascism-and-atlanticist-liberalism.

Part II

Background to the Catastrophe

1. The Whitening of European Jews and the Misuse of Holocaust Memory

In the very beginning was European antisemitism, an heir to the ancestral Christian hatred of Jews, and the most vicious variant of modern racism directed at a human group on the continent, along with the variant targeting the Romani people. Both were instances on European soil of hatred of people perceived as non-white in the sense of having a non-European origin – the same hatred that presided over the horrific treatment inflicted by Europeans on the populations of what is nowadays called the Global South. How did a people that had largely fled racism when it prevailed in Europe and taken refuge in what became the State of Israel end up identifying with white supremacism and reproducing against non-Europeans the abuses it had endured at the hands of Europeans? If we are to understand our present tragedy, this is the first riddle we must elucidate.

This essay is based on a talk that I delivered on 11 June 2022 under the same title at the Berlin conference on "Hijacking Memory: The Holocaust and the New Right", organized by the Einstein Forum and the Center for Research on Antisemitism at the Technische Universität Berlin. I finished writing it on 27 December 2023 for an edited collection based on the 2022 conference, to be published in German in 2025. The English original was first published on the Verso Blog on 21 March 2024.

***

Today it is difficult to think of the European Jews as non-white.[1] The mantra according to which the very white "Western civilization" is "Judeo-Christian" has become so ubiquitous that it has acquired the status of a common misconception, worthy of Gustave Flaubert's *Dictionary of Received Ideas*. This same mantra has been strongly buttressed lately by the way in which Western governments, starting with Joe Biden's US administration, have unconditionally supported Benjamin Netanyahu's far-right Israeli government in its retaliatory massacre of a huge number of the inhabitants of the Gaza Strip, including a staggering proportion of children, along with the devastation of most of the territory and the displacement of the vast majority of those who might yet manage to survive – all while hypocritically paying lip service to the need to spare civilians. This unconditional support stemmed from a Western identification with the Israelis in the face of the 7 October 2023 attack very similar to the "narcissistic compassion" of Europeans with Americans in the face of the 11 September 2001 attacks. I described the latter 22 years ago as "a form of compassion evoked much more by calamities striking 'people like us', much less by calamities affecting people unlike us".[2]

JEWS AS NON-WHITES

And yet, the perception of European Jews as white is quite recent by historical standards. For most of their history, Jews have been perceived in Europe as "non-white", by which is primarily meant here non-Europeans – migrants from West Asia. European languages bear witness to this perception in the now-obsolete designation of the Jews as Israelites in English and French, or their continuing designation as Hebrews in Greek, Italian, Russian, and other East European languages. Europe's Jews themselves long adhered to a self-identification as a migrant people – not one component of countless migrations that formed the modern European nations, but a specifically uprooted population that preserved its singularity through the ages in conformity with the biblical narrative.

Western and Central Europe's modernization and democratization in the nineteenth century made possible a gradual emancipation and assimilation of the Jews. This process was dangerously reversed when the Jews of the Russian Empire became increasingly scapegoated in the latter part of the century, and migrated westwards in large numbers fleeing persecution, in the context of the first major crisis of the global capitalist economy: the Long Depression of 1873–96. The combination of migration and economic crisis produced the rise of xenophobia and racism in the countries of destination – a pattern that has been recurrent ever since. The Jews were targets of the rising far-right in late nineteenth-century Europe, which continued and reached a peak in the crisis-ridden interwar years of the following century.[3] Europe's secularization and the rise of scientism in the nineteenth century translated into the secularization of this renewed hatred of the Jews: old Christian prejudices gave way to pseudo-scientific "antisemitism".

Western European Jews were at best favorably contrasted with the Eastern European migrants, and at worst lumped together with them as members of a racially inferior and maligned category.[4] Thus, the assimilation of Western European Jews was in large part reversed between the late nineteenth century and the middle of the twentieth – except that the Jews were no longer primarily seen by their haters as "Christ killers", but as members of a Semitic or Western Asian/Near Eastern race loathed by Aryan or white Europeans. The reference to an Indo-European–Aryan continuum is an ideological device embraced by Nazism that sought scientific justification for its racist worldview in linguistics. It was more acceptable to southern Europeans, such as Italy's Fascists, than the other racial theory of "white supremacism" known as Nordicism, which was closer to the spontaneous, ordinary racism in Germany and the Nordic countries.

Hitler himself was highly impressed by the views of Nordicist linguist-anthropologist Hans Friedrich Karl Günther, who explicitly refuted the racial characterization of the Jews as Semites, or even as members of a "Jewish race".[5] Günther summarized his views about the Jews in contrast with other European peoples in his 1924 book, *Rassenkunde Europas* ("Racial Studies of Europe"). It is useful to quote extensively from those ramblings, as today only specialized historians are aware of them:

> There is a range of misconceptions about Jews. They are said to belong to a "Semitic race". But there is no such thing; there are only peoples of Semitic language who show different racial

compositions ... The Jews themselves are said to be a race: "the Jewish race". This is also wrong; even a superficial look reveals that there are very different looking people among the Jews. The Jews are supposed to be a religious community. This is the most superficial error, because there are Jews of all European creeds, and particularly among the Jews with the strongest Jewish-ethnic [*jüdisch-völkisch*] views, the Zionists, there are many who do not belong to the Mosaic creed. ...

The Jews are a people [*Volk*] and, like other peoples, can be divided into several creeds and, like other peoples too, they are composed of different races. The two races, which constitute the foundation of the Jewish people, are ... the West Asian [*vorderasiatische*, also translated as "Near Eastern"] and the Oriental. There are also lighter influences of the Hamitic, Nordic, Inner Asian and Negro races, and stronger influences of the Western and, above all, East Baltic race.

Two parts of the Jewish people are distinguished: the southern Jews (Sephardim) and the eastern Jews (Ashkenazim); the former make up 1 tenth, the latter 9 tenths of the total population of around 15 million. The former mainly make up the Jewry of Africa, the Balkan Peninsula, Italy, Spain, Portugal, and part of the Jewry of France, Holland and England. These southern Jews represent an Oriental-West Asian-West Hamitic-Nordic-Negro mixture with the predominance of the Oriental race. The Eastern Jews make up the Jewry of Russia, Poland, Galicia, Hungary, Austria and Germany, probably the largest part of North American Jewry and part of the Western European. They represent a West Asian-Oriental-East Baltic-Inner Asian-Nordic-Hamitic-Negro mixture with a certain predominance of the West Asian race.

In both branches of Judaism, however, similar selection processes have apparently occurred, which have, as it were, narrowed the circle of cross-breeding combinations possible in such a racial mixture, so that physical and mental traits appear again and again in the Jewish people as a whole, which are so similar among a large proportion of Jews of all countries that the impression of a "Jewish race" can easily arise.[6]

Günther supported the Zionist "solution" to the Jewish question:

> A worthy and clear solution to the Jewish question lies in the separation of Jews from non-Jews desired by Zionism, in the parting of Jews from non-Jewish peoples. Within the European peoples, whose racial makeup is completely different from that of Judaism, the latter acts, in the words of the Jewish writer Buber, as "a wedge that Asia drove into Europe's structure, a cause of ferment and disturbance".[7]

The Buber whom Günther quoted is none other than the famous Austrian philosopher Martin Buber, who was then prominent as an ardent supporter of Zionism and admirer of Theodor Herzl. Günther borrowed from the following conclusion of an article titled, "The Land of the Jews" (1910) republished in Buber's 1916 collection, *Die Jüdische Bewegung* ("The Jewish Movement"):

> Here we are a wedge that Asia drove into Europe's structure, a cause of ferment and disturbance. Let us return to the womb of Asia, to the great cradle of nations, which was and is also the cradle of the gods, and thus return to the meaning of our existence: to serve the divine, to experience the divine, to be in the divine.[8]

Across the Atlantic, Günther-like racist ranting was widespread in the same interwar period. A prominent writer in this respect was Kenneth L. Roberts, a journalist and member of the WASP elite (he was a graduate of Cornell University) whose rant was void of the pseudo-scholarly ramblings of Günther, and is hence somewhat closer to the anti-migrant racism of our time. Roberts disseminated his views in newspapers and magazines, and published a collection of his papers in 1922 under the title *Why Europe Leaves Home*. Here is some of his prose excerpted from that book:

> Even the most liberal-minded authorities on immigration state that the Jews of Poland are human parasites, living on one another and on their neighbors of other races by means which too often are underhanded, that they continue to exist in the

same way after coming to America, and that they are therefore highly undesirable as immigrants ...

Races cannot be cross-bred without mongrelization, any more than breeds of dogs can be cross-bred without mongrelization. The American nation was founded and developed by the Nordic race, but if a few more million members of the Alpine, Mediterranean and Semitic races are poured among us, the result must inevitably be a hybrid race of people as worthless and futile as the good-for-nothing mongrels of Central America and Southeastern Europe ...

America is confronted by a perpetual emergency as long as her laws permit millions of non-Nordic aliens to pour through her sea-gates. When this inpouring ceases to be an emergency, America will have become thoroughly mongrelized ...

It must not be forgotten, moreover, that the Jews from Russia, Poland and nearly all of Southeastern Europe are not Europeans: they are Asiatics and in part, at least, Mongoloids ... There will be, of course, many well-intentioned persons to deny that the Russian and Polish Jews have Mongoloid blood in them. This fact, however, may readily be confirmed in that section of the Jewish Encyclopedia dealing with the Chazars. The Jewish Encyclopedia states that the Chazars were "people of Turkish origin whose life and history are interwoven with the very beginnings of the history of the Jews of Russia".[9]

WHITENING OF THE WESTERN JEWS

By one of history's paradoxes, the worst episode ever to befall European Jews in their centuries-long ordeal – that is, of course, the Nazi genocide of the Jews, commonly designated in English as the Holocaust – was the major catalyst of their recognition in postwar decades as a legitimate component of Western civilization on a par with the Europeans of Christian ancestry. It is chiefly in the United States that this process, and the redefinition of the Western civilization as "Judeo-Christian" were taken forward. As Peter Novick observed in 1999,

Before World War II, it was common to hear America described as a Christian country – statistically, a most defensible designation. After the war, the leaders of a no-less-overwhelmingly Christian society had accommodated Jews by coming to speak of our "Judeo-Christian traditions"; they elevated the 3 percent of American society that was Jewish to symbolic parity with vastly larger groups by speaking of "Protestant-Catholic-Jew".[10]

Mark Silk described how the "Judeo-Christian" idea emerged in the ideological fight against fascism, and how it was mainstreamed after World War II as a distinctive ideological pedigree contrasted with both variants of totalitarianism: the fascist and the communist. It thus became a major staple of Cold War ideology:

> "Judeo-Christian" and its companion terms were unstoppable. After the revelations of the Nazi death camps, a phrase like "our Christian civilization" seemed ominously exclusive; greater comprehensiveness was needed for proclaiming the spirituality of the American Way. "When our own spiritual leaders look for the moral foundations for our democratic ideals", observed Cornell's Arthur E. Murphy at the 1949 Conference on Science, Philosophy and Religion, "it is in 'our Judeo-Christian heritage', the culture of 'the West', or 'the American tradition', that they tend to find them." For his part, Murphy was contrasting America's spiritual leaders with the leaders of the Soviet Union, who proclaimed high-flying moral ideals of their own ... "Judeo-Christian" served the same purpose, highlighting, in a way that included Americans of all faiths, the godliness of the United States against the godlessness of the USSR.[11]

In her 1998 book, *How Jews Became White Folks and What That Says about Race in America*, Karen Brodkin described the correlated transformation of American Jews into mainstream partakers in the American way of life:

> American anti-Semitism was part of a broader pattern of late-nineteenth-century racism against all southern and eastern European immigrants, as well as against Asian immigrants,

not to mention African Americans, Native Americans, and Mexicans. These views justified all sorts of discriminatory treatment, including closing the doors, between 1882 and 1927, to immigration from Europe and Asia. This picture changed radically after World War II. Suddenly, the same folks who had promoted nativism and xenophobia were eager to believe that the Euro-origin people whom they had deported, reviled as members of inferior races, and prevented from immigrating only a few years earlier, were now model middle-class white suburban citizens.[12]

Hollywood and the "cultural industry" were, naturally, powerful contributors to this ideological shift, especially in their depiction of World War II and the Holocaust. The Jews represented in movies and television programs over the years have essentially been assimilated Jews – with hardly any traditionalist Eastern European Jews, especially Orthodox Jews, such as Haredi or Hasidic Jews, although they were proportionally the most affected by the Holocaust. A revealing anecdote in this regard is what Barbra Streisand faced when she tried to get Hollywood's backing for her project of making a film based on Isaac Bashevis Singer's story "Yentl the Yeshiva Boy". She was reportedly told by the Jewish production head of 20th Century Fox: "The story's too ethnic, too esoteric."[13] The 1978 TV miniseries *Holocaust* – "without doubt the most important moment in the entry of the Holocaust into general American consciousness", in the words of Peter Novick[14] – represented a fictional family of very middle-class assimilated German Jews, of course.

The whitening of American Jews went along with a shift in the mainstream political use of the Holocaust. Instead of being an extreme case of what racism of all sorts can lead to, and therefore a reference invoked in the fight against all kinds of racism, it was turned into a climax of the specific hatred of Jews alone. "Never again" was downsized from a warning against all types of racist persecution potentially leading to genocide, to a warning against anti-Jewish racism conceived as singular. As Peter Novick noted in 1999, "In recent decades, the leading Jewish organizations have invoked the Holocaust to argue that anti-Semitism is a distinctively virulent and murderous form of hatred." This contrasted with the emphasis that was put on "the common psychological roots of all forms of prejudice" in the first postwar decades, when the same leading Jewish organizations "reasoned that they could serve the cause of Jewish self-defense as well by attacking prejudice and discrimination against blacks as by tackling anti-Semitism directly".[15]

The Martinican poet Aimé Césaire's famous protest in 1950 at the Western double standard in the reaction to the fate of European Jews compared to that of non-white people was thus retrospectively validated. It was famously expressed in Césaire's *Discourse on Colonialism*, where he contended, referring to "the very distinguished, very humanistic, very Christian bourgeois of the twentieth century", that

> what he cannot forgive Hitler for is not *the crime* in itself, *the crime against man*, it is not *the humiliation of man as such*, it is the crime against the white man, the humiliation of the white man, and the fact that he applied to Europe colonialist procedures which until then had been reserved exclusively for the Arabs of Algeria, the "coolies" of India, and the "niggers" of Africa.[16]

In 1950, Césaire's claim was only partially right. As we have seen, the European Jews had not, prior to the Holocaust, been regarded as white people by a large proportion of the white "bourgeois of the twentieth century". It was only later that the Holocaust acquired in the common representation the character of a crime against white people. What remains true, however, is that the degrading and eventually genocidal treatment inflicted by the Nazis upon Jews and a few other human categories took place in the heart of Europe, not somewhere in the heart of darkness far from the sight of Europeans, where it would certainly have aroused much less condemnation in the Global North.

FROM ANTISEMITISM TO PHILO-ZIONISM

Singling out the Holocaust as irreducible to an instance of generic racism and genocide allowed another operation to take place: the identification of the state of Israel with the Jewish condition, even though it is the very antithesis of that historical condition – a Jewish-majority state based on racist discrimination against non-Jews, heavily militarized and engaged in the persecution of another people, the

Palestinians, and the occupation of their land, with periodic murderous onslaughts against them up to the massacre of genocidal proportions that is being perpetrated in Gaza at the time of writing.

This perversion of the historical record was made possible by the equation of two very different sets of attitudes: on the one hand, the racism of white Europeans, or their offshoot in other continents, against historically persecuted Jewish minorities in their midst; on the other hand, the reaction of the Palestinians and other peoples in the Global South, or originating from it, to the brutal colonial behavior of a state that insists upon its self-definition as "Jewish", thus excluding a sizeable section of its own population. This equation was achieved by designating a "new antisemitism", defined as involving criticism of the Israeli state.[17] Thus, the equation of Jews with Zionism, which had hitherto been the hallmark of Arab antisemites against progressive Arab currents insisting on the need to make a clear distinction between the two categories, has become a hallmark, not only of Zionism, for which it has been constitutive of its original pretense of speaking for the global "Jewish nation", but also of a Western "philosemitism" that morphed into unconditional support for the Zionist state, even if shyly critical at times.

Unsurprisingly, albeit paradoxically, this process reached its peak in Germany, the birthland of Nazism and of the perpetrators of the Jewish genocide. It was studied early on by Frank Stern, in his 1992 book *The Whitewashing of the Yellow Badge: Antisemitism and Philosemitism in Postwar Germany*, originally a PhD thesis defended at the University of Tel Aviv.[18] Stern's study was updated and complemented by Daniel Marwecki in his 2020 book, *Germany and Israel: Whitewashing and Statebuilding*.[19] Naturally, identification with Israel against the Palestinians and other Arabs easily becomes a vector of anti-Arab and anti-Muslim racism, upon which the dominant ideology in Israel itself is based. Hence the ease with which traditionally antisemitic far-right currents in Europe have resorted to philo-Zionism in order to "whitewash" themselves by dissolving the Jews in a generic whiteness, while continuing to regard Israel as the Jews' own and only country.

In the face of the recent sequence of events in Gaza, the German philosemitic pro-Israel stance has descended into the grotesque, as vividly described by Susan Neiman:

German denunciations of Hamas, and statements of unyielding solidarity with Israel, have become so automatic that one appeared in the cash machine of my local bank: "We are horrified by the brutal attack on Israel. Our sympathies are with the people of Israel, the victims, their families and friends." The notice displayed once when I tapped the screen, once again when I chose a language, a third time when I typed in my PIN, and finally when the money popped out of the slot. Whether from a machine or a politician, such statements do not make me feel safer. On the contrary, the repetition of vapid formulas increases my growing fears of backlash. Germany's reflexive defenses of Israel while refraining from criticism of its government or its occupation of Palestine can only lead to resentment. Most politicians will acknowledge the problem in private but feel compelled to repeat empty phrases in public – even if they know that right-wing parties are using the massacre in Israel to stir anti-immigration sentiment in Germany.[20]

Eleonore Sterling, née Oppenheimer, whose parents died in the Holocaust, put it very aptly in *Die Zeit* in 1965: "Antisemitism and the more recent idolization of the Jews have a good deal in common".[21] Both, she commented, "derive from a mental incapacity truly to respect the 'other.' Jews remain foreigners for antisemites and philosemites alike." The whitening of the Jews has thus drifted toward a highly reprehensible admiration for an Israel perceived as super-white, an outpost of white supremacism in the Middle East – the cradle of Islam, the foremost object of hatred for present-day racism in the Global North. When this outpost engages in a fury of killing and destruction against Gaza that the *Washington Post* described as being conducted "at a pace and level of devastation that likely exceeds any recent conflict",[22] the inevitable backlash is a resurgence of antisemitism centered around the Israeli state – thus, alas, turning the mantra of a "new antisemitism" into a self-fulfilling prophecy.

NOTES

1   I am grateful to Brian Klug and Stephen Shalom, who read and commented on an earlier draft of this essay.

2   That was in a book that I wrote in the wake of 9/11: Gilbert Achcar, *The Clash of Barbarisms: The Making of the New World Disorder* [2002], 2nd edn, London: Saqi/Routledge, 2006, p. 34. I continued: "Only this narcissistic compassion – going beyond legitimate compassion for any human being victimized by a barbaric act – makes it possible to understand the formidable, absolutely exceptional intensity of the emotions and passions that seized hold of 'public opinion,' beginning with opinion makers, in Western countries and the metropolises of the globalized economy in the wake of the September 11 attacks."

3   The first analysis of the rise of antisemitism in Europe in these terms was the one formulated by the young Abraham Léon (born Abram Wajnsztok) – a Belgian Trotskyist of Polish-Jewish descent – before his death at Auschwitz in 1944, at the age of twenty-six. This was in a book written in French (*La conception matérialiste de la question juive*) and translated into English under the title *The Jewish Question: A Marxist Interpretation*, New York: Pathfinder, several editions.

4   Modern political Zionism originally exploited the desire of Central and Western assimilated European Jews to stop the harmful effect that the tide of migration of their poor Eastern European coreligionists had on their own condition. This is transparent in Theodor Herzl's Zionist manifesto, *Der Judenstaat* (translated into English as *The Jewish State*), as I argued in Gilbert Achcar, "The Zionist Project's Duality: Escaping Racist Oppression and Reproducing It in Colonial Context" – the next chapter in this collection.

5   On Hans F. K. Günther, see Alan E. Steinweis, *Studying the Jew: Scholarly Antisemitism in Nazi Germany*, Cambridge, MA: Harvard University Press, 2006, pp. 25–41.

6   Hans F. K. Günther, *Rassenkunde Europas*, 3rd edn, Munich: J. F. Lehmanns Verlag, 1929, pp. 100–4. There exists a rather approximate English translation based on the second edition (1925): *The Racial Elements of European History*, trans. G. C. Wheeler, London: Methuen, 1927. The quotations here have been directly translated from the German original for better accuracy.

7   Ibid., p. 105. The correspondence between the antisemitic desire to make Germany Judenrein and the Zionist desire to move all Jews to Palestine translated into the Nazi authorities' collaboration with German Zionists in organizing the "transfer" of German Jews to Palestine (Haavara Agreement, signed 25 August 1933). This collaboration lasted until 1941 – that is, until the Nazis' shift toward the "Final Solution". The best and most reliable source on this issue is Francis R. Nicosia, *Zionism and Anti-Semitism in Nazi Germany*, Cambridge: Cambridge University Press, 2008.

8   Martin Buber, *Die Jüdische Bewegung: Gesammelte Aufsätze und Ansprachen 1900–1915*, Berlin: Jüdischer Verlag, 1916, p. 195.

9   Kenneth L. Roberts, *Why Europe Leaves Home*, New York: Bobbs-Merrill, 1922, pp. 15, 22, 97, 117–18.

10   Peter Novick, *The Holocaust in American Life*, Boston, MA: Houghton Mifflin, 1999, p. 225.

11   Mark Silk, "Notes on the Judeo-Christian Tradition in America", *American Quarterly* 36: 1 (Spring 1984), pp. 69–70. Silk went on to describe the theological consequences of this shift in perspective within American Judaism as well as within Catholicism and Protestantism, and the difference between the two Christian branches in that regard.

12   Karen Brodkin, *How Jews Became White Folks and What That Says about Race in America*, New Brunswick, NJ: Rutgers University Press, 1998, p. 26.

13   Neal Gabler, *Barbra Streisand: Redefining Beauty, Femininity, and Power*, New Haven, CT: Yale University Press, 2016, p. 190.

14   Novick, *Holocaust in American Life*, p. 209.

15   Ibid., p. 116.

16   Aimé Césaire, *Discourse on Colonialism*, transl. Joan Pinkham, with an Introduction by Robin D. G. Kelley, New York: Monthly Review, 2000, p. 36. Emphases in original.

17   See Gilbert Achcar, *The Arabs and the Holocaust: The Arab-Israeli War of Narratives*, London: Saqi / New York: Metropolitan, 2010.

18   Frank Stern, *The Whitewashing of the Yellow Badge: Antisemitism and Philosemitism in Postwar Germany*, Oxford: Pergamon, 1992.

19   Daniel Marwecki, *Germany and Israel: Whitewashing and Statebuilding*, London: Hurst, 2020.

20   Susan Neiman, "Germany on Edge", *New York Review of Books*, 3 November 2023.

21   Eleonore Sterling, "Judenfreunde–Judenfeinde: Fragwürdiger Philosemitismus in der Bundesrepublik", *Die Zeit*, 10 December 1965.

22   Evan Hill, Imogen Piper, Meg Kelly, and Jarrett Ley, "Israel Has Waged One of this Century's Most Destructive Wars in Gaza", *Washington Post*, 23 December 2023.

2. The Duality of the Zionist Project

How could the reproduction of European racist oppression by some of its victims operate in a colonial framework, as in the case of Zionism? How did the logic of European racism permeate the Zionist worldview? These are the questions this essay explores. Through a close reading of the founding manifesto of statist Zionism authored by Theodor Herzl, it sheds light on the affinities between its own logic and that of the British racist-colonialist government that issued the infamous Balfour Declaration.

I finished writing this essay in Arabic on 27 October 2017, and delivered it at the conference "100 Years after the Balfour Declaration and 70 Years after the Partition Plan", convened by the Institute for Palestine Studies in Beirut on 13–14 December 2017. I then translated it from the Arabic original, and first published it in English on the Jadaliyya *website on 3 November 2017.*

***

Occupying the dual roles of oppressed and oppressor is not rare in history. It is encountered in particular in the case of national movements embodying the quest of an oppressed nation for liberation from colonialism while this same nation, in its own country, oppresses a minority – be it national, racial, religious, or defined by any other identity – while the national movement disregards this latter oppression or, worse, endorses it under various pretexts, such as accusing the minority of constituting a "fifth column" of colonialism.[1]

Reference to the frequency of such duality is often made in order to normalize the case of Zionism, in the sense of presenting it as ordinary and similar to many other cases. The aim is usually to diminish the wrongs of Zionism, if not to excuse them, in order to represent the Zionist state as "normal", framing it as one example among many. I will seek to demonstrate here that this argument is not valid by explaining the peculiarity of the duality proper to the Zionist case.

It is undisputable that Zionism was born historically as a reaction to the protracted oppression suffered by Jewish minorities in European countries. As is well established, the condition of the Jews in Christian Europe from the Middle Ages up to the nineteenth century was much worse than their condition in Muslim-majority countries. Under self-described Christian authorities, the Jews were victims of much worse persecution than the discrimination and intermittent persecution they suffered from self-described Muslim authorities.

However, the modern era that followed the age of Enlightenment and the French Revolution of the late eighteenth century brought this persecution gradually to an end in Western Europe, with the diffusion of the modern notion of citizenship based on equal rights. With gradual democratic change, the Jews' condition improved gradually in Western Europe between the shores of the Atlantic and the eastern borders of Germany and Austria. It evolved gradually toward integration of the Jews in local societies and the end of formal discrimination. But the first major crisis that affected the world capitalist economy during the last quarter of the nineteenth century – the Long Depression, as it is called – stirred up various xenophobic tendencies. Like all social crises, it boosted the search by far-right groups for scapegoats, in order to mobilize the anger of their societies in service of their reactionary projects.

In the same period, Eastern Europe – especially its largest part, contained within the Russian Empire – was witnessing a belated expansion of the capitalist mode of production. This late capitalist transformation – whose disruptive effect was increased and complicated by its contemporaneity with more advanced capitalism in the West, as well as with the Long Depression – led to an acute social crisis featuring an accelerated rural exodus. The result was that xenophobic tendencies were boosted in Eastern Europe as well, the Jews being their primary victims in the Russian Empire, particularly in the areas that belong today to Ukraine and Poland. There, the Jews were subjected to successive pogroms, prompting many of them to migrate to Western Europe or North America.

As a result, Jews became a favored target of xenophobia in Western Europe, where they combined the character of migrant foreigners and that of people belonging to an alien religion.[2] Thus, against the backdrop of the Long Depression and its wider effects, Western Europe witnessed a revival of anti-Judaism in a new, modern guise: a racial theory pretending to base itself on anthropological sciences, and claiming that Jews – or Semites in general, including the Arabs[3] – belonged to an inferior and evil race. This was the time of the emergence of "antisemitism", which concentrated its fire on European Jews, and went along with the expansion of a fanatical brand of nationalism combined with the advocacy of colonialism. The Long Depression had indeed exacerbated the competition over the division of the globe between colonial metropolises, in the age of what is called "imperialism".

It is against this same backdrop that the modern Zionist movement was born as statist Zionism, aiming at the creation of a Jewish state unlike previous or contemporary brands of spiritual or cultural Zionism. As is well known, the founder of the movement, Theodor Herzl, was an assimilated Austrian Jew who came to his Zionist beliefs after having, as a journalist, covered the trial in Rennes, France, of the French officer of Jewish descent, Alfred Dreyfus, a victim of the surge of antisemitism in his country. This affair led Herzl to write his famous book-manifesto *The Jewish State* (*Der Judenstaat* in the original German: literally, *The State of the Jews*), which came out in 1896 and provided the base upon which the first Zionist congress was convened in the Swiss city of Basel in 1897, a year and a half after the book's publication.[4]

There is a most significant qualitative difference between the Zionist ideology as elaborated by Herzl and the national ideologies that were born in Europe during the first half of the nineteenth century, or in the colonial countries during the first half of the twentieth century. Whereas most of these ideologies belonged to democratic, emancipatory thinking, modern Zionist ideology belonged to the brand of fanatical and colonialist nationalism that was on the rise when it appeared. Indeed, whereas it is undisputable that Zionism is the result of Jewish oppression and a reaction against it – Herzl himself explained in the preface of his book how "the misery of the Jews" was the "propelling force" of the movement that he wanted to create – it is likewise undisputable that Zionism as theorized by Herzl is an ideology that is essentially framed by reactionary and colonialist thinking.

In reality, leaving aside how it was perceived by poor and harshly persecuted East European Jews, who clung to it as to a rescue board, the Zionist project elaborated by Herzl was at its core a design elaborated by an assimilated secular Austrian Jew, which sought to exclude poor religious Jews coming from Eastern Europe, whose migration to the West had disturbed the existence of their west European co-religionists. Herzl acknowledged this with striking bluntness in the introduction of his book:

> The "assimilated" would profit even more than Christian citizens by the departure of faithful Jews; for they would be rid of the disquieting, incalculable, and unavoidable rivalry of a Jewish proletariat, driven by poverty and political pressure from place to place, from land to land. This floating proletariat would become stationary. Many Christian citizens – whom we call Anti-Semites – can now offer determined resistance to the immigration of foreign Jews. Jewish citizens cannot do this, although it affects them far more nearly; for on them they feel first of all the keen competition of individuals carrying on similar branches of industry, who, in addition, either introduce Anti-Semitism where it does not exist, or intensify it where it does. The "assimilated" give expression to this secret grievance in "philanthropic" undertakings. They found emigration societies for wandering Jews. There is a reverse to the picture which would be comic, if it did not deal with human beings. For some of these charitable institutions are created not for, but against, persecuted Jews, they are created to despatch these poor creatures just as fast and far as possible. And thus, many an apparent friend of the Jews turns out, on careful inspection, to be nothing more than an Anti-Semite of Jewish origin, disguised in the garb of a philanthropist.
>
> But the attempts at colonization made even by really benevolent men, interesting attempts though they were, have so far been unsuccessful ... These attempts were interesting, in that they represented on a small scale the practical forerunners of the idea of a Jewish State.

The new idea contributed by Herzl to replace that of the failed "philanthropic" colonial enterprises that he mentioned (the most prominent was funded by the Rothschild family), was to shift from benevolent actions to a political project integrated in the European colonialist framework, aiming at the foundation of a Jewish state that would belong to this framework and reinforce it. For this, Herzl realized that Christian anti-Semites would be his project's staunchest supporters. His main argument, in the section entitled "The Plan", in his book's second chapter, is the following: "The creation of a new State is neither ridiculous nor impossible ... The Governments of all countries scourged by Anti-Semitism will be keenly interested in assisting us to obtain the sovereignty we want."

All that was needed was to select the territory upon which the Zionist project would materialize:

> Here two territories come under consideration, Palestine and Argentina. In both countries important experiments in colonization have been made, though on the mistaken principle of a gradual infiltration of Jews. An infiltration is bound to end badly. It continues till the inevitable moment when the native population feels itself threatened, and forces the Government to stop a further influx of Jews. Immigration is consequently futile unless based on an assured supremacy. The Society of Jews will treat with the present masters of the land, putting itself under the protectorate of the European Powers, if they prove friendly to the plan.

Toward the end of his book's last chapter, where he explained the "Benefits of the Emigration of the Jews", Herzl assured his readers that governments would pay attention to his scheme "either voluntarily or under pressure from the Anti-Semites". His Diaries include many observations about the complementarity between his project of sending the poor Jews out of the European continent and the desire of the anti-Semites to get rid of them. He even prophesized at the beginning of his first diary (1895) that the Jews would adapt to the brutality of the anti-Semites, imitating it in their future state:

> However, anti-Semitism, which is a strong and unconscious force among the masses, will not harm the Jews. I consider it to

be a movement useful to the Jewish character. It represents the education of a group by the masses, and will perhaps lead to its being absorbed. Education is accomplished only through hard knocks. A Darwinian mimicry will set in. The Jews will adapt themselves.[5]

In line with the plan devised by their spiritual father, Herzl, the leaders of the Zionist movement made great efforts to secure the support of one of the great European powers for their project, which had soon become exclusively aimed at Palestine. They took advantage of the land's transfer from Ottoman dominion to British dominion in the context of World War I, after the division of the Ottoman spoils between the British and the French starting from the infamous 1916 Sykes–Picot Agreement.

From that point onwards, the efforts of Zionist leaders focused on London. The leader of British Zionism, Chaim Weizmann, relied on British Jewish tycoon and former member of parliament, Lord Walter Rothschild. Their combined efforts were successful in obtaining the well-known pledge by Foreign Secretary Arthur Balfour on 2 November 1917. In his letter, Balfour insisted that "His Majesty's [King George V's] Government view with favor the establishment in Palestine of a national home for the Jewish people, and will use their best endeavors to facilitate the achievement of this object". This infamous declaration was naturally part and parcel of British imperialist calculations of that time, in the context of ongoing competition between Britain and the two allies that shared its victory in the war: France and the United States.

The historical circumstances of the Balfour Declaration were completely in accordance with the views of Zionism's "prophet" Theodor Herzl. Arthur Balfour himself was one of those anti-Semitic Christians about whom Herzl knew that they would become Zionism's best allies. The British foreign secretary was indeed influenced by Christian Zionism, the Christian current that supports the "return" of the Jews to Palestine. The true goal of this support – undeclared in most cases, but sometimes explicit – is to get rid of the Jewish presence in Christian-majority lands. Christian Zionists see in the Jews' "return" to the Holy Land a fulfillment of the condition of the Second Coming of Christ, which will be followed by the Last Judgment, leading all Jews who have not converted to Christianity to eternal suffering in Hell. In the United States, this same current today represents the staunchest base of support for Zionism in general, and of the Zionist right in particular.

When he was prime minister (1902–05), the author of the infamous Declaration, Balfour himself, promulgated the 1905 Aliens Act, whose aim was to stop the immigration to Britain of Jewish refugees fleeing from the Russian Empire. It is worth pointing here to a rarely mentioned historical fact: Edwin Samuel Montagu is the only British minister who resisted Balfour's drive toward issuing his declaration, and the only minister who manifested wholesale opposition to the Zionist project (aside from the reservations expressed by George Curzon, better known as Lord Curzon). Montagu happened to be the only Jewish member of the cabinet headed by David Lloyd George, to which Balfour belonged, and only the third Jewish minister in British history. Montagu warned that the Zionist enterprise would lead to the expulsion of the Palestinian natives, and reinforce in all other countries the currents wishing to expel Jews. In a memorandum he submitted in August 1917 to the British Cabinet, after having learned about what was to become the Balfour Declaration, he declared straightforwardly: "I wish to place on record my view that the policy of His Majesty's Government is anti-Semitic and in result will prove a rallying ground for Anti-Semites in every country in the world."[6] Montagu regarded it as

> inconceivable that Zionism should be officially recognised by the British Government, and that Mr Balfour should be authorized to say that Palestine was to be reconstituted as the "national home of the Jewish people". I do not know what this involves, but I assume that it means that Mahommedans and Christians are to make way for the Jews and that the Jews should be put in all positions of preference and should be peculiarly associated with Palestine in the same way that England is with the English or France with the French, that Turks and other Mahommedans in Palestine will be regarded as foreigners, just in the same way as Jews will hereafter be treated as foreigners in every country but Palestine.

He then added, most presciently: "Perhaps also citizenship must be granted only as a result of a religious test."

As Herzl expected, the Zionist project materialized under the protection of a great European power as part of its colonial-imperialist designs. This project could not have been made real without such protection, and without being integrated into a much larger colonial-imperialist framework. The "Jewish people" that Herzl wanted to equip with a state of its own was an "imagined" people, with no political institutions that would constitute it as a people, and without the force required in order to take part in the colonial race of the late nineteenth century.

By founding the Zionist movement, Herzl sought to create that missing political institution and steer it toward collaborating with one of the great powers. The Zionist project was thus, from the start, structurally dependent on the protection of a great power, as Herzl had foreseen. This dependence has characterized the history of the Zionist movement, and later that of its state, up to the present. It will not end as long as the state of Israel is based on colonial oppression, for the natural consequence of this is enmity with the Palestinian people and the other peoples around Palestine to a level requiring Israel's protection by an external great power. The United States has been playing this role since the 1960s.

In short, Zionism is not a "normal" movement of national liberation that shares the dual character of many such movements struggling against colonial oppression while oppressing other communities, be they national or otherwise. This is the claim of those partisans of Israel who are not fanatical to the point of denying the oppression perpetrated by the Zionist state. The truth, however, is that the Zionist movement was built upon exploitation of the oppression suffered by the Jews and reliance on help from anti-Semites in order to create a colonial state structurally integrated in the imperialist system – not a postcolonial state, as it pretends to be.

By a most unfortunate turn of history, antisemitism reached a climax in twentieth-century Europe with the Nazis' rise to power and the subsequent enaction of their genocidal project, compelling large numbers of European Jews to find refuge in Zionism, since other forms of antisemitism had slammed the doors of the United States, Britain, and other countries in their face. Thus was the Zionist state able to come into being, portraying itself as a redemptive compensation for the Nazi genocide of the Jews. These historical circumstances have allowed this state to oppress native Palestinians to a degree that went certainly way beyond what the founders of Zionism, Herzl included, had expected.

Today – a century after the Balfour Declaration, and close to seventy years after the founding of the state of Israel over 78 per cent of the territory of British Mandate Palestine, and half a century after this state occupied the remaining 22 per cent – the Zionist prime minister, Benjamin Netanyahu, is still banking on present-day antisemites in Western countries to win support for the arrogant colonial behavior of his state and government. From his reliance on Christian Zionists in the United States to his flirtation with the antisemitic prime minister of Hungary and his silence over Donald Trump's defense of the anti-Jewish, anti-Muslim US far right, Netanyahu is following Herzl's recipe, but in a way that is morally even uglier, as he does so in the shadow of the Nazi genocide, which showed the horrors that antisemitism and other types of racism may induce.

NOTES

1   It is true that foreign domination over a country often seeks to use oppressed minorities whose condition has improved as a side-effect of its presence. This does not justify in the least, of course, the oppression of the minority by the majority after liberation from foreign domination, instead of the new government limiting itself to the punishment of the individuals who collaborated with the occupiers in the perpetration of ugly crimes – be they members of the minority or of the majority – while striving to abolish the oppression from which the minority suffered historically, in order to build a new society of equal citizens.

2   The first exponent of this materialist analysis of the rise of antisemitism is Abraham Leon, *The Jewish Question: A Marxist Interpretation*, New York: Pathfinder, 1970. A Belgian Marxist anti-Zionist of Jewish descent, Leon died at Auschwitz in 1944. His French manuscript was first published as a book in 1946. (See Chapter 1, note 3.)

3   The category of Semite refers to the Semitic language family, of which Hebrew and Arabic are today the most prominent members.

4   There are several online editions of the English version of *The Jewish State*, originally published in 1946 by the American Zionist Emergency Council, New York, based on a revised translation published by the Scopus Publishing Company, New York, 1943, which was in turn based on the first English-language edition, *A Jewish State*, transl. Sylvie d'Avigdor, London: Nutt, 1896. All subsequent quotes from this book are taken from the online edition by Project Gutenberg, at gutenberg. org/files/25282/25282-h/25282-h.htm.

5   Raphael Patai, ed., *The Complete Diaries of Theodor Herzl*, trans. Harry Zohn, New York: Herzl / London: Thomas Yoseloff, 1960, vol. 1, p. 10.

6   "Memorandum of Edwin Montagu on the Anti-Semitism of the Present (British) Government" – text available on the Balfour Project website: balfourproject.org/ edwin-montagu-and-zionism-1917.

3. Zionism and Peace: From the Allon Plan to the Oslo Accords

After forty-five years of highly conflictual relations between the Zionist state of Israel and the Palestinian people on whose land it was established, there came a time when the world believed that peace had finally settled in the Holy Land – the land of Jerusalem, the City of Peace. The accords negotiated by the Israeli Zionist-Laborite government of Yitzhak Rabin and Shimon Peres with the PLO's chairman, Yasser Arafat, in Oslo. Signed with great pomp on 13 September 1993 in Washington, DC, on the White House lawn, the Oslo Accords seemed to inaugurate an era of concord and collaboration between Israel and a Palestinian state-like entity on the remaining stretches of Palestinian territory between the Jordan River and the Mediterranean Sea that Israel had conquered in the Six-Day War of June 1967.

By the end of the century, seven years later, the "peace process" that culminated in the Oslo Accords had collapsed, entering a protracted coma from which, a quarter-century later, it has not awakened. On the contrary, everything indicates that the patient is now brain dead. How did events reach this outcome, in such sharp contrast with the euphoria of 1993? The truth is that things were doomed from the beginning: the Oslo framework was not conducive to peace, as it did not provide for anything resembling the "independent Palestinian state" that the PLO was dreaming of. It instead provided for the kind of situation that became frozen after the turn of the century, in which Palestinian enclaves were surrounded by Israeli settlements and military outposts, as I explained in this essay. It was first published, in French, dated 8 September 1994, in L'Homme et la Société (Paris, No. 114, October–December 1994). This English translation by Bernard Gibbons appeared in New Politics *(New York, vol. 5, no. 3 of new series, Summer 1995), and was reprinted in my collection* Eastern Cauldron: Islam, Afghanistan, Palestine, and Iraq in a Marxist Mirror *(New York: Monthly Review Press and London: Pluto Press, 2004). I was among the few who were critics of the Oslo Accords from the start: my first text making the argument that is developed in this essay dates from December 1993, and is available in the 2004 collection.*

***

PROLOGUE: ON THE "JEWISH AND DEMOCRATIC STATE"

Contrary to the dominant perception today and the most current ideology, democracy and discrimination – religious, racial, ethnic, or sexual – are not antithetical notions.[1] The recognition of so-called democratic rights – civil and political – does not predetermine their extension; even the principle of equality of rights does not imply their real universality.[2] Thus the democratic form of a government is independent of the particular selection of the *demos*. And without going back to the slave-owning democracy of Athenian antiquity, one is aware of the fact that, in the matter of human rights, explicit universalism ruled out tacit particularisms[3] only a long time after the solemn declarations of the eighteenth century.[4]

The anteriority of the discriminatory particularisms and, perhaps, the difficulty of justifying them with regard to the democratic spirit which supposedly inspired the drafters of these declarations, have meant that they have most often remained tacit, as parts of a hidden statement. Their abolition, on the other hand, is generally explicit, in the manner of the 15th (1870) and 19th (1920) amendments to the US Constitution, which suppressed racial and sexual discrimination so far as the right to vote was concerned, although these forms of discrimination were nowhere mentioned in the original document. In fact, an explicit universalism of democratic rights was imposed on a worldwide scale, in the texts and in the dominant ideology, only after World War II – partly as a result of the confrontation with its fascist antitheses. It was consecrated by the International Declaration of Human Rights, adopted by the UN General Assembly in 1948, of which article 2, in particular, proclaimed the equality of rights – with a very extensive definition of rights – "without distinction of any kind, such as race, colour, sex, language, religion, political or other opinion, national or social origin, property, birth or other status."

Egalitarian universalism carried the day on the level of declared principles, but not always – far from it – in the realities of state and social practices. The hypocrisy then became manifest, the texts having lost any ambiguity. If the USSR and its satellites, as well as Saudi Arabia and the Union of South Africa, abstained during the vote in 1948, the three great Western democracies seated on the Security Council, although official sponsors of the declaration, would themselves infringe its proclaimed egalitarianism, not only from the point of view of gender relations, but also through racial and ethnic discrimination in the colonies, if not in the metropolis.

David Ben-Gurion was in good company, then, when he proclaimed, in the Israeli Declaration of Independence of 14 May 1948, that the new state would "ensure complete equality of social and political rights to all its inhabitants irrespective of religion, race or sex." Nonetheless, the contradiction in this precise case figures in the very text, the falseness of the proclaimed egalitarianism being only more patent. The entire Declaration of Independence was placed under the sign of the "Jewish State", the central objective of the world Zionist movement. It was not simply the State of Israel that was proclaimed, but "a Jewish State in Eretz Israel [the land of Israel], to be known as the State of Israel", which would "be open for Jewish immigration and for the Ingathering of the [Jewish] Exiles".

The contradiction between proclaimed egalitarianism and implicit discrimination had become inherent in the Zionist project of colonization when it targeted a territory already inhabited by a non-Jewish population.[5] It was necessary from that point that the "colonists" of the "Jewish Company" conceived by Theodor Herzl establish their state through the expulsion of the indigenous inhabitants, before being able to show themselves generous toward their eventual hosts: "And if it should occur that men of other creeds and different nationalities come to live amongst us, we should accord them honourable protection and equality before the law. We have learnt toleration in Europe."[6] This tension between the profession of democratic faith and the real colonialist project would characterize the thought of Ben-Gurion, disciple of Herzl and realizer of his project. The founder of the state of Israel could thus affirm, in 1937, that "the Arab inhabitants of Palestine should enjoy all civic and political rights, not only as individuals, but as a national group, just like the Jews" – and then, shortly afterwards, make this statement: "Were I an Arab ... I would rebel even more vigorously, bitterly, and desperately against the immigration that will one day turn Palestine and all its Arab residents over to Jewish rule."[7]

It is well known that, even within the frontiers proposed by the partition plan adopted by the UN in 1947, the "Jewish" state was demographically only 55 per cent Jewish.[8] It would have been very much less so within the frontiers established by the 1948 war (650,000 Jews to 877,000 Arabs), were it not for the massive exodus of Palestinians (710,000) who fled the terror and the fighting. The reasons for this exodus have been much discussed.[9] Jean-Paul Chagnollaud was completely right, however, when he affirmed that, "in a certain sense, the question hardly has any interest today, for in essence the problem is no longer why they left when one knows perfectly well why they could not return".[10]

By an implacable "ratchet effect", the Palestinian refugees were prevented by the new state from recovering their lands and their homes (which were massively destroyed, entire villages having been razed), prevented from returning (the notion of *return* is, in their case, unchallengeable) to their age old territory, which was now "open to Jewish immigration". On the other hand, the "Law of Return" of 1950 accorded Israeli citizenship automatically to all new immigrants, on condition that they were "Jewish" according to a definition that would be inexorably reduced to the most obtuse religious criteria.[11] Thus, by a cruel irony of history, the Zionist movement – fleeing a hideous European antisemitism that erected religious descent as a criterion of "racial" discrimination – had come to establish a state founded on discrimination based on the same religious criterion, with a more restrictive religious interpretation. And it was by the same inexorable logic that the Zionist "socialists" of Ben-Gurion's party came to make religious instruction compulsory in the schools.[12]

This outcome was fully prefigured in the very idea of the "State of the Jews" (*Der Judenstaat*), the original title of Herzl's book, which became the "Jewish State" in the principal European translations.[13] As many have observed, harking back to the original debate between the nationalist and secular state project of Herzl's "political Zionism", on the one hand, and, on the other, Ahad Ha'Am's "cultural Zionism" – concerned to establish in Palestine a Jewish spiritual homeland incarnating the highest spiritual values of Judaism, without sullying and degrading it through the recourse to arms rendered inevitable by the state project – the mistranslation comes close to the opposite sense. It is justified however by *the doctrinal logic of political Zionism, whose nationalism, from the point that it embraced not only the Yiddish nation,[14] but all the Jews of the planet, became inseparable from the religious reference, the sole common denominator* – not as a system of spiritual values, but in its narrowest discriminatory conception, matched with the traditional obligations and restrictions.

Much irony has been elicited from the striking contrast between the reality of the state of Israel and Herzl's determination, proclaimed in his Zionist manifesto, that the clergy (and the army!) should not "interfere in the administration of the state".[15] But the same Herzl, in the same work, betrayed quite clearly the confessional logic of his approach, when he described the organization of the immigration:

> Each group will have its rabbi, traveling with his congregation ... Local groups will afterwards form voluntarily about their rabbi, and each locality will have its spiritual leader ... They will not need to address special meetings for the purpose; an appeal such as this may be uttered in the synagogue. And thus it must be done. *For we feel our historic affinity only through the faith of our fathers, as we have long ago absorbed the languages of different nations to an ineradicable degree.*[16]

To the convergence between political Zionism and the most traditionalist religious Zionism was added another equally ineluctable convergence.[17] Rereading Herzl's work in 1946, Hannah Arendt stressed how close the "state of mind" of the founder of the Zionist movement was to that of his antisemitic environment, and how much it was inspired by the tradition of German nationalism.[18] This common state of mind in the dominant currents of political Zionism would lead to a convergence on the terrain of armed expansionism between the "socialist" Zionism of a Ben-Gurion and the "Revisionism" of a Jabotinsky – although the former had not hesitated, at the beginning of the 1930s, to compare the latter to fascism and Hitlerism.[19] The politics of power, the *Machtpolitik*, was built into the very logic of the "Jewish State" project as soon as it was decided to establish it in Palestine: it could only be achieved by force, as advocated by the "Revisionists".[20]

In 1946, Judah Magnes – a partisan with Martin Buber of peaceful coexistence between Arabs and Jews in a binational Palestine – noted bitterly that the Zionist movement had de facto adopted Jabotinsky's point of view.[21] Forty years later, Simha Flapan, former leader of Mapam, the party of the Zionist far left, attacking the legend woven by the Labor Party around the historic figure of Ben-Gurion, wrote about him in his posthumous work: "[W]here the Arabs were concerned, he espoused the basic principles of Revisionism: the expansion of the borders, the conquest of Arab areas, and the evacuation of the Arab population."[22]

On the Zionist state – a qualification very much more rigorous than that of the "Jewish" state – one of the most severe verdicts was that expressed, in 1959, by a prominent figure of the American Jewish community, James P. Warburg:

> Nothing could be more understandable than the desire of the European Jews, generated by centuries of persecution and fired by the inhuman Nazi atrocities, to escape forever from minority status ... But nothing could be more tragic than to witness the creation of a Jewish state in which the non-Jewish minorities are treated as second-class citizens – in which neither a Jew's Christian wife nor their children could be buried in the same cemetery as their father.
>
> It is one thing to create a much-needed refuge for the persecuted and oppressed. It is quite another thing to create a new chauvinistic nationalism and a state based in part upon medieval theocratic bigotry and in part upon the Nazi-exploited myth of the existence of a Jewish race.[23]

And yet! This semi-religious Zionist state, founded on religious discrimination, is undoubtedly democratic for its inhabitants of Jewish descent. Moreover, the Palestinian Arabs who hold Israeli citizenship, although second-class citizens in many respects, also undoubtedly enjoy more political rights than the inhabitants of the Arab states. We return here to our point of departure: there is not at all an antinomy between formal political democracy and the existence of constitutive discrimination in the definition of the *demos*. From this can be derived the *possibility* of a Zionist ideology of the "Jewish and democratic state", as developed by Ben-Gurion in opposition to the Revisionists.

As to the *plausibility* of this ideology with regard to the egalitarian universalism proclaimed in 1948, it is precisely conditioned by the existence of an assured Jewish majority inside the *demos* – concealing the fact that it has been constituted by the discriminatory denial to the indigenous inhabitants of an elementary right of return. The maintenance of a minority of non-Jewish citizens inside the Israeli *demos* appears, therefore, as the indispensable token, not to say alibi, of Zionist democracy and its proclaimed universalism – on the express condition that this minority remains very much a minority, and cannot put in question the "Jewishness" of the state.

Such is the rationale of the opposition of Ben-Gurion and his disciples to the program of the Zionist right, advocating the extension of the frontiers of the "Jewish" state by the pure and simple annexation of the entire territory of mandatory Palestine, if not the two banks of the Jordan – prepared thus to include a great mass of Arabs and to accommodate itself to political discrimination inside its boundaries, making a nonsense of the myth of the democratic state.[24] "Labor", wrote Simha Flapan, "presents Ben-Gurion's ideas and strategies as the other alternative to Likud's concept of a Greater Israel, pointing out that he totally rejected rule over another people and was unconditionally committed to the preservation of the Jewish and democratic character of the state."[25]

The Mapam leader added this commentary:

> Indeed, the concept of a democratic Jewish society might conceivably provide such an alternative were it free from the impulse toward territorial expansionism – for whatever reason: historical, religious, political or strategic. But the fact is that Ben-Gurion built his political philosophy precisely on these two contradictory elements: a democratic *Jewish* society in the *whole*, or in most, of Palestine.[26]

Indeed, Ben-Gurion did not hide the fact that he only accepted partition out of tactical concerns, on a provisional basis, and that his objective was "Palestine as a whole".[27] The motivation for his expansionism was the necessary space for the original Zionist project of gathering in Palestine the majority of the world's Jews, a project that he always placed above any other consideration. Thus, the disagreement between Jabotinsky's heirs and those of Ben-Gurion was never about the desirable position of the eastern frontier of the Zionist state: all were agreed that it should pass along the Jordan River and the Dead Sea, if only for "security" reasons.[28]

The disagreement concerned instead the way of settling the demographic problem within this framework, so as to preserve the "Jewishness" of the state – the concern of the Labor Party being to preserve at the same time its democratic reputation, a vital question for a state so dependent on foreign aid. It is thus highly significant that the first coalition government grouping, together the Revisionists (represented by Menachem Begin) and the socialists, was formed on the eve of the war of June 1967, and in preparation for it. When the state of Israel was later reunited with the rest of British Mandate Palestine, the divergences between the two Zionist factions recovered all of their salience.

ISRAEL'S POST-1967 DILEMMA AND THE ALLON PLAN

Contrary to what happened nineteen years earlier, and for several reasons – among them undoubtedly the desire not to share the unenviable fate of the 1948 refugees – the great majority of the Palestinian population of the West Bank and Gaza remained in their territory in 1967. The Zionist leaders found themselves confronted with a real dilemma. Having attained their objective of shifting the eastern frontier of their state to the Jordan River, they found themselves with a sizeable Palestinian Arab population under their control. In these conditions, straightforward annexation of the whole of the newly occupied Palestinian territories became impracticable: granting Israeli citizenship to their inhabitants would have imperilled the *Jewish* character of the Zionist state; refusing their citizenship would have put in question its *democratic* character.[29]

By any logic, the only solution that would permit both remaining along the bank of the Jordan River and preserving the "Jewish state", along with its democratic reputation, was to grant to the *areas of Palestinian high population density* (with the exception of East Jerusalem, annexed from the beginning for ideological reasons) the status of *enclaves* within the new frontiers of the state of Israel.[30] It was Yigal Allon, a prominent figure of the Israeli political-military establishment and of the Labor left, who elaborated this concept for a settlement, which became known as the Allon Plan.[31] He presented it to the government of Levi Eshkol, in which he was deputy prime minister, at the beginning of July 1967. It is useful to cite the author of the plan himself to clarify the key factors:

> The territorial solution must respond to three fundamental imperatives:
> a) the historic rights of the people of Israel on the land of Israel;
> b) a state with a *preponderant* Jewish majority on the national level, which is democratic on the political, social and cultural levels;
> c) defensible frontiers.
> ...
> Consequently, if it is necessary to choose between a de facto binational state with more territory and a Jewish state with less territory, I opt for the second eventuality, on condition that it has defensible frontiers.
> The alternatives are pitilessly clear.
> If we held within Israel all the territories of strong Arab density by granting their inhabitants all civic rights, we would no longer have a Jewish state. If we annexed them while refusing these rights to the inhabitants, we would cease to be a democratic society. But we want at the same time a Jewish state – with an Arab minority enjoying equality of rights – and a democratic society in the full sense of the term.[32]

In the light of these imperatives, Allon advocated the definitive acquisition by Israel of a border strip roughly 15 kilometers wide along the Jordan River, stretching west of the Dead Sea to the outskirts of Hebron, as well as the acquisition, in addition to the old city of Jerusalem, of its eastern flank up to the river – so as to reduce the

Palestinian territories of the West Bank to two separate enclaves to the north and the south of the "holy city", linked by a narrow corridor.[33]

This formula, according to Allon, "allows for an Arab solution for the population of the West Bank and leaves a sovereign corridor at its disposition between Ramallah, Jericho and the Allenby Bridge":

> This defense configuration could resist a modern army. It is meant to protect the country, not only from its direct neighbors, but also from the entire region to the east, which extends as far as the Persian Gulf and the Indian Ocean, *a fortiori* since the countries that compose it are equipping themselves massively with ultramodern offensive weapons. It creates also a *hinterland* destined to protect Jerusalem and its environs from the dangers of guerilla warfare, and gives us the possibility of settlement in the semi-deserted areas. I add that the territories that we would return will be demilitarized, and that in installing ourselves on the flank of the population of the West Bank, we will in any case neutralize its offensive potential.[34]

As to Gaza, Allon advocated that it should not be returned to Egypt, but rather attached to the West Bank enclaves, as access to the sea "with rights of circulation, but without creating a corridor", while keeping control of the south of the sector so as to control access to the Egyptian Sinai.

Yigal Allon was in no way motivated by some internationalist or pacifist generosity; his entire past as a nationalist combatant attests to this, as does his own line of argument, faithful to the Zionist tradition of Ben-Gurion.[35] At the time when he formulated his plan – that, is immediately after the 1967 war – the territories concerned had only just been conquered. The Israeli pacifists, the true "doves", proposed that they should be returned almost in their totality in exchange for peace treaties with the Arab states.[36] The Allon Plan envisaged, on the contrary, a prolonged occupation, and a process of annexation by the requisitioning of lands and the implantation of settlements, so as to physically occupy the territory that it sought to acquire definitively.

Fundamentally, *the Allon Plan was thus a plan of colonization and partial annexation*, in the name of "territorial compromise" – unlike the complete annexation advocated by the Zionist right. The debate

between the right and Labor partisans of the Allon Plan was not a matter
of hawks versus doves, but "rather of hawks and vultures", in the words
of the radical internationalist Eli Lobel.[37] But the Allon Plan was very
much more coherent and realistic than the aims of Likud. Having come
to power in 1977, Likud did not dare anyway to carry out its program to
the end, but got bogged down with the subtleties of a project of extra-
territorial Palestinian autonomy that had never convinced anybody.
The Labor Party plan thus ended up as the fundamental, de facto line
of conduct of the Zionist state in the 1967 territories – even under the
Likud, which, despite having amended it in its fashion, nevertheless
strengthened its essential tendencies.[38]

Allon hardly said anything about the ultimate fate of the Palestinian
enclaves, for reasons of elementary tactical prudence. To the extent that
his plan was precisely a long-term one, it was necessary to allow some
time for its implementation, and for the ultimate emergence of an Arab
interlocutor disposed to collaborate with the settlement dictated by
Israel, but nonetheless armed with the authority needed to be credible.[39]
Since the creation of a Palestinian state – that is, an entity enjoying
the attributes of political and military sovereignty – had always been
categorically rejected by the entire Zionist establishment, the three
possibilities envisaged for the enclaves were to reunite them with King
Hussein's Jordan, to federate them with it, or again to constitute them as
an "autonomous entity":

> I will not enter into a debate here on what is known as the
> "Palestinian entity". I am among those who think that historic
> circumstances entail its constitution even if it does not have
> roots plunged deep into the past ... Do not forget above all that
> it was in the name of the Palestinian problem that the Arab states
> unleashed war against us in 1948 ... and that, without its solution,
> one cannot hope for a real peace ...
>
> The king's idea of [Jordanian–Palestinian] federation does
> not in principle obstruct the road of direct negotiations with the
> population of these territories ... From our point of view, there is
> room for negotiations with both.[40]

This well-perceived importance of the Palestinian factor in any credible
settlement would lead successive Israeli governments to search for

Palestinian negotiating partners.[41] In 1977, Allon excluded no hypothesis in this regard, including that of dealing with the PLO if it were to mend its ways. His words have today acquired a premonitory value: "Certainly, if the PLO ceased to be the PLO, we could cease to consider it as such. Or if the tiger transformed itself into a horse, we could mount it. At that moment, we would get front-page headlines in our favor."[42]

THE WASHINGTON ACCORDS

The front-page headlines were certainly there on 13 September 1993. The media affected total surprise, as if a new miracle had just come to pass in relation to a land that, to be sure, had witnessed many others. Only the discordant voices of some critics of the accords who were well acquainted with the situation, like Edward Said, Noam Chomsky, and Meron Benvenisti, pointed out that the accords signed on the White House lawn amounted to an updated version of the Allon Plan.[43]

What, then, did the accords actually say?

It is undeniable that the texts made public – the letters, the Declaration of Principles and its four Annexes, as well as its Agreed Minutes – fit in perfectly with the broad outline of the plan formulated in 1967.[44] None of the measures in the Washington Accords contradict in any way the program set in motion by the Israeli Labor Party in relation to the West Bank and Gaza more than a quarter of a century before. This can easily be seen by examining some key points of these documents (without entering into every aspect of the question, notably the economic ones).[45]

Let us begin with what has been perceived as the most spectacular event – namely, "mutual recognition". Yasser Arafat's letter, addressed to the Israeli prime minister, says the following: "The PLO recognizes the right of the State of Israel to exist in peace and security", and "accepts U.N. Security Council Resolutions 242 and 338". The most important of these resolutions, 242 (November 1967), which the State of Israel has accepted from the beginning, had been rejected by the PLO for a long time, because it made no mention of the right of the Palestinians to return or to self-determination, and ratified the principle of "secure borders", interpreted by the Israelis as justifying their redrawing of borders and their territorial demands.[46] In exchange for this concession, the PLO obtained no mention of the right of the Palestinians to self-determination or to return – one finds only the very vague formula of "legitimate rights".

The Arafat letter affirms that "the PLO renounces the use of terrorism and other acts of violence and will assume responsibility over all PLO elements and personnel in order to assure their compliance, prevent violations and discipline violators". Because it applied only to the personnel of the PLO, this repudiation of violence and the commitment to repress it in the face of a continuing occupation was not enough for the Israeli government. A second letter, addressed to the Norwegian minister Holst and annexed to the first, stated: "the PLO encourages and calls upon the Palestinian people in the West Bank and Gaza Strip to take part in the steps leading to the normalization of life, rejecting violence and terrorism".

Through the first affirmation of his letter to Yitzhak Rabin, Arafat repudiated the PLO's basic program (the liberation of Palestine). Logically enough, he concluded that "those articles of the Palestinian Covenant which deny Israel's right to exist and the provisions of the Covenant which are inconsistent with the commitments of this letter are now inoperative and no longer valid". In reality, this amounted to saying that the Covenant itself was no longer valid. The tiger had indeed transformed itself into a horse; it could now be mounted. Rabin's letter, for its part, addresses itself to the Norwegian minister, and not to Arafat – "in light of the PLO commitments ... the Government of Israel has decided to recognize the PLO as the representative of the Palestinian people" – without any mention of rights.

The Declaration of Principles aimed

> to establish a Palestinian Interim Self-Government Authority, the elected Council for the Palestinian people in the West Bank and the Gaza Strip, for a transitional period not exceeding five years, leading to a permanent settlement based on Security Council Resolutions 242 and 338. (art. 1)

The Palestinian "Self-Government" Authority would exercise its prerogatives in the territories from which the Israeli army will choose to withdraw. The accords specify that these territories will be determined according to the principle of the withdrawal from the territories with a strong Arab population density, which is at the heart of the Allon Plan:

> [A] redeployment of Israeli military forces in the West Bank and the Gaza Strip will take place ... In redeploying its military forces, Israel will be guided by the principle that [this should be done] outside populated areas. (art. 13)

Of course, East Jerusalem, officially annexed by Israel since 1967, is not covered.[47] Moreover, not only does the accord not envisage the dismantling of any settlements, but it guarantees to the settlers and other Israelis a regime of extraterritorial rights under which they will not come under the jurisdiction of the Palestinian Authority on its own territory. The Authority is responsible only for controlling Palestinians, and this by means of its police. It will have no army, its external defense being assured by Israel (*sic*) whose army can circulate freely in the "Self-Government" territory.[48]

> In order to guarantee public order and internal security for the Palestinians of the West Bank and Gaza Strip, the Council will establish a strong police force, while Israel will continue to carry the responsibility for defending against external threats, as well as the responsibility for overall security of Israelis for the purpose of safeguarding their internal security and public order. (art. 8)

The first phase of the application of the accords affects the Gaza Strip and the region of Jericho, and it is stipulated in the Agreed Minutes "that, subsequent to the Israeli withdrawal, Israel will continue to be responsible for external security, and for internal security and public order of settlements and Israelis. Israeli military forces and civilians may continue to use roads freely within the Gaza Strip and the Jericho area" (Annex 2).

Thus, the general framework envisaged by the Washington accords is very much that of the Allon Plan: Israeli withdrawal from the populated Arab areas, except for East Jerusalem, and redeployment in the rest of the Palestinian territories occupied in 1967, with the maintenance of the settlements; the constitution of the evacuated enclaves as an autonomous Palestinian entity without full state powers, and without military means other than those necessary for internal repression; Israeli control of access to these enclaves, in particular the crossing points to Egypt and Jordan (confirmed by the accords signed later in Cairo).

Admittedly, these are for the moment interim arrangements, in expectation of a permanent status that is to be defined within five years at the latest. But this, like the interim settlement, will depend on a balance of forces – which speaks for itself. One would really have to believe in miracles to imagine that, at the end of five years of implementation of the framework envisaged by the Allon Plan – and it was obvious during the negotiations on Gaza and Jericho that the Israeli regime had no intention of giving anybody any presents – the Zionist state, out of sheer charity, would decide to evacuate the rest of Gaza and the West Bank, including East Jerusalem, to allow the creation of an "independent and sovereign" Palestinian state. This is, nonetheless, what Arafat is promising to anyone prepared to believe him. In reality, if the PLO ever manages to obtain even the dismantling of some of the settlements that the Israeli government considers to be "strategic" (that is, those which fall outside the framework of the Allon Plan), it should count itself lucky.

Meron Benvenisti, a well-known Israeli specialist on the 1967 territories, states that the PLO negotiators have already accepted two principles: "no Israeli settlement will be evacuated" and "settlement blocs – constituting a continuous expanse – will be under Israeli authority".[49] According to Benvenisti, "these settlement blocs, which include the majority of the existing settlements, will be hooked up to Israel by far-reaching road networks, along which Israel will possess the authority to perform autonomous security activities". They will divide the West Bank into "three cantons linked to each other by narrow corridors". Moreover, "the road network serving these settlement blocs will turn the Palestinian cantons into a puzzle that will not permit the [Palestinian] administration any real authority". The author concludes that the Palestinians will not be able to contest these principles, because they have already accepted them.

What is more, the peace treaty currently being negotiated between Israel and Jordan envisages agreement on a border between the two states running along the Jordan River and the Dead Sea. This treaty could therefore remove all international legitimacy from the demand for Israeli withdrawal from the whole of the West Bank, which was under Jordanian sovereignty before June 1967. The Palestinian entity being new, its frontiers with the state of Israel remain to be defined, as the Declaration of Principles stipulates.

The Allon Plan is thus well on the way to getting the consecration it expected: international and Arab recognition of the Israeli fait accompli in the West Bank and Gaza; peace in exchange for a "territorial compromise" allowing Israel to exercise direct or semi-direct sovereignty over the whole of British Mandate Palestine; the solution – some would say the liquidation – of the Palestinian problem, at little cost, and the preservation of the "Jewish and democratic state", with yet more favorable front-page headlines.

"PEACE OF THE BRAVE" OR SURRENDER?

Nonetheless, the historic context in which these accords have been concluded gives a specific meaning to the role allotted to Yasser Arafat's PLO – a meaning that was no more than a secondary consideration for Yigal Allon. For Allon, the main argument was demographic, in relation to the composition of the Israeli population. True, it did not escape the clear-sighted Zionist strategist that controlling the Arab population of the 1967 territories could ultimately pose a problem.[50] But the fact is that, until 1987 – that is, until the outbreak of the Palestinian Intifada – the tensions inside these territories had been kept at an acceptable level for the Israeli occupier.[51]

The main problem during the elaboration of the Allon Plan was posed by the Palestinians in exile, organized by the PLO, as well as by "Arab rejection", which remained steadfast in the wake of the Six-Day War.[52] The Labor Party's program of "territorial compromise" appeared, at best, as the policy of an active waiting game. Time played in favor of Israel and its territorial strategy of requisitions and settlements, faced with the impotent Arab demand for the complete restoration of the territories occupied in 1967. When King Hussein crushed the Palestinian armed movement in Jordan in 1970–71, he became a potentially valuable partner for Labor's project, having largely proved himself in the matter of control of his subjects. It was then that he formulated his project of the "United Arab Kingdom", involving his recovery of the West Bank as a federated province. However, the Arab context hardly permitted him to enter into a separate peace with the Zionist state on its own conditions – the only option that Israel ever offered to its neighbors.

The affair became more complicated when the Jordanian monarch found himself still more isolated following the 1973 war, in which he did not take part. The PLO had succeeded in reconstituting its quasi-state in Lebanon, and replaced its initial nationalist maximalism with the program of the independent Palestinian state in the West Bank and Gaza.[53] The Rabat summit of Arab heads of state in 1974 approved this new program of the Palestinian leadership, and recognized it as "sole legitimate representative of the Palestinian people". The Israeli–Arab negotiations (International Conference at Geneva, bilateral military negotiations), which followed the Yom Kippur/Ramadan War, had raised the perspective of a "negotiated settlement", but then became bogged down. The second attempt to crush the PLO degenerated into a fifteen-year war in Lebanon.

The coming to power of Likud in Israel in 1977 ruled out any prospect of a comprehensive settlement. It was out of the question that the Zionist right would envisage any kind of compromise on the Golan Heights or the Palestinian territories. Only the Sinai lost its political mystique; the neutralization of the Egyptian front under a US guarantee could in fact strengthen Likud's annexationist ambitions. Thus, the defection of Anwar Sadat led to a separate peace and the restoration to Egypt of this vast desert expanse, except for the Gaza Strip. Israeli preconditions – demilitarization and alert mechanisms under US control – ensured perfect security for this enormous "buffer zone". Likud proceeded officially to annex the Golan, which it emptied in 1967 of most of its Arab population; demographic considerations prevented them from doing the same in "Judea and Samaria" and Gaza.

The Zionist right nonetheless worked toward annexation: intensification and extension of the settlement process; pressures of every kind for a creeping expulsion of the indigenous inhabitants; a project of extra-territorial Palestinian self-government and attempts to set up a network of collaborators to this end; and efforts to increase the flow of Jewish immigration to Israel, so as to consolidate the Jewish demographic majority in the whole of Palestine. However, the 1982 invasion of Lebanon discredited Likud and led to worsened relations between Israel and its US godfather. This war nonetheless considerably weakened the PLO, just as the peace with Egypt had opened the road to the Israeli–Arab settlement.

Having left Lebanon, Yasser Arafat had praised Ronald Reagan's policies, reconciled himself with King Hussein, and quickly fallen out with Syria. After his second departure from Lebanon by sea (1983), he went to Cairo, thus breaking the official Arab boycott of Egypt. Then, in 1985, he concluded an agreement with the Jordanian monarch for common participation in negotiations with Israel, provoking dissent on the part of the PLO left-wing factions. The conditions for a settlement on the Jordanian–Palestinian front seemed to be ripening rapidly on the Arab side.

Having returned to power in the context of a coalition government with Likud, the Israeli Labor Party led by Shimon Peres had made overtures to King Hussein. Hussein increased his pressure on the PLO to accelerate the process, and believed himself strong enough to go forward without it. At the 1987 Arab summit in Baghdad the PLO was more marginalized than it had ever been. But at the end of this same year the Intifada exploded in Gaza and the West Bank, overturning fundamental aspects of the situation. For the first time in twenty years, the Palestinians of the interior became uncontrollable, and placed Israel in an extremely embarrassing situation. King Hussein, acknowledging his defeat, officially announced the abandonment of his claim to the West Bank. The PLO found itself once more in a position of strength.

Shimon Peres waged his electoral campaign in 1988 under the slogan of "territorial compromise", with an open invitation to the PLO to negotiate with Israel.[54] But he was defeated, while the Palestinian leadership, on its side, bent itself to the requirements of negotiations with the United States, being unable to negotiate with a Likud-dominated Israeli government. The situation had once more became bogged down, despite US efforts, when the Gulf crisis blew up. By considerably reinforcing the weight of the United States in regional politics, the 1991 war opened the road to the Peace Conference inaugurated in Madrid, including for the first time direct negotiations between the Israeli government and a delegation officially sponsored by the PLO.

For the Likud, led by Yitzhak Shamir, it was just a matter of temporizing so as to obtain the US green light for a $10 billion loan. Israel needed this sum to be able to absorb the million Jewish immigrants expected to arrive as a consequence of the collapse of the USSR. For Shamir, this heaven-sent immigration would allow the annexation of the 1967 territories without any demographic worries. But the Bush administration was not stupid. It kept in hand its means of financial pressure, which provided a key argument in the victorious electoral campaign of the Israeli Labor Party in 1992 under the leadership of Yitzhak Rabin.

Meanwhile, the traditional forms of struggle of the Intifada were running out of steam, giving way to Palestinian radicalization marked by the irresistible rise of the Islamic-fundamentalist Hamas movement and a multiplication of the violent actions it advocated. These attacks succeeded in seriously disturbing the Israeli sense of security on both sides of the 1967 border. Rabin first tried to repress the Palestinian fundamentalists by expelling several hundred of them to Lebanon in December 1992. But the operation boomeranged, considerably strengthening the prestige of Hamas.

Yet Rabin was convinced, with good reason, that the Palestinians of the interior – or those of them among the Palestinian delegation at the Peace Conference – under the pressure of a population in the process of radicalization, were not disposed to bend themselves to the demands of the Allon Plan, and still less to commit themselves to repress the struggle of the fundamentalists. Only the Palestinian bureaucracy of the PLO in exile would be prepared to meet these conditions – all the more so because it was on the verge of bankruptcy, the Arab oil monarchies having ceased to finance it because of its favorable attitude toward Iraq during the Gulf crisis. This was why Rabin and Peres decided to engage in direct secret negotiations with Arafat, who did not ask for anything more. These negotiations would quickly lead to the Washington Accords.

This summary of the historic context allows us to clarify the specific role allotted to the PLO in the current implementation of the final phase of the Allon Plan. The Intifada, and then the expansion of Hamas and its violent struggle in the interior (whereas the armed Palestinian exile organizations had long since ceased to threaten Israeli security seriously), have given a capital importance to a function that seemed relatively minor during the first twenty years of Israeli occupation of the West Bank and Gaza: the maintenance of order in these territories and the repression of the armed anti-Zionist struggle. The bet of the Israeli

Labor Party is that Arafat and his men are best suited to carry out this task.

This explains, in particular, the novel turn made by the Rabin government in relation to what one could call the Zionist law of the "non-return" of Palestinians in exile. Rather than negotiating with the Palestinians of the interior about what was supposed to be their self-government, the Zionist regime has decided the fate of the 1967 territories with a small group of leaders based in Tunis, behind the backs of the delegates from the interior. It accepted that a part of the PLO bureaucracy – this little state apparatus in exile – could install itself in the West Bank and Gaza to be responsible for the local population. In addition, it agreed that some thousands of exiled Palestinians, soldiers of the units of the very regular Palestine Liberation Army, would accompany the bureaucracy of the PLO to form the backbone of the Palestinian police force.[55]

The smallest details concerning "the Palestinian authority" are moreover subject to the agreement of the Israeli government: "the structure of the Council, the number of its members", its legislative and executive authority (article 7), as well as "the system of elections", and even "rules and regulations regarding election campaign" (Annex I). The meaning of this tight control of the Palestinian electoral procedure was obvious to Elias Sanbar: "Israel, a democratic state for its own citizens, is betting on an authoritarian Palestinian self-government that will muzzle its own opposition and avoid any surprise effect resulting from an always possible change of mind on the part of Palestinian public opinion."[56]

If, moreover, the Rabin government has chosen to begin with "Gaza-Jericho first", it is obviously so as to test in the powder keg of Gaza, bastion of Palestinian radicalism, the PLO's real capacity to master the situation and repress the anti-Zionist struggle – a struggle that Hamas and its allies have of course no intention of halting voluntarily.[57] The PLO must prove its repressive capacities in Gaza before being allowed to run other enclaves on the West Bank. If not, as Rabin has unceasingly stated, the accords will be abrogated. Noam Chomsky only expressed the feeling of many observers when he said, alluding to a statement by the Israeli prime minister: "Yitzhak Rabin is obviously right: the Palestinian mercenaries can govern the population without fearing recourse to the Supreme Court ... or the beautiful souls of every kind."[58]

***

In the light of the Zionist strategy defined by the Allon Plan and the mission of repressing the anti-Zionist struggle devolved to the PLO, the Israeli-Arab peace takes on a very different appearance to that presented by the dominant idyllic presentation. Rather than a "peace of the brave" and reconciliation between peoples, it appears as a peace between governments, concluded essentially on the conditions laid down by the Israeli victor – a Pax Sionista, one could say. From the point of view of the Arab peoples who have been receptive for several decades to nationalist discourse, today exploited by the Muslim fundamentalists, this peace has every chance of being perceived as surrender: the culmination of America's crushing of Iraq.[59]

But is this not the case? Is there any possible doubt about the direct link between the Gulf War and the process of settling the Israeli-Arab conflict, inaugurated by George Bush at Madrid and sealed by Bill Clinton in Washington? How can one not see in the current arrangements the establishment of the "New Arab Order" announced as the local expression of the "New World Order"? The cycle that began in 1947 with the Arabs' rejection of the award to the "Jewish state" of half of Palestine is concluding today with Arab recognition of this same state, now in control of all of Palestine – without any hope of return for the majority of its original inhabitants.

This is what Yigal Allon called "acceptance of reality".[60] When this acceptance follows forty-five years of rejection of this same reality because of its injustice, it amounts to capitulation. Lucid to the end, Allon knew that this would not amount to a "revolution in people's hearts". Such a revolution is not yet on the agenda – far from it. But Israel and the United States will have succeeded in displacing the tension from the confrontation between the Zionist state and its Arab neighbors, toward the internal confrontation in the Arab countries between states and popular opposition movements. So long as this conflict is not definitively resolved, the peace between governments will rest on shaky ground.

NOTES

1   The author wishes to thank Bernard Gibbons in London, who has kindly translated this article into English; Peter Drucker in Amsterdam, who edited the American version; and Tikva Honig-Parnass in Jerusalem and Michael Löwy in Paris, who have read the first draft and given their friendly suggestions. However, none of the friends mentioned here bears any responsibility for the views expressed in this article.

2   "We hold these Truths to be self-evident, that all Men are created equal, that they are endowed by their Creator with certain unalienable Rights, that among these are Life, Liberty, and the Pursuit of Happiness", proclaimed the United States Declaration of Independence in 1776. Blacks and Indians were de facto excluded from the ranks of men, by "the white, or European, the MAN pre-eminently so called" (Alexis De Tocqueville, *Democracy in America*).

3   The universalism–particularism antithesis belongs to the vocabulary of Christian theology. The affinities between the universalist doctrine of Redemption and that of the rights of the human person are, moreover, to be counted among the contributions of Christianity to political humanism.

4   Florence Gauthier vigorously stressed this point at the time of the bicentennial of the 1789 revolution. See Gauthier, "Le droit naturel en révolution", in Étienne Balibar et al., *Permanences de la Révolution*, Paris: La Brèche, 1989.

5   "Wanting to create a purely Jewish, or predominantly Jewish, state in an Arab Palestine in the twentieth century could not help but lead to a colonial-type situation and to the development (completely normal sociologically speaking) of a racist state of mind, and in the final analysis to a military confrontation between the two ethnic groups." Maxime Rodinson, *Israel: A Colonial-Settler State?*, New York: Monad, 1973, p. 77.

6   Theodor Herzl, *The Jewish State: An Attempt at a Modern Solution of the Jewish Question*, London: H. Pordes, 1972, p. 71. "We should there [in Palestine] form a portion of the rampart of Europe against Asia, an outpost of civilisation as opposed to barbarism" (p. 30). The reference to colonists is on p. 46.

7   Shabtai Teveth, *Ben-Gurion: The Burning Ground, 1886–1948*, Boston: Houghton Mifflin, 1987, pp. 542, 544. Rather than rehabilitating the Zionist far right, one discredits still more its democratic professions of faith in recalling, as Alain Dieckhoff does, that "the various proclamations by the Irgun [the Zionist Revisionist armed organization] always mentioned, like that published in July 1946, that the aim of the political struggle was to found an independent democratic society where equality of rights would be guaranteed for all whatever their origin and their belief." Dieckhoff, *The Invention of a Nation: Zionist Thought and the Making of Modern Israel*, trans. Jonathan Derrick, London: Hurst, 2003, p. 229. Interestingly, the English translation of Dieckhoff's book published in 2003 omitted the sentence that followed in the original French version: "It even made reference to drawing up a constitution based on the United States Declaration of Independence." Dieckhoff, *L'invention d'une nation: Israël et la modernité politique*, Paris: Gallimard, 1993, p. 264.

8   Nearly 55 per cent of the territory of British Mandate Palestine was assigned to the "Jewish state", though the Jewish residents of this territory only constituted one-third of its total population. Even allowing that all the residents – newly arrived immigrants, like indigenous inhabitants – would have enjoyed equal rights to sovereignty in the territory, the partition plan was manifestly iniquitous. In effect, the UN took up the Zionist thesis of the right of the Diaspora Jews to sovereignty in Palestine. "The authors of this partition saw this demographic relationship in a dynamic perspective: the expected immigration would very quickly allow the constitution of a Jewish majority." Jean-Paul Chagnollaud, "Palestine: l'enjeu démographique", in *Revue d'études palestiniennes* 7 (Paris, Spring 1983), pp. 27–9.

The victors in World War II, Truman's United States in particular, sought to rid themselves of the troublesome burden of the survivors of the Holocaust by diverting them to Palestine, in concert with the Zionist movement. Recall the vehemence with which the Zionists had previously opposed the Roosevelt plan to admit the refugees to other countries, including the United States. See Morris Ernst, *So Far So Good*, New York: Harper, 1948, and Alan Taylor, *Prelude to Israel*, New York: Philosophical Library, 1959. During the Holocaust, Roosevelt himself had failed to come to the aid of the Jews of Europe, as has been shown in David Wyman, *The Abandonment of the Jews: America and the Holocaust, 1941–1945*, New York: Pantheon, 1984. The same author admits, however, although in an apologetic fashion, that the Zionists deliberately chose to privilege their Palestinian project to the detriment of saving the Jews of Europe (pp. 175–7).

This was Ben-Gurion's choice, as his biographer Shabtai Teveth explains: "In spite of the certainty that genocide was being carried out, the JAE [Jewish Agency Executive, presided over by Ben-Gurion] did not deviate appreciably from its routine ... Two facts can be definitively stated: Ben-Gurion did not put the rescue effort above Zionist politics, and he did not regard it as a principal task demanding his personal leadership". *Ben-Gurion*, p. 848. Teveth attributes this attitude to what he called a "philosophy of the beneficial disaster" (p. 850), quoting Ben-Gurion, who said: "The harsher the affliction, the greater the strength of Zionism" (ibid.). In this respect, Ben-Gurion was only taking after his inspirer, Theodor Herzl, who stated in the prologue to his book-manifesto: "the present scheme ... includes the employment of an existent propelling force ... And what is our propelling force? The misery of the Jews." Herzl, *Jewish State*, p. 8.

Recently, the Zionist movement has again been inciting the departure of the Jewish population of the former USSR, and has sought to channel them toward Israel, contrary to the wish of the great majority of emigrants to go to North America. "Mr. Shamir, the Israeli prime minister, complained that the [US] administration offered them the freedom to choose their country of destination. This free choice, in effect, is unfavorable to Israel. Ninety per cent of Soviet Jews prefer to go to the United States." *Le Monde*, Paris, 4 October 1989.

9   This debate is today dominated by the work of the Israeli historian Benny Morris, *The Birth of the Palestinian Refugee Problem, 1947–1949*, Cambridge: Cambridge University Press, 1987.

10   Chagnollaud, "Palestine: l'enjeu démographique", p. 31.

11   On the odd debates in Israel about the definition of Jewish identity, see Akiva Orr, *The UnJewish State: The Politics of Jewish Identity in Israel*, London: Ithaca, 1981. See also on this subject, Nathan Weinstock, *Le Sionisme contre Israël*, Paris: Maspero, 1969, pp. 310–19.

12   This was true to the point that the teaching of the Jewish religion is even imposed on Arabs: "At the end of his studies, the Arab high school student knows much more of the history of the Jewish people than that of the Arabs. The Koran is less studied than the Torah." Doris Bensimon and Eglal Errera, *Israéliens: Des Juifs et des Arabes*, Brussels: Complexe, 1989, p. 443.

13   See the "Note" by Claude Klein preluding to his new French translation of Herzl's manifesto, *L'État des Juifs*, Paris: La Découverte, 1990, pp. 5–12.

14   "In fact, there is an identity between the emergence of Yiddish, that is its passage, or its *promotion*, from the status of 'jargon' to that of language, and the appearance of Jewish national sentiment", wrote Claude Klein (p. 135) in his excellent *Essai sur le sionisme*, published as an appendix to his translation of Herzl – ibid., pp. 117–86.

15   Herzl, *Jewish State*, p. 71.

16   Ibid., p. 54. The phrase that I stressed here conceals, and for good reason, the specificity of Yiddish, which was spoken by the overwhelming majority of Jews in Central and Eastern Europe.

In Dieckhoff's *Invention of a Nation* – a brilliant work, though not free from ambiguities and contradictions in his attempt to stress the "political modernity" of Zionism – the author stumbles in explaining the patent inadequacy of this ideology so far as secularism is concerned. He attributes this inadequacy principally to the persistence in Zionism of an "ardent longing for community life" (p. 96) – a quasi-tautological explanation. The author shows nonetheless how this inadequacy is inherent to the Zionist doctrine of the "Jewish nation", to the "invention" of which his book is devoted *without for all that ever questioning the postulate*. Indeed, only the pan-Jewish postulate explains why "the religious criterion was in the last resort the only one that could precisely define the contours of the Jewish nation, all the other parameters – cultural, subjective, etc. – being too vague or inapplicable" (p. 131). And it was the insufficiency of this same criterion to cement a nationalism which impelled Zionism to "invent" a veritable new nation, the *Israeli nation* (which Dieckhoff does not even mention), founded on a new-old language – modern Hebrew – and on the destruction, for the purposes of assimilation, of the original national particularities of the immigrants, in the first place the Yiddish language.

Thus, one can understand the paradox of Zionist nationalism, at the same time anti-assimilationist and strongly assimilationist, which considered the French model of national integration "unsuitable when applied to the detriment [*sic*] of the Jews (as in France in 1789), but perfectly valid when it enabled the Jews to rediscover a collective substratum." (p. 99). Perhaps one can thus keep in mind the fact that "Zionism also included an element of protest against, even rejection of republican modernity which had assumed for the Jews the form of civic emancipation and integration in the host societies" (p. 73).

17 The convergence between religious and political Zionism has been reflected, since Herzl, by the alliance between the two currents inside the World Zionist Organization.

18 Hannah Arendt, "The Jewish State: Fifty Years After – Where Have Herzl's Politics Led?", in Gary Smith, ed., *Zionism – The Dream and the Reality: A Jewish Critique*, New York: Barnes & Noble, 1974, pp. 67–80.

19 See Teveth, *Ben-Gurion* – Chapter 26 in particular. The Ben-Gurion–Jabotinsky meetings and their 1934 agreement (halted by the opposition of the Zionist left) were the occasion for the two men to note their "like-mindedness" (Teveth, *Ben-Gurion*, Chapter 29, p. 482). It was Ben-Gurion's Rafi that insisted in 1967 on including Menachem Begin's Gahal in the government of national unity (see note 36, below). On the convergence between Ben-Gurion and Jabotinsky–Begin, see Mitchell Cohen, *Zion and State: Nation, Class and the Shaping of Modern Israel*, New York: Basil Blackwell, 1987.

20 This is eloquently explained by Alain Dieckhoff:

> In all this an essential question arose: was building a Jewish national home compatible with scrupulous respect for democratic rules? Jabotinsky's reply was unhesitatingly negative, for an obvious reason. If the British Mandatory power applied the democratic (i.e. majority rule) principle in its full rigor, political power would automatically go to the Arabs, the largest community in numbers, and they would make haste to ban Jewish immigration and put a stop to consolidation of the socio-political infrastructure of the Yishuv [the Jewish community in Palestine]. So the national objective required non-application of the majority rule principle ... As usual Jabotinsky proclaimed without unnecessary flourishes the cold facts on which his left-wing opponents preferred to maintain hypocritical silence." (*Invention of a Nation*, p. 182)

Astonishingly, the same author shortly afterwards takes as good coin the democratic proclamations of the Irgun (see note 7, above): he uses them as an argument to refute the anathemas hurled against this organization by Hannah Arendt, who characterized it as terroristic and chauvinist, similar to fascism and Nazism. One of the main ambiguities of Dieckhoff's work, moreover, is his attempt to absolve Jabotinsky of the accusation of fascism (to be distinguished from any comparison to Nazism, which would be excessive certainly in his personal case, although justified for some of his comrades). The main argument invoked by the author is the proclaimed "liberalism" of the founder of Revisionism, which supposes an antinomy between economic liberalism and Mussolini's fascism (a debatable postulate: see Cohen, *Zion and State*, pp. 170–4). Moreover, Dieckhoff obscures the full extent of the relationship between Jabotinsky and fascist Italy, which he shunts aside later in a few lines (*Invention of a Nation*, pp. 242–3). As to the alleged "contempt" held by Jabotinsky for the cult of the Führer and the Duce (p. 209), anybody familiar with the trajectory of the "Rosh Betar" can judge its worth.

21 Judah Magnes, "A Solution through Force?", in Smith, *Zionism*, pp. 109–18.

22 Simha Flapan, *The Birth of Israel: Myths and Realities*, New York: Pantheon, 1987, p. 37.

23   The first paragraph alludes to the case of the burial of Joseph Steinberg, son of a Jewish father and a Christian mother, which made the news in 1958. Quoted in Smith, *Zionism*, p. 131.

24   In the sense Élise Marientras deploys in *Les mythes fondateurs de la nation américaine*, Brussels: Éditions Complexe, 1992. Moreover, the founding myths of the Israeli nation clearly imitate US founding myths, to the point that one could detect a narcissistic dimension in the mutual admiration between the two nations.

25   Flapan, *Birth of Israel*, p. 234.

26   Ibid., p. 236. Emphases in original.

27   See Teveth, *Ben-Gurion*, Chapters 34 and 35, as well as p. 853. Chaim Weizmann shared the same opinion – see Norman Rose, *Chaim Weizmann: A Biography*, New York: Viking, 1986, pp. 320–30). The aim was, he said, "to get a fulcrum on which to place a lever ... leaving the problems of expansion and extension to future generations" (p. 323).

28   To the argument of *Lebensraum* and the references to the Bible, there was added, after 1949, the security, or "strategic" motivation which predominated in the eyes of the Israeli political-military establishment, and whose key argument turned upon the narrowness of the strip of territory between the Mediterranean and the old Jordanian frontier (the "Green Line"), where the majority of Israelis lived.

29   Saul Friedländer has summed up the concerns of the Ashkenazi Labor establishment with admirable frankness:

> Faced with the presence of a vast Arab population inside Israel, one can conceive the reinforcement of Jewish extremist tendencies inspired as much by economic as by religious or national motives, to demand the expulsion of all the Arabs or the application of an "apartheid" regime. If these elements succeeded in imposing themselves, the Jewish state would be cut off from the world and the Jews of the Diaspora themselves. Finally, if it is probable that in contact with a vast Arab population the "Oriental" Jews would tend to integrate themselves more rapidly inside the "western" population to distinguish themselves from the Arabs, it is not entirely excluded that the poorest elements among them would be attracted by the Arab proletariat on both the social and cultural levels. The Arab population could then become an active element in the disintegration of Jewish society. (Saul Friedländer, *Réflexions sur l'avenir d'Israël*, Paris: Seuil, 1969, p. 146).

30   As this essay is devoted to the solution that finally imposed itself, this is not the place to go into the different points of view expressed, in Israel, in the debate on the fate of the territories occupied in 1967. On this subject, see, for the immediate post-1967 debate, Éli Lobel, "Palestine and the Jews", in Ahmad El Kodsy and Eli Lobel, *The Arab World and Israel*, trans. Brian Pearce and Alfred Ehrenfeld, New York: Monthly Review, 1970, pp. 63–137; Peretz Merhav, *The Israeli Left: History, Problems*, San Diego: A.S. Barnes/London: Tantivy Press, 1980, Chapters 24 and 25. For a review of the more recent debates, see Louis-Jean Duclos, "La question des frontières orientales d'Israël", in *Revue d'études palestiniennes* 9 (Autumn 1983), pp. 17–31.

Moreover, since this article deals with the Israeli–Palestinian settlement, I have not gone into the debates concerning the non-Palestinian Arab-occupied territories.

31 See Yigal Allon, *Israël: la lutte pour l'espoir*, Paris: Stock, 1977. The Allon Plan met with the approval of the United States and, remarkably, of François Mitterrand (see the extracts from Yeruham Cohen's book in Hebrew on *The Allon Plan*, reproduced in the appendix to the preceding book, pp. 243–7). Allon died in 1978.

32 Allon, *Israël*, pp. 180, 184. Emphasis in original.

33 For a detailed description of the Allon Plan, see Chagnollaud, "Palestine: l'enjeu démographique", and Alain Dieckhoff, *Les Espaces d'Israël*, Paris: FNSP, 1989, pp. 28–33. The Likud in turn divided the northern enclave (Samaria) into two sections. This is what Dieckhoff calls a *"strategy of segmentation* of the territory and of demarcation between human groups" (p. 79). Emphasis in original.

34 Allon, *Israël*, p. 189.

35 Allon was already in 1948 a partisan of the conquest of the whole of Palestine up to the Jordan River, as he himself recalled: "I say it openly: I disagreed with the way in which the war ended ... I was already convinced that we should go as far as the Judean desert and the Jordan to create the conditions of a stable defense ... while finding a solution to the problem of the Arab population" (*Israël*, p. 37). Allon had certainly conceived this "solution" well before presenting it to the Israeli cabinet. In 1967, he was the leader of Ahdut Haavodah ("Unity of Labor"), which laid claim to the whole of Palestine, as well as of the Hakibbutz Hameuhad movement, which pioneered the creation of strategic settlements in the aftermath of the "Six-Day War". It is also significant that he was in charge of the Ministry of Absorption of Immigration from 1967 to 1969.

36 See Merhav, *Israeli Left*. In the debate that raged inside the Labor Party in 1969, Allon's faction, Ahdut Haavodah, allied itself to Rafi, the rightist faction led by Moshe Dayan and Shimon Peres, against the "doves" of the party (Abba Eban and Pinhas Sapir, allied to Mapam).

37 Lobel, "Palestine and the Jews", p. 85. Subsequently, the drift to the right of Israeli society revealed by the electoral victory of the Likud would make Allon appear a "dove". Simha Flapan, the former leader of Mapam, could not fall victim to this optical illusion. In his posthumous work, he recalled that "the first settlements in the West Bank were constructed at the instigation of Yigal Allon", and that "it was again Allon who gave his agreement to the attempts of the fundamentalist rabbi Moshe Levinger to establish a Jewish community in the heart of Arab Hebron" (*Birth of Israel*, p. 239). One of the Hebron settlers carried out the massacre in the Tomb of the Patriarchs/Mosque of Ibrahim in February 1994.

38 Alain Dieckhoff gives a remarkable analysis of this process of partial annexation and the strategies that underlie it in his already cited work, *Les Espaces d'Israël*. See also Michel Foucher, "L''intersection' cisjordanienne", in *Maghreb-Machrek* 108 (Paris, April 1985), pp. 38–59.

39 "Peace will not come as a result of a 'revolution of hearts' among them [the Arabs], but as the corollary of the balance of forces and cold political realism. It will be

lucidity and the acceptance of reality which will lead them to reconciliation, negotiation and peace." Allon, *Israël*, p. 179.

40   Ibid., p. 257 – from a speech made by Allon to the Central Committee of the Israeli Labor Party in 1972, reproduced as an appendix to the book.

41   Here again, it is important not to be taken in by appearances. The stress placed on the distinction between the Palestinian West Bank and the Jordanian kingdom is not in itself indicative of the attitude of a "dove". Initially, it was the right wing of the Labor Party – Dayan and Peres, in particular – who rejected the idea of returning it to Jordan, whereas the left defended the idea of a territorial continuity between the two banks of the Jordan (see Merhav, *Israeli Left*, Chapter 24). The Likud, partisans of the annexation of the whole of the West Bank, supported Palestinian "autonomy" all the more strongly (purely administrative in the framework of Israeli sovereignty), which it placed at the heart of the Camp David agreement with Sadat's Egypt.

42   Ibid., p. 204.

43   See Edward Said, "The Morning After", in *London Review of Books* 15: 20 (21 October 1993); Noam Chomsky, "The Israel–Arafat Agreement", in *Z Magazine*, October 1993; and Meron Benvenisti's article in the Israeli daily *Haaretz*, 19 May 1994.

44   All relevant documents are available on the UN webpage *The Question of Palestine*, at un.org/unispal.

45   See on this subject the articles by Sara Roy, "La prospérité ou l'affrontement", and Mahmoud Abdel-Fadil, "Une coopération économique déséquilibrée en faveur d'Israël", both in *Le Monde diplomatique*, August 1994.

46   See Duclos, "La question des frontières orientales d'Israël", p. 21.

47   Annex I (point 1) stipulates nonetheless that "Palestinians of Jerusalem who live there will have the right to participate in the election process" (the elections to the Palestinian "Council"). That is to say, the Arab inhabitants of the old city – who have refused Israeli citizenship – will have, in some way, the status of foreign residents in their own city, holding citizenship in territories where they do not live. So far as the holy places are concerned, recall that Herzl had envisaged "a formula of extraterritoriality coming under international law" (*Jewish State*, p. 47).

48   Nathan Weinstock commented on this type of status in 1969:
The Israeli plans for the constitution of a Palestinian entity explicitly envisage that the diminished sovereignty of the Arab state would not cover any essential questions. As the Pretoria government has written in relation to Transkei: "so far as defense, foreign affairs and certain judicial questions are concerned, the guardian republic of the new state must remain responsible for the moment" ... in other words, it amounts to the creation of an indigenous protectorate under the authority of the dominant nation: a Bantustan ... (*Le Sionisme contre Israël*, p. 520).

49   Article already cited; quotations taken from the monthly bulletin *News from Within*, Alternative Information Center, Jerusalem, June 1994.

50   "I understood that it was neither politically nor morally necessary to control the Arabs of this territory. Moreover, even if we wanted to, we could only do it at the

point of a bayonet, and that only for a time – we are well placed to know it." Allon, *Israël*, p. 174.

51   See Dieckhoff, *Les Espaces d'Israël*, pp. 195–7.

52   Maxime Rodinson, *Israel and the Arabs*, New York: Pantheon, 1968 (the title of the French original is *Israel and the Arab Rejection*).

53   Alain Gresh's book *The PLO: The Struggle Within: Towards an Independent Palestinian State*, trans. A. M. Berrett, London: Zed Press, 1985, is devoted to this programmatic evolution. See also Nadine Picaudou, *Le Mouvement national palestinien: genèse et structures*, Paris: L'Harmattan, 1989.

54   See his article published in *Le Monde*, 23 September 1988: "The PLO must, in the final analysis, choose between two options: support from Syria ... or dialogue with Jordan ... It is only with Jordan that the PLO can work out a policy of negotiation with Israel."

55   The Palestinian police force will consist of "police officers recruited locally and from abroad (holding Jordanian passports and Palestinian documents issued by Egypt). Those who will participate in the Palestinian police force coming from abroad should be trained as police and police officers." Annex II of the Declaration of Principles, point 3c.

56   "L'autogouvernement palestinien: premiers défis", p. 107, in Ghassan Salamé, ed., *Proche-Orient: les exigences de la paix*, Brussels: Complexe, 1994, pp. 101–10. See also the article by Alain Gresh, "Israéliens et Palestiniens sur un terrain miné", in *Le Monde diplomatique*, January 1994.

57   The choice of Jericho, a small and relatively peaceful town, is purely symbolic: it is close to the Allenby Bridge – the crossing point to Jordan, prefiguring a Jordanian–Palestinian confederation – and is also on the edge of the "sovereign corridor" envisaged by the Allon Plan.

58   Quoted from a French translation of an article by Noam Chomsky, "L'accord d'Oslo, vicié au départ", in *Courrier International* (Paris), 3 March 1994. The same opinion was recently expressed by Amos Perlmutter, who formulated this prediction as to the key instrument of the new regime: "Arafat will have to rely heavily on his security services, *Mukhabarat*, the old terrorist machine that has protected him from the Israelis, dissident Palestinians and Arab foes for so long. As a result, the police will have some military functions, while the security services, rather than the political parties, human rights organizations or other institutions, will become the foundation of Arafat's political power and administrative domination." ("Arafat's Police State", in *Foreign Affairs*, July–August 1994, p. 10).

59   In an article with a revealing title – "An Agreement of Surrender", in *Haaretz*, 12 May 1994 – Meron Benvenisti writes: "one can clearly recognize that Israeli victory was absolute and Palestinian defeat abject", adding: "It is also easy to understand the depth of disappointment of those Palestinian leaders from the Territories who considered the Agreement shameful to the point of discrediting their people as a whole."

60   See note 39, above.

4.   On the Electoral Victory of Hamas

On 25 January 2006 the second – and, at the time of writing, last – election was held to the Palestinian Legislative Council, which was created under the framework of the Oslo Accords. It took place ten full years after the first election, which included years of armed confrontation that started in September 2000, and led to the reoccupation of parts of the West Bank by Israeli armed forces. Yasser Arafat was forced by Washington in 2003 to create a position of prime minister and hand it to Mahmoud Abbas. Abbas succeeded him as president of the Palestinian National Authority, after Arafat's death under suspicious circumstances in 2004. Abbas was perceived by the majority of Palestinians as Washington's choice, and bore the main responsibility for the corruption that had by then come to characterize the PNA. Hamas thus won the PLC election with 44.5 per cent of the vote, securing 74 seats out of 132.

This text was written on 27 January 2006, and first published the next day as a guest editorial on Informed Comment, *the blog of the University of Michigan's Professor Juan Cole.*

***

1. The sweeping electoral victory of Hamas is but one of the products of the intensive use made by the United States in the Muslim world since the 1950s of Islamic fundamentalism as an ideological weapon against both progressive nationalism and communism.[1]

This was done in close collaboration with the Saudi kingdom – a de facto US protectorate almost from its foundation in 1932. The promotion of the most reactionary interpretation of the Islamic religion, exploiting deeply rooted popular religious beliefs, led this ideology to fill the vacuum left by the exhaustion by the 1970s of the two ideological currents it served to fight. The road was thus paved in the entire Muslim world for the transformation of Islamic fundamentalism into the dominant expression of mass national and social resentment, to the great dismay of the United States and its Saudi protectorate. The story of Washington's relation with Islamic fundamentalism is the most striking modern example of the sorcerer's apprenticeship.[2]

2. The Palestinian scene was no exception to this general regional pattern, though it followed suit with some delay. Although the Palestinian guerrilla movement came to the fore initially as a result of the exhaustion of more traditional Arab nationalism and as an expression of radicalization, the movement underwent a very rapid bureaucratization, fostered by an impressive influx of petrodollars, and reaching levels of corruption that have no equivalent in the history of national liberation movements. Still, as long as it remained – in the guise of the PLO – what could be described as a "stateless state apparatus seeking a territory", the Palestinian national movement could still embody the aspirations of the vast majority of the Palestinian masses, despite the numerous twists, turns and betrayals of commitments with which its history is littered.[3] However, when a new generation of Palestinians took up the struggle in the late 1980s, with the Intifada that started in December 1987, their radicalization increasingly began to take the path of Islamic fundamentalism. This was facilitated by the fact that the Palestinian left, the leading force within the Intifada in the first months, squandered this last historic opportunity by eventually aligning itself one more time behind the PLO leadership, thus completing its own bankruptcy. On a smaller scale, Israel had played its own version of the sorcerer's apprentice by favoring the Islamic fundamentalist movement as a rival to the PLO prior to the Intifada.

3. The 1993 Oslo agreement inaugurated the final phase of the PLO's
    degeneration, as its leadership – or, rather, the leading nucleus of
    this leadership, bypassing the official leading bodies – was granted
    guardianship over the Palestinian population of the West Bank
    and the Gaza Strip. This came in exchange for what amounted
    to a capitulation: the PLO leadership abandoned the minimal
    conditions that were demanded by the Palestinian negotiators from
    the 1967 occupied territories, above all an Israeli pledge to freeze
    and reverse the construction of the settlements that were colonizing
    their land. The very conditions of this capitulation – which doomed
    the Oslo agreements to tragic failure, as critics very rightly predicted
    from the start – made certain that the shift in the popular political
    mood would speed up.

    The Zionist state took advantage of the lull brought to the 1967
    territories by the Palestinian Authority's fulfillment of the role of
    police force by proxy ascribed to it by drastically intensifying the
    colonization, and building an infrastructure designed to facilitate its
    military control over these territories. Accordingly, the discrediting
    of the PA increased inexorably. This loss in public support
    increasingly hampered its ability to crack down on the Palestinian
    Islamic fundamentalist movement – as was required from it, and
    as it began attempting as early as 1994 – let alone its ability to
    marginalize the Islamic movement politically and ideologically.
    Moreover, the transfer of the PLO bureaucracy from exile into the
    1967 territories, as a ruling apparatus entrusted with the task of
    surveillance over the population that waged the Intifada, quickly
    caused its corruption to reach abysmal levels – something that the
    population of the territories had not before seen first-hand. At the
    same time, Hamas, like most sections of the Islamic fundamentalist
    mass movement – in contrast with the "substitutionist", strictly
    terrorist organizations of which al-Qaeda has become the most
    spectacular example – was keen on paying attention to popular
    basic needs, organizing social services, and cultivating a reputation
    of austerity and incorruptibility.

4. The irresistible rise of Ariel Sharon to the helm of the Israeli state
    resulted from his September 2000 provocation that ignited the
    Second Intifada – an uprising that, because of its militarization,

lacked the most positive features of the popular dynamics of the first Intifada. A PA that, by its nature, could definitely not rely on mass self-organization, and chose the only way of struggle it was familiar with, fostered this militarization. Sharon's rise was also a product of the dead end reached by the Oslo process: the clash between the Zionist interpretation of the Oslo framework – an updated version of the 1967 Allon Plan, by which Israel would relinquish the populated areas of the 1967 occupied territories to an Arab administration, while keeping colonized and militarized strategic chunks – and the PA's minimal requirements of recovering all, or nearly all, of the territories occupied in 1967, without which it knew it would lose its remaining clout with the Palestinian population.

The electoral victory of war criminal Ariel Sharon in February 2001 – an event as much "shocking" as the electoral victory of Hamas, at the very least – inevitably reinforced the Islamic fundamentalist movement, which was his counterpart as an agent of radicalization in the context of a still-born historic compromise. All of this was strongly propelled, of course, by the (very resistible, but unresisted) accession to power of George W. Bush, and the unleashing of his wildest imperial ambitions thanks to the attacks of 11 September 2001.

5. Ariel Sharon played skillfully on the dialectics between himself and his Palestinian true opposite number, Hamas. His calculation was simple: in order to be able to carry through unilaterally his own hard-line version of the Zionist interpretation of a "settlement" with the Palestinians, he needed two conditions: a) to minimize international pressure upon him – or, rather, US pressure, the only pressure that really matters to Israel; and b) to demonstrate that there was no Palestinian leadership with which Israel could "do business". For this, he needed to emphasize the weakness and unreliability of the PA by fanning the expansion of the Islamic fundamentalist movement, knowing that the latter was anathema to Western states. Thus, every time there was some kind of truce, negotiated by the PA with the Islamic organizations, Sharon's government would resort to an "extrajudicial execution" – in plain language, an assassination – in order to provoke these organizations into retaliation by the means they specialized in: suicide attacks, their "F-16s", as they

say. This had the double advantage of stressing the PA's inability to control the Palestinian population and enhancing Sharon's own popularity in Israel. The truth of the matter is that the electoral victory of Hamas was the outcome that Sharon's strategy was very obviously seeking, as many astute observers did not fail to point out.

6.   As long as Yasser Arafat was alive, he was able to use the remnant of his own historical prestige. Contrary to what many commentators have said, the seclusion of Arafat in his last months by Sharon did not "discredit" the Palestinian leader: as a matter of fact, Arafat's popularity was at an all-time low before his seclusion, and recovered in strength after it started. In fact, Arafat's leadership has always been directly nurtured by his demonization by Israel, and his popularity rose again when he became Sharon's prisoner. This is why the United States and Israel's nominee for Palestinian leadership, Mahmoud Abbas, was not able to take over effectively as long as Arafat was alive. It is also why both the Bush administration and Sharon would not let the Palestinians organize the new elections that Arafat kept demanding, as his representativeness was challenged very hypocritically in the name of "democratic reform". The very nature of the "democrats" supported by Washington and Israel under this heading is best epitomized by Mohammed Dahlan, the most corrupt chief of one of the rival repressive "security" apparatuses that Arafat kept under his control, in a pattern familiar to autocratic Arab regimes.

7.   The electoral victory of Hamas was a resounding slap in the face for the Bush administration. As the latest illustration of the sorcerer's apprenticeship that US policy in the Middle East has so spectacularly exemplified, it is the final nail in the coffin of its neocon-inspired, demagogic and deceitful rhetoric about bringing "democracy" to the "Greater Middle East". It is, of course, too early to make any safe prediction regarding what will happen on the ground. It is possible, however, to make a few observations and prognoses:

a)   Hamas does not have a social incentive for collaboration with the Israeli occupation, at least not in any way resembling that of the PLO-originated PA apparatuses: it has actually been thrown into disarray by its own victory, as it would certainly have preferred the much more comfortable posture of being a major parliamentary opposition force to the PA. Therefore, it requires a lot of self-deception and wishful thinking to believe that Hamas will adapt to the conditions laid out by the United States and Israel. Collaboration is all the less likely given that the Israeli government, under the leadership of the new Kadima party founded by Sharon, will continue his policy, taking full advantage of the election result, which suits its plans so well, and making impossible any accommodation with Hamas. Moreover, Hamas faces a rival that outbids it in radicalism represented by Islamic Jihad, which boycotted the election.

b) In order to try to rescue the very sensitive Palestinian component of overall US Middle East policy that it managed to steer into dire straits, the Bush administration will very likely consider three possibilities:

i. One would be a major shift in the policies of Hamas, bought by and mediated by the Saudis; this, however, is unlikely for the reason stated above, and would be time-consuming and uncertain.

ii. Another would be fomenting tension and political opposition against Hamas in order to provoke new elections in the near future, taking advantage of the vast presidential powers that Arafat had granted himself and Mahmoud Abbas inherited – or simply by having the latter resign, thus forcing a presidential election. For such a move to be successful, or meaningful at all, there is a need for a credible figure who could regain a majority for the traditional Palestinian leadership; but the only figure having the minimum of prestige required for this role is presently Marwan Barghouti, who – from his Israeli jail cell – made an alliance with Dahlan prior to the election. It is therefore likely that Washington will exert pressure on Israel for his release.

iii. A third possibility would be the "Algerian scenario" – referring to the interruption of the electoral process in Algeria by a military junta in January 1992 – which is already envisaged, according to reports in the Arab press: the repressive apparatuses of the PA would crack down on Hamas, impose a state of siege and establish a military-police dictatorship. Of course, a combination of the last two scenarios is also possible, postponing the crackdown until political conditions are created that are more suitable for it.

Any attempt by the United States and the European Union to starve the Palestinians into submission by interrupting the economic aid they grant them would be disastrous for both humanitarian and political reasons, and should be opposed most vigorously.

The Bush administration's catastrophic management of US policy in the Middle East, on top of decades of clumsy and shortsighted US imperial policies in this part of the world, has not yet borne all of its bitter fruits.

NOTES

1   Stephen Shalom edited this article and made useful suggestions.
2   I have described this at length in my book *The Clash of Barbarisms: The Making of the New World Disorder*, trans. Peter Drucker, 2nd edn, London: Saqi/Routledge, 2006.
3   For an analysis of the PLO, see Gilbert Achcar, *Eastern Cauldron: Islam, Afghanistan, Palestine and Iraq in a Marxist Mirror*, New York: Monthly Review/ London: Pluto, 2004.

5.   The Crisis in Gaza

As predicted in the previous essay, the George W. Bush administration tried to oust Hamas from power in 2007, a year after its electoral victory, by staging a coup led by Mohammed Dahlan (see David Rose, "The Gaza Bombshell", in the April 2008 issue of Vanity Fair*), described above as "the most corrupt chief of one of the rival repressive 'security' apparatuses that Arafat kept under his control". The coup was thwarted in the Gaza Strip, Hamas's stronghold, but led to the partition of the 1967-occupied Palestinian territories and the proto-state that the Oslo Accords had created into two competing authorities, that of Mahmoud Abbas and the PLO in the West Bank and that of Hamas in Gaza.*

Thereafter, Gaza would suffer repeated fits of unrestrained Israeli violence, at a level far more destructive than previous onslaughts on the OPTs – a pattern stemming from the "Dahiya Doctrine" of disproportionate violence, first put into practice during Israel's 2006 onslaught on Lebanon. The first major episode of such violence against Gaza took place over three weeks, between the end of 2008 and 18 January 2009. Close to 1,300 Palestinians were killed and only thirteen Israelis – a ratio of 100:1 that would become familiar thereafter.

As can be seen in this interview, this unprecedented, murderous fury prompted me to foretell what would happen fifteen years later, with the genocidal war on Gaza.

This interview was conducted on 10 January 2009 by Daniel Finn for the now-defunct Irish Left Review, *and first published on the* Review's *website on 15 January 2009. Readers will judge to what extent the analysis developed in this interview was verified during the war that unfolded after 7 October 2023. They will also judge how relevant my discussion of Palestinian liberation strategy was.*

***

DANIEL FINN: What do you think are the chief goals of Israeli strategy at present in their assault on the Gaza strip?

GILBERT ACHCAR: Well, that's a complicated question actually, because there are different levels involved. Seen through a wide angle, it is part of an ongoing struggle between Israel on the one hand and both Hamas and Hezbollah on the other, a struggle which reached a previous peak in 2006, when during the summer Israel was simultaneously waging a war against Gaza and another one, a major onslaught, on Lebanon. That was related to the global strategy of the Bush administration in its confrontation with Iran, with the conception prevailing in Washington that Hamas and Hezbollah are tools of the Iranian state, and therefore part of an alliance of forces that should be smashed if ever US hegemony in the region, as well as Israeli security, are to be stabilized. It is therefore a further stage in the same ongoing war that has been unfolding for the last few years.

Now, if we narrow the focus, the fact that this has been launched at this very moment, starting on 27 December, is of course related to shorter-term political considerations: on the one hand, the Bush administration will soon be out of the scene, and although the Israeli government have no real reason to fear a major change in US policy in the Middle East, if we judge from all the signs given by the Obama team, there remains the prospect that the new administration will get into talks with Iran, as Obama said he would during the electoral campaign. In that case, US backing for a tough stance in the confrontation with Iran might be diluted. Taking that into consideration, one reason why the campaign is being launched right now is to spare the next administration the need to cope from the beginning with a major crisis in the Middle East. So, there was relief in the Obama team that this is done under Bush.

The problem is that the operation went on much longer than expected, as is now a recurrent pattern in Israel's aggressions: bygone indeed are the days of the "Six-Day War". Ideally for the Israeli government – and there were a lot of comments about this possibility some months ago – there should have been a strike against Iran itself before the Bush administration left the scene. However, that became impossible for a number of reasons related to the deep trouble in which the Bush administration finds itself: not only the general political weakness of a lame-duck president, but also the economic crisis, which makes any kind of military confrontation with Iran at this point something that would certainly be harmful to the interest of the global economy. Instead of these strikes against Iran that it was wishing for, Israel is attacking Hamas, which it sees as a proxy for Iran.

And then there are even narrower perspectives involved, which are electoral considerations in Israel. As you know, new Israeli elections are to be held soon, and parties represented in the Israeli coalition government – Ehud Olmert's and Tzipi Livni's Kadima, on the one hand, and Ehud Barak's Labor party, on the other – are facing strong competition from Likud, the far-right wing of the mainstream Zionist scene in Israel. In a sense, this onslaught on Gaza is a way to preempt the overbidding upon which Netanyahu would certainly have built his electoral campaign.

So, if you take all these issues into consideration, you get an overdetermination, i.e. a multiplicity of reasons for this operation to be launched right now. All the rest, the rockets launched by Hamas and all that, are just pretexts, in the same way that the abduction of two soldiers by Hezbollah in July 2006 was but a pretext used by Israel to launch a premeditated full-scale aggression.

DANIEL FINN: The last major round of confrontation between Israel and Hamas and Hezbollah, in 2006, ended in a major setback for the Israeli state and all kinds of recriminations among the political and military elites. Do you think Israel now has a realistic chance of overturning that setback and talking up a victory, or does it face another defeat?

GILBERT ACHCAR: Well, here lies the reason why the situation is extremely dangerous and worrying right now. Think about it: this onslaught started on 27 December, so that means we are some two weeks into the fighting, and you already have a heavier death toll in absolute numbers than what you had in Lebanon after the first two weeks of intensive bombing. If you take it in relative numbers, knowing that the Lebanese population is close to three times larger than that of Gaza, then it is much, much heavier. What is very worrying and dangerous about the present situation is precisely that, because of the previous fiasco in Lebanon in the summer of 2006, Israel cannot afford another fiasco of the same kind. They cannot afford a new one, for both strategic reasons and opportunistic or short-term ones – small-fry political calculations, that is.

On the one hand, the Israeli state stands to lose a lot of its so-called military credibility if it faces a new fiasco, especially that the enemy they are facing this time, i.e. Hamas in Gaza, is certainly much weaker than what Hezbollah is and was in Lebanon. Hezbollah is certainly stronger in the Lebanese Shiite community than Hamas is in Gaza, where you have a bitter contest between Hamas and the PA/Fatah, and you have a few other groups competing for the same constituency. Beyond that, of course, for very obvious reasons, Hezbollah had many more weapons than Hamas has in Gaza, which is a small strip of land surrounded from all sides and under heavy surveillance. They can smuggle some light weapons, not major weapons, into Gaza, whereas in Lebanon, Hezbollah could build up an important arsenal – even more easily since it was done with Syria's backing.

So, if Israel gets into a second fiasco even against Hamas, which is much weaker than Hezbollah, then this will be seen necessarily as a major disaster, worse than the 2006 one for Israel. Not to mention – and this is the second point – the petty consideration. If the ruling coalition in Israel comes out from the present war with another fiasco, its parties won't even need to go to elections. Netanyahu would stand to defeat them completely and they know that. So, they cannot afford a fiasco for these two reasons combined, and this is what makes the situation very, very worrying. They might develop the syndrome of the wounded beast, getting more ferocious than they are already. The level of Israeli atrocity is increasing war after war. The Thirty-Three-Day War in 2006 was already the most brutal aggression in the long history of Israeli wars, the most brutal utilization of power by Israel, carpet-bombing whole regions of Lebanon, civilian areas.

The pretext, then as now, is that fighters are hiding among the population. This is the most hypocritical argument: What do they want them to do, to regroup in some wasteland with signposts saying

"Bomb us here"? This is preposterous. The truth is that Israel is trying to crush mass political parties, which are armed, of course, but they need to be armed because they are permanently under threat. These are armed popular movements. Most of their armed members are not professional fighters living in barracks. When you take all these aspects of the problem into consideration, there are very, very serious grounds for the mounting, increasing worries that are expressed by international humanitarian agencies.

A lot of people now sense that the population of Gaza is really under threat of massive extermination. This is not the usual kind of exaggeration, it is a sober assessment when you face such a level of violence and brutality, day after day, with more and more so-called accidents in which concentrations of civilians are targeted with mass-murder as a result. The only alternative to a fiasco for Israel is to push forward its ground offensive in the populated areas. The worst-case scenario becomes therefore quite possible, and that would mean thousands and thousands of people killed, not to mention the maimed and wounded, and that is absolutely frightening.

DANIEL FINN: If Hamas is going to be seen as a victor, even a partial victor, coming out of this latest confrontation with Israel, what does it have to do? Is it enough for Hamas to survive? Do they just have to keep standing?

GILBERT ACHCAR: *If* Hamas manages to come out of this war standing up, that is. The fact is that due to the geographical conditions, they have already suffered proportionally a certainly higher rate of casualties in their ranks than Hezbollah did in 2006. The day when Israeli bombing started, the very first day, if you remember, it targeted buildings of the Hamas security force, and the death toll was immediately very heavy. But if at the level of leadership and basic structure they manage to come out preserving more or less their existence without giving any major concession or, let's say, no major concession that is not reciprocated, like, "We stop firing rockets but we get guarantees that you, Israel, stop shooting at us and stop embargoing us, strangulating us" – if they come out of this war with a deal of this kind, this would mean an Israeli fiasco, and this would be seen for them as a political victory in the same way that Hezbollah achieved one in 2006.

But right now, at the time we are speaking, this is purely hypothetical because we cannot predict how things will evolve. What is actually clear is that, at the regional level, if not at the world level, this Israeli onslaught has tremendously increased Hamas's popularity. We cannot take it for granted, however, that the same applies to the Palestinians in Gaza, precisely because of this competition between Hamas and Fatah. On this there are mixed reports. Of course, Fatah supporters will say "Hamas have put us in this terrible situation, we are suffering because of them; of course, Israel is the first to blame, but...", this same "but" that we have heard from some Arab regimes. This is what the Egyptian government, which is very obviously colluding with this Israeli onslaught, expressed from the very start, and that is what we heard here and there from Arab allies of the United States, the same rhetoric we heard in 2006, the same blame that was put on Hezbollah for Israel's onslaught on Lebanon. The final political outcome for Hamas remains to be seen. It is, I think, too early now to make any assessment for what it will be in the long run, or even in the medium term. For the time being, as I said, the only certain thing is for Hamas at the regional level an increasing popularity, which is the almost automatic outcome that you get every time Israel singles out an Arab target and starts striking at it. The target becomes automatically popular because of the hatred for Israel and its permanent aggression in the region: any victim of Israel, and especially any force resisting Israel, is sure of achieving popularity in the region.

DANIEL FINN: There has been talk over the last week of a certain amount of discontent among a younger generation of Fatah. There have been reports that Marwan Barghouti has sent messages from his prison cell critical of the statements made by Mahmoud Abbas. Do you think that is likely to take on any substantial form with the current leadership of Fatah being undermined? Do you think there's any chance of the Fatah leadership changing course?

GILBERT ACHCAR: Barghouti is in a sense a reserve card for Fatah. Mahmoud Abbas has already burnt his cards to a great degree. He doesn't have any credibility anymore, but appears as a servile man, a secondary pawn in this regional game. He is not popular even within Fatah, so it is clear that Fatah will be in need of another leading figure immediately, or very soon, and Barghouti would be an alternative. But since he is in jail, his fate much depends on Israel – and on Washington, to be sure. Now, to know how Barghouti would behave if ever he was liberated from jail is hard to tell. The main problem is what kind of relation he would have with the US and their number-one Palestinian stooge Mohammed Dahlan. Dahlan and Barghouti were in electoral alliance in the January 2006 election. Does it mean that they will maintain a collaboration and form a cohesive, dominant team in the post-Abbas Fatah, or will they be in competition? It remains to be seen.

DANIEL FINN: As you said, the Egyptian regime, in particular, and to a greater or lesser extent also all of the pro-US Arab regimes, have been seen as complicit with Israel, particularly the Mubarak government. If there is further escalation, if Israel behaves, as you described it, like a wounded animal, using more and more brutal methods against the Palestinians living in Gaza, how difficult is it going to prove for the Egyptian government to be able to contain anger among its own people, which already seems to be very substantial.

GILBERT ACHCAR: Well, they are not only "seen" as complicit. They are actually complicit with Israel. They were told about the onslaught before it started, and this was reported in the press. The day the onslaught started, the Arabic daily published in London, *Al-Quds al-Arabi*, ran an article by their correspondent in the West Bank explaining that Israeli foreign minister Tzipi Livni, who had been in Cairo the day before, had told the Egyptian authorities that Israel was going to launch an operation against Hamas. General Omar Suleiman, the head of Egyptian intelligence, asked her that Israel target specifically Hamas fighters, and take care to spare civilians. Well, the onslaught started on the same day the article came out, and it started by targeting police barracks in Gaza. So, on the face of it, it was an onslaught sparing civilians and specifically targeting armed forces. This proves beyond a shadow of a doubt that they were told that this would happen, and they did not even tell Hamas, which was taken by surprise when the onslaught started, hence the initial heavy death toll in the ranks of its armed forces.

The Egyptian government and other pro-US Arab regimes wish very much for a weakened Hamas. They are not for wiping out Hamas, as they know that it would entail a huge and traumatizing human cost, if it were possible at all. They would like a weakened Hamas that would have no choice then but to sever its links with Iran and be obliged to depend on them for its survival. This is what they wish. They want a tamed Hamas, and therefore look for Israel to do the taming. So, Israel has to teach Hamas a lesson and then Egypt and, behind Egypt, the Saudis and the Jordanians will say to Hamas: "Look, you have no other choice but to cooperate with us; either you join the game under our conditions, and sever all links with Iran and Syria, or you will have to face Israel alone and the possibility that it crushes you."

Now, if the Israeli operation backfires, they will turn coats immediately, of course, by pure opportunism. They will turn coats and start bashing Israel and multiply statements of condemnation, which don't go very far. The Egyptian regime could upgrade its disagreement with Israel on the issue of international troops on the Egyptian side of the border with Gaza, which Israel is demanding and Cairo is rejecting. There are issues of this kind which could be blown out of proportion, allowing Cairo and fellow Arab regimes to pretend that they do confront Israel, but in a responsible way because they know Israeli military strength and care for the welfare of the people, and therefore they are not like those crazy guys of Hamas, etc. This is their kind of hypocritical discourse.

DANIEL FINN: Hezbollah organized some very substantial rallies in Lebanon in solidarity with Hamas, and in solidarity with the people of Gaza. Is their support likely to remain political, or is there any prospect, as some people have speculated in rather alarmist terms, that Hezbollah might open a second front against Israel on the Northern border.

GILBERT ACHCAR: I don't think there is any prospect of this kind. It seems that the three rockets fired from Lebanon into northern Israel yesterday were launched by one of the small Palestinian groups linked to Damascus. Hezbollah immediately denied any responsibility, and the Lebanese coalition government, where Hezbollah is represented, condemned unanimously the firing of these rockets. The reality, at this stage, is that you have huge demonstrations and manifestations of political solidarity, but Hezbollah have also drawn the lesson from 2006. If you remember, after the Thirty-Three-Day War in 2006, the secretary-general of Hezbollah, Hassan Nasrallah, said in an interview that, had he known that Israel would react the way it reacted to the abduction of its two soldiers on 12 July, Hezbollah wouldn't have done it. He meant: "Had I known that they would destroy my country and kill 1,500 of my people, I wouldn't have given them a pretext for that." This is what he meant, addressing human feelings.

At the same time, we know that, for Israel, the abduction was but a pretext: had no soldiers been abducted, Israel would have found – or created – whatever pretext in order to do what they tried to do at that time. Hezbollah accepted UN Security Council Resolution 1701, which meant deployment not only of Lebanese troops to Southern Lebanon but also international forces, the UNIFIL – although this is not exactly in the interest of Hezbollah, since these forces are heavily composed of NATO forces, and are therefore a potential threat to Hezbollah itself. They had to accept them nevertheless, because the alternative was to carry on with that horrible war, and there were human limits on that level. Hezbollah cannot therefore take what would appear to be a completely irresponsible initiative in opening a second front – especially if it gets no green light for that from both Damascus and Tehran.

On the other hand, how can one expect the Lebanese to open a second front, when the Palestinians on the West Bank themselves, including Hamas, are not opening one: Hamas did not fire rockets from the West Bank. This, by the way, shows how serious an error was Hamas's decision to seize full power in Gaza alone, thus separating the two Palestinian territories. Not that they should not have preempted the coup that Dahlan was busy organizing against them with US and Israeli backing, but they should not have wiped out all Fatah presence in PA institutions in Gaza as they did. Whereas the strategic need is for the struggle to be built on a pan-regional level, the Palestinian scene itself has been fragmented into two segments. This is a pity.

These events also bring into discussion the whole issue of the strategic choices of weapons. Hamas is resisting heroically, no doubt, but we cannot compare the conditions in Lebanon with the conditions in Palestine. During the years when you had the Israeli occupation of Lebanon, Hezbollah was waging a war of attrition against the occupation, mainly in occupied Lebanese areas. It even reached with the occupier in April 1996, through US mediation, an agreement which stipulated that "Armed groups in Lebanon will not carry out attacks by Katyusha rockets or by any kind of weapon into Israel. Israel and those cooperating with it will not fire any kind of weapon at civilians or civilian targets in Lebanon. Beyond this, the two parties commit to ensuring that under no circumstances will civilians be the target of attack, and that civilian-populated areas and industrial and electrical installations will not be used as launching grounds for attacks." The geographical nature of the Lebanese terrain and the presence of Israeli forces in Lebanese populated areas made a strategy of popular resistance possible, and this triumphed eventually, with Israel evacuating Southern Lebanon in what looked like a debacle in 2000.

In the case of Gaza however, Israeli troops had withdrawn from the interior of the Strip and were encircling it. It doesn't make much sense strategically to confront them militarily by launching rockets into populated areas in southern Israel. The point is that, with regard to the occupied Palestinian territories, if you drew up a balance-sheet of the Palestinian struggle against the Israeli state since 1967, it is very clear that the peak efficiency of the Palestinian struggle was reached in 1988 with the so-called Revolution of the Stones, the first Intifada – without firearms, suicide bombing, rockets, anything of the kind, just mass mobilization. This is what was most terrible for Israel: it put the Israelis in terrible political difficulty.

There is a lesson to be drawn here. These are matters of strategic understanding which not all forces in the region are sufficiently taking into consideration. There is today a lot of religious-inspired maximalism in the Palestinian struggle, as there was yesterday nationalist-inspired maximalism, but hardly any realistic assessment of the conditions in designing a strategy. Not a strategy of capitulation in the name of "realism", of course, like that of the PLO – I mean the PA, Arafat and now Mahmoud Abbas – but a strategy of resistance and liberation, of popular resistance to impose on Israel whatever strategic goal is feasible under the present conditions. And what remains possible in the prevailing objective conditions is to get Israel to withdraw from the 1967 occupied territories, with the possibility for these territories to organize their own government democratically, to enjoy at least political sovereignty – which is not the case presently, when you see how Israel and its Western backers reacted to Hamas's electoral victory.

Beyond this immediate goal, the only sensible long-term strategy has to involve a disruption in the Israeli society itself. It cannot be designed as purely from without Israeli society, as have been both the PLO's strategy and that of Hamas. There is no possibility to defeat Israel militarily from without: no possibility in conventional terms, because its weaponry is much stronger than all surrounding Arab states, not to mention the fact that no part of this environment is willing to confront Israel – not only Egypt and Jordan, but Syria too. A "popular war" for the liberation of the whole of historical Palestine does not make sense, because Israelis are the overwhelming majority in the pre-1967 territory. This is not like an occupying army, whether the US in Vietnam or Afghanistan or Iraq, or Israel in Lebanon. Beyond that, everyone knows that Israel is a nuclear power since the late 1960s. Any thinking aiming at destroying the Israeli state from without is therefore irrational, in all senses of the term.

So, aside from the requisites of internationalism, i.e. the kind of victory over the Zionist state that is desirable, there is no sensible strategy to defeat it anyway that does not take in account the necessity for a major disruption within Israeli society itself, with a major faction of Israeli society actively opposing the bellicose policies of the Israeli government and fighting for a lasting, peaceful settlement based on justice, self-determination and an end to all kinds of discrimination. This is a major, hugely important prerequisite. That is why the Intifada in 1988 was so important: it created a real, deep crisis within Israeli society.

But what we are seeing now is a very high degree of cohesion and unanimity among the Israelis in the most ferocious, severe and brutal aggression of their history, and that is something which bodes ill. In such conditions, even when you get fiascos like the one in 2006, what do they produce? Not a break of major chunks of the Israeli population away from its government's policy, let alone with Zionism, and their turning anti-war like major portions of the German population in the First World War or the US population during the Vietnam War, but what you get are rather further shifts to the right. That is why the whole picture is very gloomy in the region because, as I said, if this offensive ends in a fiasco, which is what we wish, we know in advance that this means Netanyahu, who is even worse than the present guys. Where all this will end is very difficult to see.

DANIEL FINN: It does appear to be a very dangerous time for the Palestinians, and perhaps as dangerous a time as it has faced since 1967.

There's talk in Israel media circles, in establishment circles, about handing over the Gaza strip to Egyptian authority, handing over populated areas of the West Bank to Jordan. And if that plan or something similar was put into practice, that would surely be fatal for Palestinian national aspirations for many years to come. What steps do you think could be taken by forces within Palestinian society to improve the prospects of the national movement?

GILBERT ACHCAR: I don't really see things as you described them. First of all, the Jordanian monarchy itself would be rather scared today if it had to resume control of the West Bank. When this was a real prospect, it had already taken into account the rising militancy of the Palestinians, which is why the plans designed by previous King Hussein were federative in nature – that is, plans giving the West Bank, or the West Bank and Gaza, some degree of self-government. But the problem now is that the Jordanian monarchy cannot rely on the likes of Mahmoud Abbas to tame the Palestinian population. They know that they are facing a very radicalized population and that a new junction, a new merger between the Palestinians on the West Bank and Palestinians in Jordan, where they already constitute a majority of the population, would be very dangerous for the Jordanian monarchy. That's the problem.

A renewed merger of the West bank with Jordan would definitely be in the interest of the Palestinians, because the so-called independent state in the West Bank and Gaza does not make sense. This is where I fully agree with those who criticize the two-state solution: a so-called independent state does not make sense in the West Bank, if it is to be held hostage between Israel and Jordan as vice and hammer. Therefore, the Palestinian people need the necessary breathing space and outlet provided by Jordan, not to mention the human and familial continuities between the two banks of the River Jordan. There is a natural historical unity of human community between the two banks, and for that community to be able to exert self-determination you need a different kind of government in Jordan, a really democratic one and not one where the majority of the population are oppressed by a regime that stirs up ethnic divisions of a tribal nature, as is the case right now.

This is why I don't think that the prospect of a renewed merging of the two banks is one that the Jordanian government is enthusiastic for, or even actively considering. In 1988 King Hussein officially severed the links between his kingdom and the West Bank. Why did he do so? Very simply because in 1988 you had the Intifada in full swing, and he understood that the kind of West Bank that the monarchy ruled over since the deal that his father cut with the Zionists in 1948 – the West Bank that his monarchy was able to rule more or less without major trouble until 1967, and that came under Israeli occupation afterwards – had become unmanageable in light of the Intifada. It became a hot potato – too dangerous to handle; and that is why he severed the links officially, and abandoned any claims to the West Bank.

DANIEL FINN: Do you think the Palestinian political stage is likely to remain the property of Hamas and Fatah for the foreseeable future, or do you think that some of the marginal forces at present have any chance of establishing themselves to a greater extent?

GILBERT ACHCAR: Well, I don't really see any such prospect presently. I mean, there are no real challengers for the time being to the two major actors, which are Fatah and Hamas. Other existing forces, especially the Palestinian left, lost credibility throughout the years, after having lost so many opportunities. So, one cannot expect a sudden miraculous development, whereby some new force arises, which we haven't heard of yet and which would take some time to mature anyway. What you will have under the present conditions are further evolutions from within the two polar forces in Palestinian society – a struggle between different factions within Fatah, and the same for Hamas. Neither of these two forces, because they are big forces and have mass constituencies and memberships, is monolithic. Changes from within them are presently more likely than any unexpected rise of new forces from without.

Now, that being said, I wish very strongly that a third force could rise, one which would be a progressive movement based on the left-wing tradition that exists among the Palestinians and that is far from being negligible, even in Gaza, although it is not strong enough to be a counterweight to Fatah or Hamas. I wish very much that some Palestinian left-wing force could emerge as a real major player on the scene. But, to be frank, for the time being, aside from hope or wish, this is not a realistic prospect. We don't see any premise for that.

Part III

Gaza, Nakba, Genocide

6. Initial Comments on Hamas's 7 October Counter-Offensive

This initial reaction to the Hamas-led Al-Aqsa Flood attack of 7 October 2023 was first published on my blog (gilbert-achcar.net) the next day. In the fog of war and polemics, at a time when little was known for certain about some horrendous details of the operation, a very large number of supporters of the Palestinian cause in the Arab world, to which I originally belong, as well as in the West, were hailing Hamas's operation.

In reaction to that, I acknowledged that the attack was "amazing and highly daring" ("amazing" in the sense of "astonishing", to be sure, not in the positive sense that can be associated with this word), in a prelude to my warning that "this new chapter will end with a terrible cost for the Palestinians in general, the Gazans in particular, and Hamas specifically"; and that, whatever it might achieve for the Palestinian cause "would have been achieved at a hugely disproportionate cost for the Palestinians". I then went on to criticize the logic that presided over the operation, asserting that, instead, mass political action is the only rational Palestinian liberation strategy.

I was nevertheless criticized by some supporters of Israel for having called this attack a "counter-offensive" – even though it came as a response to Israel's long-term siege of the Gaza Strip and repeated murderous onslaughts on it – and, above all, for comparing it to the 1943 Warsaw Ghetto Uprising, although the comparison was specifically and only about both historical events being a "quasi-desperate act of bravery" due to the "huge military disproportion" – which meant that the attackers in both cases were facing a very high risk of death. In this regard, it is little known that more Palestinian participants in the Hamas-led attack than Israelis were killed on 7 October – "Israel has said some 1,500 terrorists are believed to have been killed by security forces as the attack and the Israeli response unfolded, leaving authorities with thousands of corpses to process", according to the Times of Israel on 11 November 2023 (ToI staff, "Israel Revises Death Toll from Oct. 7 Hamas assault, Dropping It from 1,400 to 1,200").

Two days later, on 10 October 2023, my weekly Arabic column in the London-based Al-Quds al-Arabi bore the title "Al-Aqsa Flood risks to sweep Gaza Away". Here is a translation of its last paragraph:

> Ever since the establishment of the State of Israel, the Zionist right has been dreaming of completing the Nakba of 1948 with a new mass expulsion of Palestinians from the land of Palestine between the sea and the river, including the Gaza Strip. There is no doubt that they now see what happened last Saturday [7 October 2023] as a shock that will allow them to drag the rest of the Zionist society behind them in implementing their dream – in the Strip first, while waiting for the opportunity to implement it in the West Bank ... It is very likely that the [Zionist state] will not be satisfied this time with anything less than destroying the Strip to an extent that exceeds everything we have seen to date, in order to reoccupy it at the lowest possible Israeli human cost and cause most of its population to flee to Egyptian territory – all under the pretext of completely eradicating Hamas from Gaza. It is therefore to be greatly feared that the Al-Aqsa Flood will eventually sweep away the entire Gaza Strip, just as the natural flood swept away the Libyan city of Derna a month ago, but on a much larger scale.

***

The counter-offensive launched by Hamas against Israel on 7 October 2023, a day after the fiftieth anniversary of another Arab surprise attack on Israel – the October 1973 War – is a much more spectacular feat than the latter. Whereas, fifty years ago, the two Arab states of Egypt and

Syria launched a conventional war to attempt to recover the territories that Israel had seized from them six years earlier, in the June 1967 War, the new counter-offensive launched by Hamas evokes the boldness of the biblical David in his fight against the giant Goliath. Combining rudimentary air, sea and land means – the equivalent of David's sling – Hamas's fighters executed an amazing and highly daring offensive all along the border zone between the Gaza strip and the Israeli state.

In the same way that Israel's arrogant self-confidence in the face of its Arab neighbors was shattered in 1973, the security and impunity that it has been taking for granted in dealing with the Palestinian people and combatting Palestinian guerrillas have been severely and irreversibly impaired. From that angle, Hamas's October counter-offensive is to the Israeli population and state a powerful reminder of their vulnerability, and of the fact that there can be no security without peace and no peace without justice.

Whatever one may think of Hamas's decision to launch such a massive operation against the Israeli state, thus inevitably unleashing the Israeli government's massive, murderous retaliation, and inciting it to attempt to wipe Hamas and its allies from the Gaza Strip, at a huge cost to civilians, the fact remains that this counter-offensive has already and undoubtedly dealt a heavy blow to the unbearable haughtiness of the Israeli racist far-right government, and their belief that Israel could ever reach a "normal" state of coexistence with its regional environment while persecuting the Palestinian people and inflicting upon them a protracted Nakba of territorial dispossession, ethnic cleansing and apartheid.

No less unbearable is the precipitousness with which Western governments (and a Ukrainian government that ought to know better about the legitimate fight against foreign occupation) have expressed their solidarity with Israel, very much in contrast with their muted reactions to Israel's brutal onslaughts on the Palestinian population. The Israeli flag was projected on Berlin's Brandenburg Gate on the evening of 7 October, in a contemptible display of fawning over the state of Israel, the usual hallmark of misdirected German redemption-seeking for Nazi crimes against European Jews through endorsing Israel's crimes against the Palestinians. This becomes even worse at a time when Israel's government is composed of the whole gamut of Jewish far-right forces, including people whom Daniel Blatman, a prominent Israeli Holocaust historian, did not hesitate to aptly describe in *Haaretz* (10 February 2023) as neo-Nazis!

No less contemptible are the attempts at "analyzing" Hamas's offensive as an Iranian plot to derail the ongoing US-fostered rapprochement between the Saudi kingdom and the Israeli state. Even if it were true that Tehran wished to derail that rapprochement instead of using it to enhance its own claim of monopoly over anti-Zionism – a very disputable hypothesis indeed – this denial of Palestinian agency by way of conspiracy theory is the exact equivalent of every oppressive government's reaction to popular revolt. It postulates that there are no sufficient grounds for the oppressed people to revolt against their oppression, and that any such move is necessarily inspired by the invisible hand of some foreign government.

Anyone familiar with what the Palestinian people have been enduring for decades, and aware of the kind of open-air prison that the Gaza Strip has become ever since it was occupied in 1967 and then evacuated by Israeli troops in 2005 – an open-air prison that is periodically the target of a murderous Israeli "turkey shoot" – can easily understand that the only reason why such a quasi-desperate act of bravery as Hamas's latest operation does not happen more frequently is the huge military mismatch between the Palestinian David and the Israeli Goliath. Indeed, Gaza's latest counter-offensive brings to mind the 1943 Warsaw Ghetto Uprising.

There can be no doubt that this new chapter will end with a terrible cost for the Palestinians in general, the Gazans in particular, and Hamas specifically – much higher than the cost endured by the Israelis, as has unfailingly been the case in every round of fighting between Israel and the Palestinians. And whereas it is not difficult to understand the "enough-is-enough" logic behind Hamas's counter-offensive, it is much more doubtful that it will help advance the Palestinian cause beyond the blow to Israel's self-confidence mentioned above. This will have been achieved at a hugely disproportionate cost to the Palestinians.

The very idea that such an operation, however spectacular it was, could achieve "victory" can only stem from the religious type of magical thinking that is characteristic of a fundamentalist movement like Hamas. The distribution by its information service of a video showing the movement's leadership praying to thank God on the morning of

7 October is a good illustration of this thinking. Unfortunately, no magic can alter the fact of Israel's massive military superiority: the result of Israel's new ongoing war against Gaza is certainly going to be devastating.

The 9/11 attacks on New York and Washington dealt the arrogance of the United States a spectacular blow. Eventually, they tremendously enhanced George W. Bush's popularity, enabling him to launch eighteen months later the occupation of Iraq that was his ambition. Likewise, Hamas's October counter-offensive has already succeeded in reunifying a previously deeply divided Israeli society and polity, and will allow Benjamin Netanyahu to implement his wildest plans to inflict massive terror on the Palestinians, to precipitate their forced displacement.

On the other hand, if Hamas's leadership had been betting on Lebanon's Hezbollah – and Iran behind it – to join the war at a level that would really put Israel in jeopardy, this bet would have been very risky indeed. Not only it is far from certain that Hezbollah would take the high risk of massively entering a new war with Israel, but such a situation, if it were to happen, would inevitably bring Israel to resort unrestrainedly to its massive destructive power (which includes nuclear weapons), thus bringing about a catastrophe of historic magnitude.

Against an oppressor that is far superior in military means, the only truly efficient method of struggle for the Palestinian people is by choosing the terrain on which they can circumvent that superiority. The peak of Palestinians' effectiveness in their struggle was reached in 1988, during the First Intifada, in which the Palestinians deliberately avoided the use of violent means. This led to a deep moral crisis in Israel's society and polity, including its armed forces, and was a key factor in leading the Israeli Rabin–Peres leadership to negotiate the 1993 Oslo Accords with Yasser Arafat – however flawed these accords were, due to the Palestinian leader's indulgence in wishful thinking.

The Palestinian struggle must rely primarily on mass political action against Israel's oppression, occupation and settler-colonial expansion. The new underground armed resistance organized by young Palestinians in Jenin or Nablus can be an efficient adjunct to the people's mass movement, provided it is predicated on the latter's priority and conceived in such a way as to incentivize it. The regional support that the Palestinian people should rely upon is from tyrannical governments like that of Iran, but from the peoples fighting against these oppressive regimes. Herein lies the true potential prospect for Palestinian liberation, which needs to be combined with the emancipation of Israeli society itself from the logic of Zionism, which has inexorably produced its polity's ever-expanding drift to the far right.

7. The Impending Catastrophe and the Urgency of Stopping It

My next article on 7 October and the Israeli bombing of Gaza, first published on my blog on 16 October 2023, reflected upon the impending catastrophe announced in its title, forewarning that "What looms on the horizon is nothing less than a second stage of the Nakba – the Arabic word for 'catastrophe' that is the name given to the forced displacement of most of the indigenous Palestinian population from the territories that the newborn Israeli state managed to conquer in 1948".

The article pointed to the qualitative difference in the perception of the ongoing events and their representation between the Global South and the Global North. Without denying the atrocious character of the Hamas-led attack on 7 October, it emphasized the fact that whatever label could be attached to it applied at a much higher degree to Israel's treatment of the Palestinian people.

***

In the last few days, Gaza has epitomized the global North–South divide more than any other conflict in contemporary history. The indecent unanimity of Western governments in unreservedly expressing their unconditional support of the Israeli state – at the very moment when the latter had already and quite obviously embarked on a campaign of war crimes against the Palestinian people of unprecedented magnitude in the seventy-five-year history of the regional conflict – has been truly sickening. Since 7 October, these governments have been outbidding each other in this endeavor – from projecting the Israeli flag on Berlin's Brandenburg Gate, London's parliament, Paris's Eiffel Tower and Washington's White House, to sending military hardware to Israel, as well as dispatching US and UK naval reinforcements to the Eastern Mediterranean in a gesture of solidarity with the Zionist state, and prohibiting diverse forms of expression of political support for the Palestinian cause, thus curtailing elementary political freedoms.

All this is happening at a time when the usual imbalance in Western media reporting on Israel/Palestine has reached a peak. As usual, grieving Israelis, women in particular, have been profusely shown on screens, incomparably more than grieving Palestinians have ever been. Hamas's Operation Al-Aqsa Flood occasioned a flood of images of violence against unarmed people, with a special focus on a rave similar to those commonly organized in Western countries, so as to accentuate the "narcissistic compassion ... evoked much more by calamities striking 'people like us', much less by calamities affecting people unlike us".[1] The much larger-scale Israeli violence that has been pounding civilians in Gaza since Hamas launched its operation has been much less reported, let alone condemned. Even as blatant a war crime as the total blockade in water, food, fuel and electricity inflicted upon a population of 2.3 million, and the no less blatant violation of humanitarian law consisting in ordering more than a million civilians to leave their city or face death under the rubble of their dwellings, is all but condoned by prominent Western political leaders and major Western media.

It is as if they had reconstituted the International Society for the Suppression of Savage Customs for which Joseph Conrad's fictional Kurtz (in *Heart of Darkness*) had written a report ending with the terrifying postscript: "Exterminate all the brutes!" Kurtz's prescription has indeed found an equivalent in Israeli minister of "defense" Yoav Gallant's sinister announcement: "I have ordered a complete siege on the Gaza Strip. There will be no electricity, no food, no fuel, everything is closed ... We are fighting human animals and we are acting accordingly."[2]

Unsurprisingly, the Western media have echoed Israel's media in depicting Hamas's operation as the deadliest attack targeting Jews since the Holocaust, continuing the usual pattern of Nazification of the Palestinians in order to justify their dehumanization and extermination. The truth, though, is that, however dreadful some aspects of Hamas's operation were, they are not a continuation of Nazi imperialist violence in any meaningful historical perspective. They are inscribed instead in two very different historical cycles: that of the Palestinians' struggle against Israeli colonial dispossession and oppression, and that of the struggle of the peoples of the Global South against colonialism. The key to the mindset behind Hamas's action is not to be found in Adolf Hitler's *Mein Kampf*, but in Frantz Fanon's *Wretched of the Earth* – the best-known interpretation of the feelings of the colonized, by a political thinker who was also a psychiatrist. Fanon reflected on the struggles of the colonized against French colonialism – the Algerians in particular. The parallels are striking:

> The colonized, who have made up their mind to make such an agenda into a driving force, have been prepared for violence from time immemorial. As soon as they are born it is obvious to them that their cramped world, riddled with taboos, can only be challenged by out and out violence ...
>
> The violence which governed the ordering of the colonial world ... will be vindicated and appropriated when, taking history into their own hands, the colonized swarm into the forbidden cities. To blow the colonial world to smithereens is henceforth a clear image within the grasp and imagination of every colonized subject. ...
>
> The outcome, however, is profoundly unequal, for machine-gunning by planes or bombardments from naval vessels outweigh in horror and scope the response from the colonized. The most alienated of the colonized are once and for all demystified by this pendulum motion of terror and counterterror. They see for themselves that any number of speeches on human equality cannot mask the absurdity whereby seven Frenchmen killed or wounded in an ambush at the Sakamody pass sparks the indignation of civilized consciences, whereas the sacking of the Guergour *douars*, the Djerah *dechra*, and the massacre of the population behind the ambush count for nothing.[3]

Were some of the acts committed by Hamas fighters during Operation Al-Aqsa Flood "terroristic"? If by "terrorism" is meant the deliberate assassination of unarmed people, they certainly were. But then, the deliberate killing of thousands upon thousands of Gazan civilians over the past seventeen years – since 2006, only a few months after Israel evacuated the Gaza Strip to control it from without, in the belief that the cost would be lesser than that of controlling it from within – that is terrorism, too. State terrorism has indeed caused much more casualties in history that terrorism by non-state groups.

Likewise, were some of the acts committed by Hamas fighters acts of "barbarism"? Undoubtedly so, but they were no less undoubtedly part of a clash of barbarisms. Allow me to quote here from what I wrote about this more than twenty years ago, in the wake of the 9/11 attacks:

> Taken separately, each barbarous act can be judged equally reprehensible from a moral standpoint. No civilized ethic can justify deliberate assassination of non-combatants or children, whether indiscriminate or deliberate, by state or non-governmental terror ...
>
> Nevertheless, from the point of view of basic fairness, we cannot wrap ourselves in a metaphysical ethic that rejects all forms of barbarism equally. The different barbarisms do not carry the same weight in the scales of justice. Admittedly, barbarism can never be an instrument of "legitimate self-defense"; it is always illegitimate by definition. But this does not change the fact that when two barbarisms clash, the stronger, the one that acts as the oppressor, is still the more culpable. Except in cases of manifest irrationality, the barbarism of the weak is most often, logically enough, a reaction to the barbarism of the strong. Otherwise, why would the weak provoke the strong, at the risk of being crushed themselves? This is, incidentally, why the strong seek to hide their culpability by portraying their adversaries as demented, demonic and bestial.[4]

The most crucial issue with Hamas's conception of the fight against Israeli occupation and oppression is not moral, but political and practical. Instead of serving Palestinian emancipation and winning over to its cause an increasing number of Israelis, Hamas's strategy facilitates the nationalist unity of Jewish Israelis and provides the Zionist state with pretexts for increased suppression of Palestinian rights and existence. The idea that the Palestinian people could achieve its national emancipation by way of armed confrontation with an Israeli state that is far superior militarily is irrational. The most effective episode in Palestinian struggle to this day was unarmed: the 1988 Intifada provoked a deep crisis in Israel's society, polity and armed forces, and won for the Palestinian cause massive sympathy in the world, Western countries included.

Hamas's latest operation – the most spectacular attack it has ever launched against Israel – has provided an opportunity for much more than the usual pattern of brutal murderous retaliation in a protracted cycle of violence and counter-violence. What looms on the horizon is nothing less than a second stage of the Nakba – the Arabic word for "catastrophe" that is the name given to the forced displacement of most of the indigenous Palestinian population from the territories that the newborn Israeli state managed to conquer in 1948. The present Israeli government, which includes neo-Nazis,[5] is led by the leader of Likud, and is thus the heir to the political groups that perpetrated the most infamous massacre of Palestinians in 1948: the Deir Yassin massacre. Benjamin Netanyahu led the opposition to Ariel Sharon, and resigned from the Israeli cabinet run by Sharon in 2005, when the latter opted for Israel's "unilateral disengagement" from Gaza. Soon after, Sharon quitted Likud, which Netanyahu has led ever since.

The Israeli far right, led by Likud, has been relentlessly pursuing its goal of a Greater Israel that encompasses the entire territory of British-mandate Palestine between the Mediterranean Sea and the Jordan River, including both the West Bank and Gaza. Only a few days before Hamas's operation, Netanyahu, during his speech at the UN General Assembly, brandished a map of Greater Israel – a deliberate signal that did not go unnoticed.[6] That is why the injunction given to the population of Northern Gaza to move southward is much more than the usual hypocritical excuse for the deliberate destruction of civilian-populated areas, while laying the blame at Hamas's door by accusing it of hiding among civilians (an absurd accusation indeed: How could Hamas exist in the wilderness, out of urban concentrations, without being wiped away by far superior Israeli means of remote warfare?).

What we are witnessing is in all likelihood the prelude to a second round of displacement of Gazans toward the Egyptian Sinai, with the intention of committing the second major act of territorial conquest combined with ethnic cleansing since the Nakba, under the pretext of eradicating Hamas. The Palestinians immediately remembered the 1948 exodus, when they fled war only to be prevented from returning to their towns and villages. They have understood that they are now facing in Gaza a second instance of forced displacement – a prelude to further dispossession and settler-colonization. This second stage of the Nakba will be much bloodier than the first: the number of Palestinians killed at the time of writing is already nearing the number of those killed in 1948, and this is but the beginning of the Israeli onslaught. Only massive popular mobilization in the United States and Europe to induce Western governments to pressure Israel into stopping before it fulfils its sinister war aims could prevent this dreadful outcome. This is extremely urgent. Make no mistake: the impending catastrophe will not be contained in the Middle East, but will certainly spill over into Western countries, as has been happening for several decades – on a yet more tragic scale.

NOTES

1   Gilbert Achcar, *The Clash of Barbarisms: The Making of the New World Disorder*, trans. Peter Drucker, 2nd edn, London: Saqi/Routledge, 2006, p. 34.
2   Emanuel Fabian, "Defense Minister Announces 'Complete Siege' of Gaza: No Power, Food or Fuel", *Times of Israel*, 9 October 2023.
3   Frantz Fanon, *The Wretched of the Earth*, trans. Richard Philcox, New York: Grove, 2004, pp. 3, 5–6, 47.
4   Achcar, *Clash of Barbarisms*, p. 89.
5   Ayelett Shani, "Israel's Government Has Neo-Nazi Ministers. It Really Does Recall Germany in 1933", *Haaretz*, 10 February 2023.
6   Liveblog, "Netanyahu Brandishes Map of Israel that Includes West Bank and Gaza at UN Speech", *Times of Israel*, 22 September 2023.

8.   7 October in Historical Perspective

A few months after writing the previous article, I returned to discussing the conflicting narratives about the Hamas-led attack, to demonstrate how it fully fitted within the history of anticolonial struggles, and plainly belonged to it, rather than to the history of Nazi crimes against the Jews. This was in my closing keynote speech at the conference on "The instrumentalization of antisemitism, or how an essential struggle is diverted toward a bad cause", held on 2 March 2024 at the Université libre de Bruxelles. The conference was organized by Institut Marcel Liebman, Union des progressistes juifs de Belgique, Association belgo-palestinienne, Bruxelles-Laïque, Cercle du Libre Examen and Actions in the Mediterranean. This article develops this aspect of my speech, and was first published in the original English on the Historical Materialism *website, on 7 May 2024.*

***

Seven months after Hamas's Al-Aqsa Flood attack across the fence surrounding the Gaza Strip on 7 October 2023, the provisional balance-sheet is daunting.

A PROVISIONAL BALANCE-SHEET

According to the available figures, on 7 October 1,143 mostly Israeli persons were killed – 767 civilians, including thirty-six children and seventy-one foreigners, and 376 military and security people – while close to 250 persons were abducted. On the same day, according to Israeli sources, more than 1,600 fighters among the assailants were killed on the spot, and close to 200 persons were detained. Since 7 October, according to Gazan sources, close to 35,000 Palestinians have been killed, among whom an estimated 40 per cent were children, i.e. 14,000, to whom should be added up to 20,000 persons believed to be buried under the rubble, along with close to 78,000 wounded, many with very serious injuries. The vast majority of the 2.4 million Gazans have been displaced, and the Strip's entire population is suffering from increasing famine, inflicted upon them by Israel's severe limitation of the amount of aid entering the enclave.

Most of Gaza's dwellings have been destroyed, in what is certainly the most destructive bombing campaign of this century, and probably the most destructive ever in terms of intensity (combining extent and speed), barring the use of nuclear weapons. In fact, whereas the atomic bomb dropped on Hiroshima had a blast of 15 kilotons of TNT, Israel's armed forces have already dropped close to five times this tonnage over Gaza's 365 square kilometers. Needless to say, at the time of writing, all of these figures are provisional, and still increasing by the day.

WHAT WAS 7 OCTOBER THE CONTINUATION OF?

Israel's immediate reaction to the 7 October attack was not only to call it the largest killing of Israelis in a single day, which is indisputable, but also "the largest massacre of Jews since the Holocaust" – a much more disputable description, loaded with an implicit political statement. And yet the latter description has become a mantra in Western countries, repeated for instance by French president Emmanuel Macron who, on 7 February 2024, called 7 October "the largest antisemitic massacre of our century", during a ceremony honoring forty-two holders of French citizenship who had been among those killed close to Gaza's border on that day.

For anyone bearing in mind the dreadful balance-sheet depicted above, the implicit analogy between the 7 October attack and the Nazi massacre of Jews must sound quite inappropriate, since it completely disregards the actual balance of forces, as well as the identity of the oppressors and oppressed in each case. As several experts on antisemitism and the Holocaust rightly noted in their collective "Open Letter on the Misuse of Holocaust Memory":

> It is understandable why many in the Jewish community recall the Holocaust and earlier pogroms when trying to comprehend what happened on October 7 – the massacres, and the images that came out in the aftermath, have tapped into deep-seated collective memory of genocidal antisemitism, driven by all-too-recent Jewish history.
>
> However, appealing to the memory of the Holocaust obscures our understanding of the antisemitism Jews face today, and dangerously misrepresents the causes of violence in Israel-Palestine. The Nazi genocide involved a state – and its willing civil society – attacking a tiny minority, which then escalated to a continent-wide genocide. Indeed, comparisons of the crisis unfolding in Israel-Palestine to Nazism and the Holocaust – above all when they come from political leaders and others who can sway public opinion – are intellectual and moral failings.[1]

This is notwithstanding the fact that, whatever resemblances one may identify between Hamas and the Nazis, there are certainly more similarities between the latter and Israel's far-right Zionist government, dominated by Likud – a party with a fascist pedigree[2] – and including ministers whom Israeli Holocaust historian Daniel Blatman, a professor at the Institute for Contemporary Jewry at the Hebrew University in Jerusalem, did not hesitate to describe as "neo-Nazi" in the Israeli daily *Haaretz*.[3]

7 OCTOBER IN CONTEXT

For having articulated on 24 October the rather obvious and banal truth that 7 October "did not happen in a vacuum", UN Secretary-General

Antonio Guterres was accused by Israel of "justifying terrorism", while Israel's ambassador at the UN demanded his resignation.[4] Pointing to the post-1967 occupation, Guterres had explained that "the Palestinian people have been subjected to 56 years of suffocating occupation. They have seen their land steadily devoured by settlements and plagued by violence; their economy stifled; their people displaced and their homes demolished. Their hopes for a political solution to their plight have been vanishing."[5]

He had also commented that "the grievances of the Palestinian people cannot justify the appalling attacks by Hamas. And those appalling attacks cannot justify the collective punishment of the Palestinian people." And yet, even Benny Gantz, Benjamin Netanyahu's political opponent and a supposedly "moderate" member of Israel's post-7 October war cabinet, stated that the UN secretary-general "condones terror", adding that "terror apologists cannot speak on behalf of the world" – thus tacitly approving the demand formulated by Israel's envoy.

Those reactions by Israeli officials were but further instances of the denial of reality common to all occupying powers in modern times, ever since the prevailing ethics and international law of modern times condemned occupation of another people's territory. In fact, not only did 7 October "not happen in a vacuum"; it was entirely predictable that a flare-up of violence would occur at some point, in the Gaza Strip in particular. In December 2009, two years into the blockade imposed by Israel on Gaza after the withdrawal of its troops in 2005 and the enclave's takeover by Hamas in 2007, and a few months after Israel's first major campaign of bombing of the enclave (2008–09), Larry Derfner put the right questions to his fellow Israeli citizens in the *Jerusalem Post*:

> The question we have to ask ourselves is this: If anybody treated us like we're treating the people in Gaza, what would we do? ...
>
> It's not that we can't imagine life in Gaza. It's that we are determined not to try to imagine. If we did, we might not stop there. Next we might try to imagine what it would be like if our country were in the condition in which we left Gaza. And sooner or later we might try to imagine what we would do if we were living over here like they're living over there.

    Or not even what we would do, just what we would think –
about the people, about the country, that did that to us and that
wouldn't even allow us to begin to recover after the war was over.
That blockaded our borders and allowed in only enough supplies
to keep us at subsistence level, to prevent starvation and mass
epidemics.[6]

The truth is that portraying Hamas as primarily motivated by
antisemitism and akin to the Nazis is but the continuation, in the
present new intensive episode of the "Arab-Israeli war of narratives",
of an old, proven narrative stratagem inaugurated by the post-1945
exploitation of the figure of Amin al-Husseini to present the Zionist
conquest of Palestinian land in 1948 as World War II's ultimate battle.[7]
Thus, the last episode of colonial conquest in modern times could be
presented as the latest battle against Nazism.

    This stratagem works well in those parts of the world that bear
the guilt of the Nazi genocide of European Jews: populations whose
ancestors were perpetrators, direct accomplices or bystanders, including
those who slammed their countries' doors in the face of Jewish refugees.
The same stratagem does not work, however, for most of humankind,
which, based in the Global South, had little stake in World War II,
and has always perceived the Palestinians as continuators not of Nazi
imperialism, but of the long, bloody series of colonial victims.

HISTORICAL FLASHBACK: ANGOLA 1961

In the aftermath of 7 October, my friend Michel Cahen, a French
specialist of the history of Portuguese-speaking Africa, drew my
attention to a historical episode that took place in Angola in 1961, and
bears a striking resemblance to the ongoing events in the Middle East.
Intrigued, I researched the matter, and found that the parallel goes way
beyond the moment of 7 October alone.

    In 1961, against the background of major progress in decolonization
on the African continent, resentment against die-hard Portuguese
colonialism tremendously increased in Angola, especially after the
neighboring Republic of Congo (later the Democratic Republic of
Congo) had achieved its independence from Belgian colonial rule in

the previous year, prompting Portuguese colonial authorities to increase their repression of the Angolan independence movement. Anticolonial armed struggle was progressing in Africa's remaining colonial dominions, and Angola was no exception. One of its anticolonial movements was the Union of Angola's Peoples (UPA), whose leader, Holden Roberto, had links with both the Algerian National Liberation Front – whose name it would adopt later to become the National Liberation Front of Angola (FLNA) – and with the CIA.

On 15 March 1961, UPA fighters crossed the border from Congo into northern Angola, joined by many local natives. A ragtag mass of four to five thousand men, a few of them armed with rifles and most with machetes, went on the rampage, killing in unspeakably horrendous ways several hundred, and perhaps as many as one thousand (there are no precise figures) white colonists – men, women, babies and children – along with many more Angolans of other ethnicities or of mixed race (*mestiços*). As Maria da Conceição Neto wrote sixty years later,

> [T]he images of slaughtered whites, mestiços and blacks would become the centrepiece of Portuguese propaganda to discredit the attackers as "terrorists" and "barbarians" without any political objective. To this day, these are the most widespread images about "the 15th of March", immediately creating a barrier to understanding what has happened ...[8]

The Portuguese government of far-right dictator António de Oliveira Salazar – who personally took the ministry of defense in hand for the purpose – launched a massive retaliatory campaign, including extensive use of the air force. In a few months, tens of thousands – over 50,000 by the end of the year, according to Nkwelle Ekaney – had been killed among the black population, several villages having been burned and razed across a vast area.[9] A major weapon used by the Portuguese air force in perpetrating this genocidal massacre was napalm, provided by the US administration of John F. Kennedy.[10]

Two more elements of the historical record are relevant here. First, The UPA/FLNA would carry on as a CIA-backed rival of the Soviet-backed People's Movement for the Liberation of Angola (MPLA). However, far-right Portugal was a founding member of NATO. Therefore, as Roberto himself later explained to a Swedish researcher,

We could not receive assistance from the Western countries, because of NATO and the relations with Portugal. We had no support. The little support that we could count upon was from African and Arab countries, such as Tunisia. And Israel, which was very important for us. The Israeli government helped us at that time.

TOR SELLSTRÖM: With weapons?

HOLDEN ROBERTO: With weapons. It was with the help by Golda Meir.[11]

Second, Frantz Fanon – who had encouraged Roberto to launch armed struggle[12] – commented on the Angolan events in the chapter entitled "Grandeur and Weakness of Spontaneity", in his famous 1961 book *The Wretched of the Earth* in the following terms:

On March 15, 1961, we recall, the Angolan peasants in groups of two or three thousand attacked the Portuguese positions. Men, women, and children, armed and unarmed, courageously and enthusiastically hurled themselves en masse in wave after wave against the regions dominated by the colonists, the military, and the Portuguese flag. Villages and airports were surrounded and suffered numerous attacks, but thousands of Angolans were mowed down by colonialist machine gun fire. The leaders of the Angolan uprising soon realized that they would have to adopt different tactics if they really wanted to liberate their country. The Angolan leader, Roberto Holden, therefore, has recently reorganized the Angolan National Army using the model of other liberation wars and guerrilla warfare techniques.[13]

IN CONCLUSION

Which of these two historical sequences is more similar to the Hamas-led anti-Israeli 7 October, and the ensuing onslaught led by the Israeli far-right government: a Nazi-led anti-Jewish rampage, followed by the destruction of European Jews perpetrated by the same Nazis; or the

UPA-led anti-Portuguese rampage, and the ensuing onslaught led by the Portuguese far-right government with the complicity of the United States?

Were the UPA-led Angolans of 15 March primarily motivated by anti-white racism, or by hatred of Portuguese colonial oppression? Likewise, were the Hamas-led Palestinians of 7 October primarily motivated by antisemitism, or by hatred of Israeli colonial oppression? The answers to these questions should be obvious to anyone who is not blinded by anti-Palestinian, anti-Arab or anti-Muslim racism, and "narcissistic compassion" for whitened Israelis.[14]

NOTES

1   Omer Bartov, Christopher R. Browning, Jane Caplan, Debórah Dwork, David Feldman, et al., "An Open Letter on the Misuse of Holocaust Memory", website of the *New York Review of Books*, 20 November 2023.

2   See, among many other sources, Noam Rotem, "The Israeli Right's Historic Ties to European Fascism", *+972 Magazine*, 14 April 2016.

3   Ayelett Shani, "Israel's Government Has Neo-Nazi Ministers. It Really Does Recall Germany in 1933", *Haaretz*, 10 February 2023.

4   ToI Staff and AFP, "Israel Demands UN Chief Resign after He Says Hamas Attacks 'Did Not Occur in Vacuum'", *Times of Israel*, 24 October 2023.

5   Ibid.

6   Larry Derfner, "Rattling the Cage: A Taboo Question for Israelis", *Jerusalem Post*, 30 December 2009.

7   See Gilbert Achcar, *The Arabs and the Holocaust: The Arab-Israeli War of Narratives*, 2nd edn, London: Saqi, 2025; Gilbert Achcar, "Israel's Propaganda War: Blame the Grand Mufti", *Le Monde diplomatique*, English edn, May 2010.

8   Maria da Conceição Neto, "Março de 1961 – O início da guerra no Norte de Angola", *Publico*, 22 July 2021. On the role of images, see also Giselda Brito Silva, "As revoltas na Baixa de Cassange e o direito à memória e história nas lutas de libertação de Angola: entre o 04 de janeiro e o 15 de março de 1961", *Cadernos do Tempo Presente* 12: 2 (July–December 2021), at periodicos.ufs.br/tempo/article/view/17075/12488.

9   Nkwelle Ekaney, "Angola: Post-Mortem of a Conflict", *Présence Africaine*, nouvelle série 98, 2nd quarter of 1976, pp. 211–33, at jstor.org/stable/24349794.

10 See David Birmingham, *A Short History of Modern Angola*, New York: Oxford University Press, 2015, p. 72.

11 Holden Roberto interviewed by Tor Sellström, website of *The Nordic Africa Institute* (Sweden), at nai.uu.se/library/resources/liberation-africa/interviews/holden-roberto.html.

12   See the biographies of Frantz Fanon by David Macey, *Frantz Fanon: A Biography*, London: Verso, 2012, pp. 386–7, and Adam Shatz, *The Rebel's Clinic: The Revolutionary Lives of Frantz Fanon*, New York: Farrar, Straus & Giroux, 2024, pp. 248–9.

13   Frantz Fanon, *The Wretched of the Earth*, trans. Richard Philcox, New York: Grove, 2004, p. 85.

14   See Chapter 1, above.

9. Two Gaza Scenarios: Greater Israel vs. Oslo

Less than two weeks beyond 7 October and the beginning of the ensuing Israeli onslaught on Gaza, before its ground invasion, I wrote this assessment of the two alternative scenarios being prepared for the Strip – first published on the website of New Lines *magazine on 23 October 2023. After explaining the terrible logic that would inevitably lead to the full destruction of Gaza, I described the two possible – and competing – outcomes of Israel's reoccupation of the Strip.*

***

Announced as imminent several days ago, after over 1 million inhabitants of the northern half of the Gaza Strip were given only twenty-four hours to flee south, the Israeli armed forces' land onslaught on Gaza has yet to start, at the time of writing. Despite attempts to convey a contrary impression, this delay reflects the fact that Israel's political leadership and military command had no oven-ready plan for the invasion of Gaza on the scale they have been contemplating since the assault launched by Hamas on 7 October. The Israeli armed forces could hardly have been anticipating a reoccupation of Gaza, which they evacuated eighteen years ago. The successive operations they launched against the strip in 2006, 2008–09, 2012, 2014, and 2021 – to mention only the largest ones – have all been limited, essentially consisting of bombing, along with limited ground assaults in 2009 and 2014. But the extraordinary scale and traumatizing effect of 7 October made it impossible for Israel's leaders to set a lesser goal than the total eradication of Hamas from Gaza and the "pacification" of the strip.

This is a formidable challenge, for not only does the invasion of such a densely populated territory involve urban warfare of a kind that is highly risky for the assailant, but it poses most acutely the problem of what to do with the conquered territory the day after. The issue is not only military, needless to say; it is also, even primarily, political. The tight interdependency of political and military considerations is especially clear in the present situation. The scale of violence that is unavoidable in the pursuit of Israel's proclaimed goals will inevitably provoke a political fallout, which will impact the conduct of the war itself.

The most obvious factor in the equation is that Israel's tolerance for losses among its troops is very limited, as illustrated most spectacularly by the exchange in 2011 of Israeli soldier Gilad Shalit, held captive in Gaza, for over 1,000 Palestinian prisoners. This makes it impossible for the Israeli army to launch ground assaults under conditions that impose a heavy cost in soldiers' lives, like the assaults that Russian troops (regular ones and/or those affiliated with the Wagner paramilitary service) have been launching in Ukraine since 2022 – not to mention extreme cases like Iran's "human waves" during its 1980–88 war with Iraq. Thus, the Israeli army's superiority is at its maximum in terrains such as Egypt's Sinai desert or the Syrian Golan Heights, where buildings are scarce and firepower from a distance is decisive. Conversely, when Ariel Sharon, Israel's minister of defense at the time, ordered his troops to enter besieged Beirut in early August 1982, they had to abandon the attempt the next day. It was only after the negotiated evacuation of Palestinian fighters from Beirut that Israeli forces managed to storm the city, in mid-September. They withdrew by the end of the same month after a nascent Lebanese urban resistance movement started to target them.

A corollary of this is that the only way for Israel's army to invade any part of so dense and vast an urban landscape as the Gaza Strip with minimal Israeli losses is to flatten the areas that it strives to occupy by way of intensive bombing before launching the ground offensive. This is indeed what started in the immediate aftermath of 7 October, with a level of damage that, in both extent and intensity, went way beyond prior Israeli bombing campaigns, from Lebanon in 2006 to the successive wars on Gaza. Flattening vast swaths of urban territory was not possible for the Israeli military in any of the previous wars – not for lack of destructive power, of course, but for the absence of the necessary political conditions.

This was most obvious in 1982, when the Israeli siege of Beirut provoked a major international outcry and political crisis inside Israel itself, where the opposition to the Likud government of Menachem Begin and Ariel Sharon came out in massive protests. In the previous wars against Gaza, Israel's armed forces had no intention of reoccupying part of Gaza anyway. This time around, this intention is on clear display, and the shockwaves from the unprecedented killing of huge numbers of Israeli civilians as well as soldiers are of such a magnitude that both the Israeli public and Israel's traditional international backers are explicitly or implicitly approving the reoccupation of Gaza in its entirety. What can the eradication of Hamas and the analogy with the Islamic State group mean, short of conducting a search and sweep operation in the whole of the strip?

As the *Financial Times* recently reported, based on interviews with military experts,

> Israel's army will deploy its so-called "doctrine of victory", which requires the air force to have a deep bank of pre-vetted targets destroyed in rapid order. It is already in play, with fighter jets intensely bombing large swaths of Gaza, pausing only to refuel, often in mid-air. The campaign is meant to outpace the ability of Hamas to regroup and, according to a person familiar with the discussions that created the 2020 doctrine, to "achieve maximum goals before the international community puts political pressure to slow down".[1]

This is the military scenario that is brewing. Now comes the political dimension. If the military goal is indeed to reoccupy Gaza in order to eradicate Hamas, the next questions, naturally, are: For how long? And to replace Hamas with what? There is much more room for disagreement on these two questions of political strategy than on the military strategy, whose parameters are much narrower, since they depend on objective considerations and the nature of the military means at hand. The two opposite poles of the political divergence translate into two scenarios that we might call the Greater Israel scenario and the Oslo scenario.

The Greater Israel scenario is the one that appeals most to Benjamin Netanyahu and his acolytes on Israel's far right. The Likud Party is heir to the Zionist far right, known as Revisionist Zionism, whose armed offshoots perpetrated the Deir Yassin massacre, the most infamous mass murder of Palestinians in 1948, amid what the Arabs call the Nakba ("catastrophe"). On the 78 per cent of the territory of British Mandate Palestine that Zionist armed forces managed to conquer during the war of that year (the Zionists had been granted 55 per cent by the partition plan approved by a nascent United Nations Organization, then dominated by countries of the Global North), 80 per cent of the Palestinian population were uprooted. They had fled the war, frightened by atrocities such as Deir Yassin, and were never to be allowed to return to their homes and land. And yet the Zionist far right never forgave mainstream Zionism, which was then led by David Ben-Gurion, for having agreed to stop the war before conquering 100 per cent of British Mandate Palestine between the Mediterranean Sea and the Jordan River.

During his recent speech at the UN General Assembly in New York, only two weeks before 7 October, Netanyahu brandished a map of the Middle East showing a Greater Israel that included Gaza and the West Bank. Even more relevant to the new Gaza war was the fact – hardly mentioned in the global media – that Netanyahu had resigned from the Israeli cabinet led by Sharon in 2005 in protest against the latter's decision to withdraw from Gaza. (Sharon had succeeded Netanyahu as the head of Likud in 1999, following the latter's electoral defeat to the Labor Party, then led by Ehud Barak. Sharon then managed to win the next election, in 2003, and offered the ministry of finance to Netanyahu.)

Much more an army man than a politician, Sharon was attentive to the military's plea for a withdrawal of troops from the unruly Gaza, with a preference for controlling the strip from outside. He saw no prospect for an annexation of Gaza similar to what has been occurring in the West Bank since its occupation in 1967. He therefore judged that it would be wiser to let the Palestinian Authority, established by the 1993 Oslo Accords, take care of Gaza, while focusing on the West Bank – a much more prized and consensual Zionist goal.

Oslo required the withdrawal of Israeli troops only from those West Bank areas densely populated by Palestinians, while allowing Israel to maintain control of most of the territory. To show his contempt for the Palestinian Authority, Sharon opted for a unilateral "disengagement" from Gaza in 2005 – without, that is, preparing this move with the Palestinian Authority. Two years later, Hamas seized power in the strip.

Netanyahu protested Sharon's disengagement, leading the opposition to Sharon within Likud. He gathered enough support to incite him to quit the party, and found a new one that same year, 2005. Netanyahu has led Likud ever since. He maneuvred his way to the prime ministership in 2009 by playing on the fragmentation of the Israeli political scene – an art at which, as the consummate opportunist, he excels – and remained in office until June 2021. By the end of 2022, he was back at the helm, heading the most far-right government in Israel's history – a country where several successive governments since Likud's first victory in 1977 have been labeled the "most right-wing in history", in an unending drift to the right. Netanyahu nodded to Donald Trump's (and Jared Kushner's) "peace plan" in 2020 only because he knew full well that the Palestinians could not accept it. He likely saw this inevitable rejection as a good pretext for a unilateral annexation of most of the West Bank at some later point.

The prospect of reconquering Gaza required a major upheaval that was not on the horizon. No one could have expected that it would be created, all of a sudden, by Hamas's "Al-Aqsa Flood" operation. It was indeed the Israeli equivalent of 9/11. In fact, 7 October was twenty times more deadly than 9/11 relative to each country's population, as Netanyahu pointed out to Joe Biden during the latter's visit to Israel on 18 October. Just as 9/11 created the political conditions that allowed the Bush administration to realize its pet project of invading Iraq, Israel's 7 October created the political conditions for Gaza's reconquest – something that Netanyahu had long desired, but that was too wild and out of bounds to be openly discussed up to that point. Whether this goal is attainable remains to be seen, of course, but it is what the Zionist hard right aspires to.

The repeated calls by Israel's political and military authorities to Gaza's inhabitants to flee southwards, toward the border with Egypt, and their eagerness to convince Cairo to open the door to the Sinai Peninsula and take in the bulk of Gaza's population (2.3 million people), are thus rightly understood by the Egyptians as an invitation to let the Gazans settle in Sinai for the indefinite future – just as the

Palestinians displaced from their land in 1948 and 1967 have been turned into permanent refugees in neighboring Arab countries. On 18 October, Egyptian President Abdel Fattah El-Sisi poured cold water on this idea, cunningly advising Israel to give refuge to the Gazans in the Negev desert, within its own 1948 territory, if it was truly seeking to grant them only temporary shelter.[2]

Greater Israel is not a unanimous ambition of Israel's leaders, however – not even after 7 October. It has some support in the United States, from the far right of the Republican Party and among Christian Zionists. But it is certainly not supported by the bulk of the US foreign policy establishment, the Democrats in particular. The Biden administration – well known to have little sympathy for Netanyahu, who in 2012 openly backed Mitt Romney for president against Barack Obama (and Biden, his vice president) – sticks to the prospect, created by the Oslo Accords, of a Palestinian rump state, providing an alibi to sideline the Palestinian cause and clear the way for the development of links and collaboration between Israel and the Arab states.

This is why Biden told CBS on 15 October that "it would be a big mistake" for Israel to occupy Gaza. The US president did not mean that the invasion of the entire strip in order to eradicate Hamas would be a mistake. On the contrary, he clearly stated: "Going in but taking out the extremists ... is a necessary requirement." Asked then, "Do you believe that Hamas must be eliminated entirely?" Biden replied:

> Yes, I do. But there needs to be a Palestinian authority. There needs to be a path to a Palestinian state. That path, called "the two state solution", has been US policy for decades. It would create an independent nation next to Israel for 5 million Palestinians who live in Gaza and on the West Bank of the Jordan River.[3]

The purpose of Biden's daylong visit to Israel was not only to enhance his political profile for the 2024 presidential election, ensuring that Trump, right-wing Republicans and evangelical Christian Zionists could not outflank him in their military support for Israel. (Note that in doing so, Biden was going against the views of a majority of US citizens, and especially the majority of Democrats, who favor a more balanced approach to the Israeli-Palestinian conflict.) Nor was Biden's purpose only to negotiate a token humanitarian gesture in order to pretend that his administration was doing all it could to alleviate the unfolding disaster. His purpose was also, and perhaps primarily, to convince the Israeli polity – with or without Netanyahu – of the necessity of sticking to the Oslo perspective. He aimed to boost this endeavor by meeting with Mahmoud Abbas, the head of the Palestinian Authority, and with the king of Jordan. But the destruction of the Al-Ahli Arab Hospital on the eve of his visit thwarted his plan.

The clearest indication yet that part of the Israeli military-political establishment sees eye to eye with the Biden administration has been provided by Ehud Barak, former chief of the general staff of the Israeli armed forces and former prime minister. He fine-tuned the Oslo scenario in an interview with the *Economist*:

> Mr Barak believes that the optimal outcome, once Hamas's military capabilities have been sufficiently degraded, is the re-establishment of the Palestinian Authority in Gaza ... However he warns that Mahmoud Abbas, the Palestinian president, "cannot be seen to be returning on Israeli bayonets". There will, therefore, need to be an interim period during which "Israel will capitulate to international pressure and hand Gaza over to an Arab peacekeeping force, which could include members such as Egypt, Morocco and the United Arab Emirates. They would secure the area until the Palestinian Authority could take control."[4]

The fact that the Oslo process stalled shortly after being launched with great pomp in 1993 – which led to the outbreak of the Second Intifada in 2000, followed by Israel's temporary reoccupation of those parts of the West Bank that it had evacuated in favor of the Palestinian Authority – does not seem to deter Washington and its allies from regarding it as the only feasible settlement. They probably believe that some sort of territorial swap, like the one that was envisaged in the Trump-Kushner "peace plan", might eventually reconcile the annexation of the West Bank areas, where settlements have been proliferating, with granting the Palestinians a fragmented "independent state" on 22 per cent of their ancestral land west of the Jordan River.

Ultimately, the two scenarios – Greater Israel and Oslo – are predicated on Israel's ability to destroy Hamas to a degree sufficient to prevent it from controlling Gaza. This entails the conquest of most of the strip, if not all of it, by Israel's armed forces – a goal they could only achieve by destroying most of Gaza, which would come at an enormous human cost.

The *Washington Post* recently quoted Bruce Hoffman, a counter-terrorism expert and professor at Georgetown University, who pointed to the eradication of the Tamil Tigers in the northern part of Sri Lanka as the only type of success achievable in such endeavors. The Tigers were wiped out in 2009 after a military offensive by Sri Lanka's armed forces that involved the killing of up to 40,000 civilians, according to UN estimates. "God forbid that that sort of carnage unfolds today", Hoffman told the *Post*. "But, if you're determined to destroy a terrorist organization, you can. There's a ruthlessness that goes with it."[5]

The world's attention, however, is incomparably more focused on what happens in the Middle East than it was on what happened in Sri Lanka. The question therefore becomes what the Israeli army can achieve before a combination of losses in personnel and international pressure forces it to stop – not to mention the possibility of a regional conflagration involving Lebanon's Hezbollah, with Iran's backing. So, it is by no means certain that either of the two scenarios will materialize. Israel's military has cautiously drafted a minimal plan consisting of creating a new, extended buffer zone inside Gaza all along its borders, further aggravating the strip's condition as an "open-air prison".

The only certainties are that Israel's new onslaught on Gaza is already deadlier and more destructive than all previous episodes in the tragic seventy-five-year history of the Israeli-Palestinian conflict, and that the situation will deteriorate exponentially. This will only add to the destabilization of what is already the most unstable region of the world, and plays a major role in destabilizing the Global North itself – with waves of refugees and the spillover of violence. Yet again, the shortsightedness and double standards of the United States and its European allies are going to blow back in their faces – this time with even more tragic consequences.

NOTES

1   Mehul Srivastava and John Paul Rathbone, "Military Briefing: 'Everything You Can Imagine and Worse' Awaits Israeli Army in Gaza", *Financial Times*, 12 October 2023.

2   "Sisi Rejects Displacement of Palestinians into Sinai, Suggests Transfer to Israel's Negev Desert", *Arab Weekly*, 19 October 2023.

3   Scott Pelley, "President Joe Biden: The 2023 60 Minutes Interview Transcript", CBS News, 15 October 2023.

4   "Ehud Barak Blames Benjamin Netanyahu for 'the Greatest Failure in Israel's History'", *Economist*, 15 October 2023.

5   Dan Lamothe, "Israeli Ground Offensive in Gaza Could Be a 'Bloodbath', Analysts Say", *Washington Post*, 15 October 2023.

10. The Israeli Far Right's Plans for Expulsion and Expansion

This article describes the Israeli far right's plans as they evolved historically into the onslaught on Gaza. Translated from the French original by George Miller, it was first published in Le Monde diplomatique, English edition, *in December 2023.*

***

It is often said that wars are easier to start than to finish. Israel's war in Gaza is already proving to be a particularly telling demonstration of this formula. Hamas's Al-Aqsa Flood operation of 7 October has given Israel's far right, which dominates the government Benjamin Netanyahu formed in late 2022, the ideal opportunity to implement its plan for a Greater Israel that includes the West Bank and Gaza – in other words, the whole of British Mandate Palestine.

The political-ideological lineage of the Likud party, which Benjamin Netanyahu has run since 2005 (and before that in 1996–99) can be traced back to a fascist-inspired strain of "revisionist Zionism" that emerged in the interwar period. Before Israel's foundation, this movement campaigned for the Zionist project of incorporating the entire territory of the British mandate on both banks of the Jordan, including Transjordan, which Britain granted to the Hashemite dynasty in 1921, creating present-day Jordan. Later, having focused its ambition on mandatory Palestine, the movement criticized Laborite Zionism, led by David Ben-Gurion, for having stopped fighting in 1949, before it took the West Bank and Gaza.

For Ben-Gurion and his comrades, this was simply unfinished business: Israel occupied both territories in 1967. Since then, Likud has consistently sought to outdo the territorial ambitions of Laborite Zionism and its allies when it comes to these territories. But in 1967, instead of fleeing the fighting, as had happened in 1948, most residents of the West Bank and Gaza remained on their land and in their homes. They had learned the lesson of 1948: 80 per cent of the Palestinians, who had lived in the territory that formed the state of Israel the following year and represented 78 per cent of mandatory Palestine, had left in search of temporary refuge. That turned out to be permanent, as the new state denied them their right of return. This dispossession is at the heart of what Arabs call the Nakba ("catastrophe").

As there was no exact repeat of the Palestinian exodus in 1967 (though 245,000 Palestinians, mostly refugees from 1948, did flee to the other side of the Jordan), the Israeli government's desire to annex the territories was jeopardized by demographics: annexing them and granting their inhabitants Israeli citizenship would endanger Israel's Jewishness; annexing them *without* granting such a right would undermine its democracy (an "ethnic democracy", according to Israeli sociologist Sammy Smooha) by formalizing apartheid. The solution devised for this problem – known as the Allon Plan, after Yigal Allon, the deputy prime minister who came up with it in 1967–68 – was to take long-term control of the Jordan Valley and areas with a low concentration of Palestinians in the West Bank, and to give Jordan administrative control over more populous areas.

LIKUD'S QUEST FOR ANNEXATION

Likud opposed this plan, and kept pushing for the annexation of the two newly occupied territories and their complete colonization, not limiting themselves to the areas targeted under the Allon Plan in Judea and Samaria (the biblical names of the regions of which the West Bank is a part). Likud won the 1977 election, which meant that, less than thirty years after Israel's founding, the Zionist far right was in power. It would remain in control for most of the next forty-six years, including more than sixteen under Netanyahu, all the while shifting further right.

In late 1987 the Palestinian popular uprising known as the first Intifada challenged Likud's hegemony and the prospect of a Greater Israel. The Labor Party returned to power in 1992 under Yitzhak Rabin, more determined than ever to implement the Allon Plan. Jordan officially relinquished administration of the West Bank in 1988, in the midst of the Intifada, and was replaced by the PLO as Israel's partner for dialogue. The PLO leadership agreed to temporarily abandon its previously non-negotiable conditions: the eventual withdrawal of the Israeli army from all Palestinian territories occupied in 1967 and the ultimate dismantling of the settlements, a process which would begin with the halting of their expansion. This enabled the Oslo Accords, signed in Washington by Rabin and Yasser Arafat in September 1993 and presided over by Bill Clinton.

In 1996 Likud, led by Netanyahu, returned to power, but was again defeated three years later by Ehud Barak's Labor Party. Netanyahu had to resign, and was replaced by Ariel Sharon, who led Likud to victory in 2001, following his provocative visit to the Temple Mount/Haram al-Sharif in Jerusalem in autumn 2000, setting in motion the Second Intifada. In 2005 Sharon implemented Israel's unilateral withdrawal from the Gaza Strip, and dismantled the few settlements that had been established there. He thus pleased his military, who had struggled to control this densely populated territory. Sharon's main aim was to annex as much of the West Bank as possible, pursuing the option outlined by the Allon Plan in maximalist, unilateral fashion.

Netanyahu, who was Sharon's finance minister, resigned from the government in protest at the withdrawal from Gaza. He cited security reasons, while playing up to Likud's hardline base and the settler movement. Sharon, now at odds with his own party, quit in autumn 2005, clearing the way for Netanyahu's comeback. In 2009 Netanyahu became prime minister again – a post he held until June 2021, breaking Ben-Gurion's record. He returned to the role yet again in December 2022 by forming an alliance with two parties of the religious Zionist ultraright.

The Jewish Power (Otzma Yehudit) party, led by Itamar Ben Gvir, is directly descended from Kach, founded by Jewish supremacist Meir Kahane, who advocated the immediate "transfer" of Arabs from the "land of Israel" – in other words, the ethnic cleansing of the entire territory from the Mediterranean to the Jordan.[1] Bezalel Smotrich, leader of the Religious Zionist Party, made headlines in October 2021 when he told Arab deputies in the Knesset, "It's a mistake that Ben-Gurion didn't finish the job and didn't throw you out in 1948."[2]

FURTHER SETTLEMENT EXPANSION

The current Israeli government is thus dominated by politicians committed to realizing a Greater Israel through the annexation of the territories conquered in 1967 and the expulsion of their indigenous populations. But such a plan could only be accomplished in normal times by a long-term course of action with no guarantee of success: creeping annexation of the West Bank by the expansion of settlements, and harassment of its inhabitants – both of which become markedly worse since the establishment of the far-right government and the economic strangulation of Gaza.

Like the George W. Bush administration, which was full of figures who had urged Bill Clinton to invade Iraq but were unable to implement this project out of the blue, the far right needed a strong political pretext. It is in this respect that comparisons between the 9/11 attacks in the US and Hamas's operation on 7 October are especially relevant. Netanyahu emphasized this analogy when US president Joe Biden made a visit in support of Israel on 18 October. The Al-Aqsa Flood was immediately exploited by the entire Israeli far right to push for the implementation of their expansionist plan.

This clearly caught the Israeli army unprepared. War plans in response to the 7 October attack had to be hastily drawn up, which explains the delay in launching the Gaza ground offensive. The three weeks between Hamas's operation and the start of the invasion on 27 October were, however, used to intensively bombard urban population centers so that the ground offensive could be executed at the lowest cost in lives of Israeli soldiers – and, consequently, at the highest cost in lives of Palestinian civilians, many of them inevitably being children.

The Israeli government's disregard for harm to civilians, shared by the war cabinet established on 11 October, was expressed most bluntly by defense minister Yoav Gallant, a "moderate" member of Likud and

Netanyahu rival, who announced on 9 October that he had ordered a complete siege of the Gaza Strip, which he justified by describing the enemy as "human animals". There have been plenty more such declarations from members of the government and influential figures in Israeli political and intellectual life,[3] to the point that a 300-strong lawyers' collective filed a complaint against Israel on 9 November at the International Criminal Court alleging that its actions in Gaza amounted to genocide – a charge that implies deliberate intent.[4]

ISRAEL'S POSTWAR PLANS FOR GAZA

The same complaint also highlighted "population transfers", given the massive displacement of the Gazan population underway within the enclave. Israel's intention is more clearly manifest in this respect. In the aftermath of 7 October, the Israeli intelligence ministry – led by another Likud member, Gila Gamliel, and coordinated between the external service, Mossad, and the internal one, Shin Bet, under the auspices of the prime minister – put together a plan for Gaza that was finalized on 13 October, and revealed two weeks later on the Israeli dissident site Mekomit. Titled "Options for a Policy Regarding Gaza's Civilian Population", the paper considers three alternatives: (a) the population remaining in Gaza and the import of Palestinian Authority rule; (b) the population remaining in Gaza along with the emergence of a local Arab authority (to be set up by Israel); and (c) the evacuation of the civilian population from Gaza to Sinai.[5]

The document suggests that the first two options present "significant deficiencies", as neither is capable of producing the "necessary deterrent effect" in the long term. Option (c), however, "will yield positive, long-term strategic outcomes for Israel, and is an executable option. It requires determination from the political echelon in the face of international pressure, with an emphasis on harnessing the support of the United States and additional pro-Israeli countries for the endeavor."

Each scenario is then described in some detail. Option (c), favored by the intelligence ministry, begins with the evacuation of "the non-combatant population from the combat area", followed by their transfer to Egyptian Sinai. Initially, refugees would be sheltered in tent cities.

"The next stage includes the establishment of a humanitarian zone to assist the civilian population of Gaza and the construction of cities in a resettled area in northern Sinai", while maintaining a security perimeter – "a sterile zone" – on both sides of the border.

The paper then describes how the transfer of the Gazan population would be carried out. It advocates calling for the evacuation of civilians from the combat zone while concentrating airstrikes on northern Gaza to clear the way for a ground offensive that would start from the north and continue until the entire Gaza Strip was under occupation. In doing so, "it is important to leave the travel routes to the south open to enable the evacuation of the civilian population toward Rafah", where the only Egyptian border crossing is located. The paper notes that this option fits into a global context where "large-scale migration from war zones (Syria, Afghanistan, Ukraine) and population movement is a natural and sought-after outcome due to the dangers associated with remaining in the war zone".

THE ORDER TO MOVE SOUTH

On 13 October, the day this intelligence document was finalized, the Israeli army told people in northern Gaza to move south. On 30 October, the *Financial Times* reported that Netanyahu had lobbied European governments to put pressure on Egypt to allow Gazan refugees to cross to Sinai.[6] Though it received the backing of some attendees at the European summit on 26–27 October, the idea was judged unrealistic by France, Germany and the UK.

According to Israel's intelligence ministry, "Egypt has an obligation under international law to allow the passage of the population". In exchange for its cooperation, it would receive financial aid to alleviate its current economic crisis. However, despite a debt burden which is costing his country nearly 10 per cent of GDP just to service, Egypt's president Abdel Fattah El-Sisi has categorically rejected any transfer of the Gazan population to Egypt. His government even organized a billboard campaign declaring: "No to the liquidation of the Palestinian cause at Egypt's expense".

The reason for this refusal is certainly not sympathy for that cause. The Egyptian president spelled it out during German chancellor Olaf

Scholz's visit to Cairo on 18 October, to sound him out on this option. Sisi emphasized that the transfer of the Gazan population to Sinai would make Egypt "a base for attacks against Israel", jeopardizing relations between the countries.[7] The Egyptian government knows how explosive the Palestinian issue can be, especially as the ongoing war has made it yet more volatile. Likewise, the Jordanian government, alarmed by the intensification of settler attacks and IDF operations in the West Bank since 7 October, has warned against any displacement of Palestinians across the Jordan.

Israeli supporters of expelling Gazans may nevertheless be counting on the concentration of people fleeing the invasion forces becoming so great that the Egyptian border guards at the crossing are overwhelmed. Moreover, Egypt's refusal prompted the intelligence minister, Gila Gamliel, on 19 November to call on the international community to take in the Palestinians from Gaza and pay for their "voluntary resettlement" around the world, rather than mobilize funds for the reconstruction of the enclave.[8]

Washington, however, has been unequivocal in its opposition to the forced relocation of Palestinians from Gaza. While providing unwavering support for the Israeli offensive, US officials have repeatedly warned their ally against a long-term reoccupation of the Strip and forced displacement of its population to Egypt.

WHO WILL DECIDE GAZA'S FUTURE?

On 15 October, in a CBS interview, President Biden clearly indicated that he opposed a new occupation of Gaza, while conceding that it was essential for Israel to invade the Strip to eradicate Hamas.[9] This explains Washington's refusal, echoed by several other Western governments, to call for a ceasefire while the latter objective remains unfulfilled. In short, Washington and its allies approve of the temporary occupation of Gaza to root out Hamas, but want it to be followed by an Israeli military withdrawal.

The option that Washington advocates is the relaunch of the Oslo peace process, which has been stalled since the Second Intifada at the turn of the century. "There needs to be a path to a Palestinian state", Biden told CBS. To achieve this, he wants power in Gaza to be handed over to the Ramallah-based Palestinian Authority. In an op-ed in the *Washington Post* on 18 November, Biden reaffirmed his preference for a two-state solution, and called for a united Gaza and West Bank under a "revitalized" Palestinian Authority. This is the option favored by most Western governments, but also by Moscow, Beijing and most Arab states. It is supported by some of the Israeli opposition – which has also, however, backed Netanyahu's announcement that Israel will remain "indefinitely" in charge of security inside Gaza.[10] This is the position of the current Israeli opposition leader, Yair Lapid, whose party refused to join the war cabinet.[11]

The futility of trying to resurrect the Oslo process and create a Palestinian state is evident in light of its glaring contradiction with what Israel has announced. Moreover, a Palestinian state created within the framework of the Oslo accords could only be a Bantustan dependent on Israel's goodwill. This is far from the minimum conditions without which no peaceful settlement could be accepted by the Palestinians: total withdrawal of Israel from all territories occupied in 1967, dismantling of settlements, and provision for the return of refugees. These conditions were set out in the "Prisoners' Document", produced in 2006 by Palestinian political leaders held in Israeli jails and approved by almost all Palestinian political organizations, including PLO member groups and Hamas.

The greater fear is that the ongoing war will in fact lead to a second Nakba, as the Palestinians quickly apprehended and as Israeli politicians have openly announced, with the additional problem of refugees on Egyptian soil or, at very least, of "internally displaced persons" in camps in southern Gaza. It is obvious, moreover, that the very objective of eradicating an organization embedded in the population as Hamas is in Gaza could not be achieved without a massacre of huge proportions. All this demonstrates the irresponsibility of Western governments' eagerness to express unconditional support for Israel. It will inevitably backfire on their interests and their own security. For now, the real endgame in Gaza will be determined by the evolution of fighting on the ground and international pressure on Israel.

NOTES

1   Sylvain Cypel, "Itamar Ben Gvir, l'ascension d'un fasciste israélien vers le pouvoir", *Orient XXI*, 5 December 2022; Ruth Margalit, "Itamar Ben-Gvir, Israel's Minister of Chaos", *New Yorker*, 20 February 2023.

2   Jeremy Sharon, "How Bezalel Smotrich Rode Unfiltered Radicalism and Unforgiving Politics to Power", *Times of Israel*, 30 November 2022; Louis Imbert, "Bezalel Smotrich, the Extremist Settler, Is Making His Mark on the Israeli Government", *Le Monde*, 9 March 2023.

3   An eye-opening montage of video clips has been put together on X by *5 Pillars*, a Europe-based Muslim news site, at x.com/5Pillarsuk/status/1722564050154840439.

4   Human Rights League, section for the department of Aube, "Plainte pour génocide présentée à la Cour Pénale Internationale (CPI) le jeudi 9 novembre 2023 – la justice est la réponse à la violence" (Compliant of genocide presented to the ICC, Thursday, 9 November 2023), 15 November 2023.

5   Mekomit's website is at mekomit.co.il. The paper was translated into English by the Jewish-Arab +*972 Magazine*: "Expel all Palestinians from Gaza, Recommends Israeli Gov't Ministry", 30 October 2023.

6   Henry Foy, Leila Abboud, Donato Paolo Mancini, and Andrew England, "Netanyahu Lobbied EU to Pressure Egypt into Accepting Gaza Refugees", *Financial Times*, 30 October 2023.

7   Nayera Abdallah, Nadine Awadalla, and Mohamed Wali, "Egypt's Sisi Rejects Transfer of Gazans, Discusses Aid with Biden", Reuters, 18 October 2023.

8   Gila Gamliel, "Victory Is an Opportunity for Israel in the Midst of Crisis", *Jerusalem Post*, 19 November 2023.

9   Scott Pelley, "President Joe Biden: The 2023 60 Minutes Interview Transcript", CBS News, 15 October 2023.

10   Alexandra Hutzler, "Netanyahu to ABC's Muir: 'No Cease-Fire' without Release of Hostages", ABC News, 7 November 2023. Israel's president, Isaac Herzog, confirmed this aim in an interview with the *Financial Times* on 16 November: Andrew England and James Shotter, "Israel Will Maintain 'Very Strong Force' in Gaza, Says President".

11   Victoria Kim and Matthew Rosenberg, "Israel Signals Future Role in Gaza as Fighting Enters Second Month", NYT Live, 7 November 2023.

11. The First Joint US–Israeli War

The degree of Washington's involvement in Israel's genocidal war on Gaza is unprecedented. Never before has the United States been so fully involved in jointly waging a war with its Israeli ally, short of openly providing boots on the ground. This article was, to my knowledge, the first to describe the onslaught on Gaza as the first joint US–Israeli war in history. Translated from the French original by Lucie Elven, it was first published on the blog of Le Monde diplomatique, English edition, *on 22 January 2024.*

***

The Israeli military forces' war on Gaza, following Hamas's 7 October attack, is the first Israeli war in which Washington is a cobelligerent. The United States openly supports the war's proclaimed goal, and is blocking calls for a ceasefire at the United Nations – all while providing arms and ammunition to Israel and acting to dissuade other regional actors from intervening in the conflict to help Hamas.

The United States did not give Israel military support at its creation: it presented itself at first as an impartial arbiter between Israel and its Arab neighbors, ordering an embargo on arms packages to both that remained in force until the end of Dwight Eisenhower's presidency (1953–61). In the early years, Israel had to rely on West Germany and France for its funding and arming. The situation changed when

John F. Kennedy, faced with radicalized Arab nationalism led by Nasser's Egypt and setbacks to US influence in the Middle East, decided to rely on Israel, and began to send it arms.

This was the beginning of a "special relationship" that would prove very special indeed: between its creation in 1948 and the start of 2023, Israel received more than $158 billion in US aid, including more than $124 billion in military aid, which makes it the largest cumulative recipient of US funding since World War II.[1] Every year the United States provides Israel with military aid to the tune of almost $4 billion.

AN AIRLIFT OF WEAPONRY

Yet Washington did not openly support Israel's war against its Arab neighbors in 1967 (it could not endorse the invasion of the West Bank at the expense of Jordan, another ally). During the October 1973 war, the "special relationship" did translate to an airlift of weaponry to Israel – the goal, however, was to help it contain the offensive launched by Egypt and Syria. Once Israel managed to redress the situation to its advantage, Washington exercised strong pressure on it to end hostilities. The United States did not openly support the Israeli invasion of Lebanon in 1982, and intervened as a mediator for the evacuation of Palestinian Liberation Organization combatants in Beirut. Nor did it support the war launched by Israel against Lebanon in 2006, or its subsequent successive offensives against Gaza.

This time, though, US support for Israel has been explicit and massive. In the aftermath of 7 October, Washington decided to send two US carrier battle groups into the eastern Mediterranean, led by the aircraft carriers USS *Eisenhower* and USS *Ford*, a marine intervention unit, and an amphibian assault group led by the USS *Bataan* in the Black Sea and the USS *Florida* nuclear submarine, which carries cruise missiles. At the same time, Washington alerted its air bases in the region, and urgently delivered military equipment to Israel, including missiles for the Iron Dome aerial defense system.

ERADICATING HAMAS

Washington thus provided regional cover to Israel, so that it could devote the bulk of its forces to a war against Gaza whose stated objective, from the outset, has been the eradication of Hamas. The United States and other Western states have openly supported this goal. The fact is, however, that the eradication of a mass organization that has governed a small, very densely populated territory since 2007 cannot go ahead without a massacre of genocidal proportions. This is especially true since the Israeli army had the clear intention of minimizing losses in its own ranks during the invasion, which called for the intensive use of remote strikes, the flattening of urban areas in order to avoid urban guerrilla warfare, and therefore the maximization of civilian deaths.

US responsibility in this massacre includes providing Israel with a large portion of the means to commit it. As of late November, Washington had sent its ally 57,000 artillery shells and 15,000 bombs, including more than 5,400 BLU-117s and 100 BLU-109 ("bunker buster") bombs, which weigh 2,000 lb (almost a ton) each.[2] The *New York Times* reported military experts' astonishment at Israel's "liberal" use of these 2,000-pound bombs, each of which can flatten a tower several floors high, and which contributed to making Israel's war against Gaza a massacre of civilians "at a historic pace".[3] By 25 December, the United States had provided Israel with 244 arms deliveries by cargo plane, as well as twenty shipments by boat.[4] In addition, the *Guardian* revealed that Israel had been able to draw on the vast stockpile of US weapons already "pre-positioned" in the country.[5]

To finance all of this, on 20 October the Biden administration made an extra-budgetary request of $105 billion to Congress, including $61.4 billion for Ukraine ($46.3 billion in military aid), $14.1 billion for Israel ($13.9 billion in military aid) and $13.6 billion for the fight against illegal immigration at the border. The US president believed he could wrangle a green light from the Republican right for Ukraine by tying that aid (a bone of contention) with causes dearer to them; but by the end of 2023, Biden had still not succeeded in having his request approved. The Republican right has used Biden's strategy against him by demanding even more drastic measures at the border, putting him in an uncomfortable position with his own party.

DELIVERY OF SHELLS

In order to provide Israeli Merkava tanks with 45,000 artillery shells for $500 million, the Biden administration has bypassed Congress by passing an emergency measure on 9 December, providing a package of 14,000 shells for $106.5 million. It repeated this maneuvre on 30 December for $147.5 million, provoking the anger of Democrats calling for more controls on the supply of arms packages to Israel. For all this, Biden bears a direct share of responsibility for the massacre perpetrated by Israeli forces in Gaza. His exhortations for Israel to be more "humanitarian" ring hollow, and are easily dismissed by critics as hypocrisy. His disagreement with Israeli prime minister Benjamin Netanyahu on the plan for the day after the war does not change the two governments' joint responsibility for the war itself.

Ultimately, Biden – who during his 2020 presidential campaign promised to reverse course on his predecessor's markedly pro-Israel politics, notably by reopening the US consulate in East Jerusalem and the PLO office in Washington – did none of this. Instead, he followed in Donald Trump's footsteps, first by focusing on encouraging Saudi Arabia to join the Arab states that had established diplomatic relations with Israel under Trump's aegis, then by giving unconditional support to Israel in its invasion of Gaza. In so doing, he has managed to anger his own Democratic Party – which is today more sympathetic to the Palestinians than to the Israelis (by 34 per cent to 31 per cent), according to a poll published on 19 December – without satisfying the Republicans either.[6] In the end, 57 per cent of Americans disapprove of Biden's handling of the conflict, according to the same poll.

NOTES

1   Congressional Research Service, "US Foreign Aid to Israel", *CRS Report*, Washington, 1 March 2023.
2   Jared Malsin and Nancy A. Youssef, "US Sends Israel 2,000-Pound Bunker Buster Bombs for Gaza War", *Wall Street Journal*, 1 December 2023.
3   Lauren Leatherby, "Gaza Civilians, under Israeli Barrage, Are Being Killed at Historic Pace", *New York Times*, 25 November 2023.
4   "244 US Cargo Planes, 20 Ships Deliver over 10,000 Tons of Military Equipment to Israel – Report", *Times of Israel*, 25 December 2023.

5   Harry Davies and Manisha Ganguly, "Gaza War Puts US's Extensive Weapons Stockpile in Israel under Scrutiny", *Guardian*, 27 December 2023.
6   Jonathan Weisman, Ruth Igielnik and Alyce McFadden, "Poll Finds Wide Disapproval of Biden on Gaza, and Little Room to Shift Gears", *New York Times*, 19 December 2023.

12.   Gaza: Is There Any Plan for "the Day After"?

Written in May 2024, close to eight months after the beginning of Israel's onslaught on Gaza, this article draws a provisional balance-sheet of the catastrophe, which had acquired increasingly obvious genocidal proportions, and locates it in the historical trajectory of Israel's emancipation from the obligations of international humanitarian law. It also updates the assessment of prospects for post-war Gaza. Translated from the French original by Charles Goulden, it was first published in Le Monde diplomatique, English edition, *in June 2024.*

***

Nearly eight months after Israel launched reprisals for the 7 October attack by Hamas's military wing, Izz al-Din al-Qassam, across the security barrier that surrounds the Gaza Strip, "disproportionate force" – the dissuasion strategy Israel first deployed in Lebanon in 2006 – has acquired a new meaning.

Better known as the "Dahiya doctrine", after the south Beirut suburbs where Hezbollah was based (*dahiya* is suburb in Arabic) – which was largely destroyed by Israeli shelling in 2006 – it was first publicly set out in 2008 by its author, General Gadi Eizenkot, then head of the Israeli military's Northern Command, later chief of staff (2015–19), and now an observer member of the war cabinet formed on 11 October. In the words of reserve colonel Gabi Siboni, it requires the Israeli military to "act immediately, decisively, and with force that is disproportionate to the enemy's actions and the threat it poses" with the aim of "inflicting damage and meting out punishment to an extent that will demand long and expensive reconstruction processes".[1]

"Disproportionate" feels euphemistic when applied to the Israeli offensive in Gaza. According to the UN Office for the Coordination of Humanitarian Affairs (UNOCHA), deaths between 2007, when Hamas took control of the Gaza Strip, and 7 October 2023 totaled 6,904 Palestinians and 326 Israelis – a ratio of 21:1.[2] According to Israeli sources, Hamas's October attack killed 1,143 (mostly Israelis): 767 civilians and 376 military and security personnel.

Apart from the 1,600 Palestinian fighters killed on 7 October, according to the same sources, forty-five times more Palestinians have already died during the Israeli military's attack on Gaza than Israelis died on 7 October, including fatalities reported by the Palestinian health ministry (steadily rising) and people still thought to be buried under rubble (more than 10,000 according to an estimate quoted by UNOCHA).

A joint report by the European Union, World Bank and United Nations states that over 290,000 housing units had been damaged or destroyed by the end of January, leaving more than 1 million of the enclave's 2.3 million people homeless.[3] The devastation is such that the UN special rapporteur on the right to adequate housing suggested adding "domicide" to the list of crimes against humanity.[4] According to Charles Mungo Birch, chief of the UN's Mine Action Service (UNMAS) in the Palestinian territories, there are 37 million tons of rubble in Gaza – more on a strip of land 41 kilometers (25 miles) north–south than along the 965-kilometer (600-mile) front in Ukraine.[5] UNMAS estimates the debris could take fourteen years to clear.[6]

A "HISTORIC PACE" OF KILLING

The language used to describe Israel's relentless violence quickly escalated. Apart from South Africa taking Israel to the International Criminal Court for genocide, the mainstream US media have since last year focused on the unprecedented intensity of the bombardment. In late November the New York Times said that civilians in Gaza were being killed at a "historic pace", citing UN reports that more children had died there in seven weeks than in all major conflict zones worldwide in 2022 across two dozen countries, including Ukraine.[7] In December the *Washington Post* called the war "one of this century's most destructive", and in January Associated Press quoted political scientist Robert Pape of the University of Chicago as saying it was "one of the most intense civilian punishment campaigns in history".[8]

The damage to Israel's image is huge – something Samy Cohen of the Centre for International Research at Sciences Po in Paris linked to the "disproportionate response" strategy back in 2009: "If you harm civilians, the whole world turns against you. But the Israeli military don't seem to have understood how sensitive global public opinion is to civilian losses."[9] At the time, he decried the Israeli military's large-scale use of "non-precision munitions", repeated in Gaza today: the *Washington Post* reported last December that almost half of Israeli airstrikes involved unguided bombs.[10]

However, the horrifying number of Palestinian victims is also due to the use of bombs which, though fitted with guiding systems, are of a size that should be banned in urban warfare. The *New York Times* report cited above noted that nearly 90 per cent of munitions used in Gaza in the first two weeks of the war (the most intensive phase of the bombardment) were satellite-guided bombs weighing half a ton or a ton. In a densely populated area, no matter how precisely these bombs may be aimed, they will cause immense damage. The *Times* reported that experts were astonished by Israel's "liberal" use of them, one of them saying that to find a historical comparison one would "have to go back to Vietnam, or the Second World War".

This level of intensity would not be possible without help from the United States.[11] Between 2019 and 2023, it supplied 69 per cent of Israel's military imports (Germany providing 30 per cent).[12] Apart from a much larger number of smaller bombs delivered to Israel since last October, the United States had, as of December, supplied more than 5,000 Mark 84 or BLU-117 bombs weighing close to one ton (2,000 lb).[13] The spat between Joe Biden and Benjamin Netanyahu in early May concerned the suspended delivery of 1,800 additional Mark 84 bombs and 1,700 Mark 82s, each weighing half a ton (1,000 lb).

Both men knew this would not affect the Israeli military's capacity to complete their occupation of Gaza by invading Rafah (nearly 15 per cent of its total area), into which more than half of the population had been driven. Netanyahu melodramatically declared that Israel was prepared to fight with its fingernails – though the Israeli military's chief spokesman, Rear-Admiral Daniel Hagari, said they had what they needed for their planned missions, including the invasion of Rafah.[14]

ISRAEL STILL GETTING THE ARMS IT NEEDS

The White House national security communications advisor and retired rear-admiral, John Kirby, explained: "Everybody keeps talking about pausing weapons shipments. Weapons shipments are still going to Israel. They're still getting the vast, vast majority of everything that they need to defend themselves."[15] Biden has repeatedly emphasized that the suspended delivery only concerns the Mark 84 and 82 bombs.[16]

On 14 May, the United States announced it would send more than $1 billion worth of additional arms to Israel, including $700 million in tank ammunition and $60 million in mortar shells: this confirmed that Biden's show of reluctance was largely symbolic, aimed at distancing Washington from the expected massacre in Rafah at a time when talk of genocide was spreading among American universities, Democratic voters and Democrats in Congress.

Several congressional Democrats had called for a State Department report on compliance with human rights law among countries supplied with US weapons. Published shortly after the arms shipment suspension was announced, it sat on the fence, concluding that it was "reasonable" to assess that Israel had used weapons supplied by the United States in ways inconsistent with international human rights law, but that there was not enough concrete evidence to link specific weapons to violations in such a way as to warrant halting their supply.[17] Ultimately, Biden has not only failed to silence critics on the left, but given Republicans, including Donald Trump, an opportunity to mount a full-scale attack on him for serving Hamas's interests.[18]

Biden had already shown unconditional support for Israel's response and its goal of eradicating Hamas, making no distinction between the political organization and its military wing, and failing to take account of the fact that it is a mass movement and has governed the Gaza Strip since 2007. His comparison of Hamas after 7 October to ISIS rather than Hezbollah, with which it has far more in common, was intended to justify the eradication of Hamas and distract from accusations of genocide. On 15 October, Biden told CBS's Scott Pelley that, while another occupation of Gaza would be a mistake, "going in" and "taking out the extremists" was necessary.[19] When Pelley asked, "Do you believe that Hamas must be eliminated entirely?"?' he replied, "Yes, I do."

The administration's position on the invasion of Rafah was similar, not opposing it outright, but demanding assurances that it would not lead to slaughter – an amber light rather than red. Israel got the message, amplified by growing anger worldwide, and encouraged those previously told to take refuge in the Rafah area to move to an expanded "humanitarian zone" at Al-Mawasi, on the coast west of Khan Younis.

FAR RIGHT AIMED AT A SECOND NAKBA

The decision to move people away from the Egyptian border, on which Rafah is the sole crossing, highlights the failure of the Israeli far right's plan to bring about a second Nakba, with a mass expulsion of Gazans into Sinai. The problems the Israeli military already face in controlling the territory confirm that a new total, long-term occupation is not an option.[20]

Netanyahu is once more facing the dilemma that led to the 1993 Oslo Accords. With growing pressure around the world for a Palestinian state, especially from the United States (right across the political spectrum: Trump himself in January 2020 presented establishing a Palestinian state in the West Bank and Gaza as the "deal of the century"), he will find it hard to continue rejecting this option, which he has until now boasted of blocking.

The trouble is that Netanyahu, like the rest of Israel's political class, and like Biden, has no faith in the ability of Mahmoud Abbas's Palestinian Authority (PA) to keep the people of Gaza under control. It has failed to do that even in the West Bank, despite the Israeli military's presence and its frequent intervention in zone A, which the PA is supposed to govern. This is why support is growing for the solution that Israel's former Labor prime minister, Ehud Barak, advocated from the start.

On 15 October the *Economist* reported:

Mr Barak believes that the optimal outcome, once Hamas's military capabilities have been sufficiently degraded, is the re-establishment of the Palestinian Authority in Gaza ... However he warns that Mahmoud Abbas, the Palestinian president, "cannot be seen to be returning on Israeli bayonets". There will, therefore, need to be an interim period during which "Israel will capitulate to international pressure and hand Gaza over to an Arab peacekeeping force, which could include members such as Egypt, Morocco and the United Arab Emirates".[21]

However, in early May the *New York Times* revealed that, according to anonymous sources (including three Israeli officials), senior officials in Netanyahu's office are discreetly looking at a proposal made last November by business leaders close to the prime minister, under which Israel and Arab states could share oversight of Gaza.[22] The *Financial Times*, quoting Western sources, reported that the three states named by Barak were open to the idea of joining a peacekeeping force in Gaza.[23] But no Arab state will back such a project without the establishment of a Palestinian state. Saudi Arabia, without signaling any readiness to put troops on the ground, is making it a condition of normalizing relations with Israel.

Normalized relations with the Saudi kingdom would be a significant consolation prize, allowing Netanyahu to confront his far-right coalition partners, were he to decide to make a U-turn. He could then negotiate, on the grounds of national interest, remaining at the head of a national unity government that would exclude the far right but include his rival Benny Gantz, who agreed to join the war cabinet last October. Otherwise Netanyahu could face a split within his own Likud party; defense minister Yoav Gallant is in favor of the oversight-sharing proposal. It is therefore likely he will eventually come around to the idea, which would please Biden, who sees it as the ideal solution.

One thing, however, is certain: there is no question of Israel handing the PA – no matter how "revitalized", as Biden put it last November[24] – full control of Gaza, as it did in 2005. At most, the Israelis are looking at a similar scenario to the West Bank, where the Israeli military surround zone A (governed by the PA) and intervene when they see fit. Even before this latest invasion of Gaza, Israeli ministers had announced plans to create a buffer zone within the enclave.[25] It is a done deal: as well as clearing a kilometer-wide strip along the border, Israel has established strategic control corridors through Gaza, similar to the way it has carved up the West Bank.[26] Anyone who thinks this will solve the Palestinian problem is indulging in wishful thinking.

NOTES

1   Gabi Siboni, "Disproportionate Force: Israel's Concept of Response in Light of the Second Lebanon War", *INSS Insight* (Tel Aviv University), 2 October 2008.

2   UN Office for the Coordination of Humanitarian Affairs (UNOCHA), "Data on Casualties", at ochaopt.org/data/casualties.

3   European Union, World Bank, United Nations, "Gaza Strip Interim Damage Assessment: Summary Note", 29 March 2024.

4   Balakrishnan Rajagopal, "Domicide: The Mass Destruction of Homes Should Be a Crime against Humanity", *New York Times*, 29 January 2024.

5   Lisa Schlein, "Explosives Clearance Enables Aid to Reach Victims of War in Gaza", *Voice of America News*, 1 May 2024.

6   Reuters, "UN Official Says It Could Take 14 Years to Clear Debris in Gaza", 26 April 2024.

7   Lauren Leatherby, "Gaza Civilians, under Israeli Barrage, Are Being Killed at Historic Pace", *New York Times*, 25 November 2023.

8   Evan Hill et al., "Israel Has Waged One of This Century's Most Destructive Wars in Gaza", *Washington Post*, 23 December 2023; Julia Frankel, "Israel's Military Campaign in Gaza Seen as among the Most Destructive in Recent History, Experts Say", Associated Press, 11 January 2024.

9   Samy Cohen, "Tsahal ou la stratégie de la 'riposte disproportionnée'" ("Tsahal or the Strategy of 'Disproportionate Response'"), *Les Cahiers de l'Orient* 96: 4 (2009), p. 85.

10   John Hudson et al., "Unguided 'Dumb Bombs' Used in Almost Half of Israeli Strikes on Gaza", *Washington Post*, 14 December 2023.

11   See Chapter 11, above.

12   Pieter D. Wezeman et al., "Trends in International Arms Transfers, 2023", Stockholm International Peace Research Institute, March 2024.

13   Robin Stein et al., "A *Times* Investigation Tracked Israel's Use of One of Its Most Destructive Bombs in South Gaza", *New York Times*, 21 December 2023.

14   Julian Borger and Jason Burke, "'We Will Fight with Our Fingernails' Says Netanyahu after US Threat to Curb Arms", *Guardian*, 10 May 2024.

15   "On-the-Record Press Gaggle by White House National Security Communications Advisor John Kirby", White House, Washington, 9 May 2024.

16   Kevin Liptak, "Biden Says He Will Stop Sending Bombs and Artillery Shells to Israel if It Launches Major Invasion of Rafah", CNN, 9 May 2024.

17 Julian Borger, "US Finds Israel's Use of Weapons in Gaza 'Inconsistent' with Human Rights Law, but Will Not Cut Flow of Arms", *Guardian*, 10 May 2024.

18 Toluse Olorunnipa and Jacqueline Alemany, "Biden's Isolation Grows as Gaza Report Both Criticizes and Clears Israel", *Washington Post*, 10 May 2024.

19 Scott Pelley, "President Joe Biden: The 2023 60 Minutes Interview Transcript", CBS News, 15 October 2023.

20 Jared Malsin and Summer Said, "Hamas Shift to Guerrilla Tactics Raises Specter of Forever War for Israel", *Wall Street Journal*, 15 May 2024.

21 "Ehud Barak Blames Binyamin Netanyahu for 'the Greatest Failure in Israel's History'", *Economist*, 15 October 2023.

22 Patrick Kingsley, "Israeli Officials Weigh Sharing Power with Arab States in Postwar Gaza", *New York Times*, 3 May 2024.

23 Andrew England and Felicia Schwartz, "US Encouraging Arab States to Join Multinational Postwar Force in Gaza", *Financial Times*, 15 May 2024.

24 Will Weissert, "Biden Says 'Revitalized Palestinian Authority' Should Eventually Govern Gaza and the West Bank", Associated Press, 18 November 2023.

25 James Shotter and Neri Zilber, "Israel Plans Buffer Zone in Gaza After Hamas War", *Financial Times*, 19 October 2023.

26 Louis Imbert et al., "How Israel Is Reshaping the Gaza Strip", *Le Monde*, 11 May 2024; Loveday Morris et al., "What Israel's Strategic Corridor in Gaza Reveals about Its Postwar Plans", *Washington Post*, 17 May 2024.

13. Netanyahu's Bloody Onward March

With the completion of the first year since Israel's onslaught on Gaza began, in the wake of the Hamas-led attack of 7 October 2023, Benjamin Netanyahu embarked on the next phase of his intensive war drive, targeting the Lebanese Hezbollah – Iran's main regional auxiliary – while escalating Israel's direct confrontation with Iran proper. By inflicting a crippling blow on Hezbollah – soon to be compounded by the collapse of the Assad family's regime in Syria, another key ally of Tehran and the indispensable conduit for its delivery of weapons to Hezbollah – Netanyahu appeared as personally triumphant, while Israel reached the historical peak of its regional supremacy. With Donald Trump's election and the prospect of his return to the White House, the Israeli prime minister's delight was complete. Translated from the French original by Jeremy Sorkin, this article was first published in Le Monde diplomatique, English edition, *in November 2024.*

***

Over the past several months, Israeli prime minister Benjamin Netanyahu has regained his domestic standing, once again demonstrating an astounding ability to get away with anything – the secret to his remarkable political longevity. Approval among the furthest-right segment of Israelis had already been mounting since spring, as he resisted US pressure (if one can call it that) to sign a ceasefire agreement with Hamas that would bring back the remaining hostages.

In May, ignoring Washington's pleas, he sent his troops into Rafah and the border region with Egypt, thereby eliminating the main appeal a ceasefire would have held for Hamas. By then refusing to pull back from Rafah even temporarily, as recommended by Israel's military chiefs and defense minister Yoav Gallant (his foremost rival within Likud), Netanyahu sabotaged any serious chance of a deal with the Palestinians. Egypt, meanwhile, was furious to have lost the upper hand it had previously had over the Rafah crossing.

This was Netanyahu clearly snubbing President Biden, to whom he had no intention of handing a tidy truce complete with freed hostages, among them Americans, whose return would have offered a welcome opportunity for a photograph at the White House. By ungratefully rebuffing Biden, he was also helping Donald Trump's campaign. Netanyahu's calculations did not change when Kamala Harris was substituted as the Democratic candidate: he had good reason to fear Harris might move closer to Barack Obama's Middle East policy than that of her current boss.

Soon after Netanyahu took office in March 2009, he began working with Republican politicians to complicate things for Obama, who had entered the Oval Office two months earlier. Years later he relied on the same playbook, as Biden (now president) and the Pentagon started turning instead to Gallant – welcomed in Washington several times during the Gaza war – and being more critical of Netanyahu. Republicans invited him to give his fourth address to Congress (breaking Winston Churchill's record). When he spoke on 24 July 2024, the absence of Vice-President Harris (the constitutionally delegated Senate president) was perceived as her way of distancing herself.

Netanyahu's most recent decisions were surely influenced by the candidate switch and an initial Harris surge in the polls. Taking his time had seemed reasonable, as a victory for Trump – who would likely cut him even more slack than Biden – looked increasingly likely. But with the rise of Harris, who might rein him in, he had no time to waste.

WAITING FOR THE MOMENT TO STRIKE

Beyond grabbing more Palestinian land – following the expansionist vision of the Zionist right wing he represents – Netanyahu's priority is

Iran. In 1979 the danger from Egypt was neutralized when it signed a peace treaty with Israel. That same year, Iran's revolution led it to break with the West – the dawn of its status as Israel's archenemy and only existential threat. From the start, the Islamic Republic assumed a hostile posture toward the "Great Satan", and promised the destruction of its partner, Israel. Embroiled during the 1980s in a deadly war with Iraq, and cut off from arms supplies by embargoes, Iran gradually built its own regional ideological-cum-military network that could serve as a proxy against the United States and its allies in the Middle East. As it sought to expand its influence beyond Shias (its own community and most important audience) to the broader Arab and Muslim worlds, the theocratic regime's anti-Israel stance became a key selling point.

As part of this effort, it fostered a relationship with the (Sunni) Muslim Brotherhood. The group had broken off ties with Riyadh in 1990, refusing to support the US deployment of troops in Saudi Arabia ahead of the Gulf War against Iraq, which had invaded Kuwait. Hamas, the Brotherhood's Palestinian division, naturally received the most attention from Tehran, which simultaneously strengthened its connection with a competing Brotherhood offshoot, the (Palestinian) Islamic Jihad.

Israel has been obsessed with Iran since the early 2000s, when it became clear that the country had secretly restarted the nuclear program begun under the shah. Tel Aviv is certain that the goal is to develop nuclear weapons, which would end the regional monopoly it has held on such arms since the 1960s. Combined with an annihilation complex shaped as much by the Holocaust as by Israel's relatively small size, the specter of a nuclear Iran explains its leaders' determination to hit the enemy – and especially its nuclear infrastructure – hard.

A few days before Obama was sworn in, the *New York Times* published an investigation by David Sanger, its chief Washington correspondent. He described how, since early 2008 – George W. Bush's final year in office – the Israeli government had been urgently requesting that Washington send an emergency order of GBU-28s (two-ton, six-meter-long guided "bunker busters") and give it authorization to fly over US-occupied Iraq to strike Natanz, Iran's main nuclear facility.[1] Fearing that this might endanger American troops, the Bush administration refused. But it had already ordered fifty-five such bombs for Israel the year before, with fulfillment scheduled for 2009. While

Obama authorized their delivery soon after his inauguration,[2] this did little for his relationship with Netanyahu, which deteriorated as the US president publicly criticized the expansion of Israeli settlements in the West Bank.

But it was Iran that was the biggest bone of contention between the two leaders. In a way, Obama's bunker-buster shipment had increased pressure for limitations on its nuclear program. But Netanyahu agreed with Saudi Arabia, another of Tehran's sworn enemies, that even if an agreement was reached – loosening the economic chokehold on Iran – it would neither stop the country from secretly pursuing a nuclear weapons program nor from expanding its regional influence. (Several factors helped this second ambition: the West's fiasco in Iraq and the extraction of US troops, completed in 2011; the civil war that broke out in Syria that same year, after a popular uprising; and the Yemeni civil war that began in 2014.) Much to their chagrin, an accord was signed in Vienna in 2015.

WHO WANTED TO SEE TRUMP ELECTED?

Netanyahu and the Saudi rulers were thus delighted to see Donald Trump elected in 2016. The president's first international trip, in May 2017, was to Riyadh. By October, Trump had begun the process of fulfilling his campaign promise to quit the Iran nuclear deal, despite entreaties from the European signatories (Germany, France, the UK, and so on), and the withdrawal became official on 8 May 2018. Trump opened the final year of his term with the January 2020 assassination in Baghdad of Qasem Soleimani, commander of the Quds Force, the foreign operations division of Iran's Revolutionary Guard.[3]

Just as Trump had been the anti-Obama, hell-bent on unpicking one after another of his predecessor's achievements, Biden portrayed himself as the anti-Trump in the 2020 presidential campaign. Regarding the Middle East, he promised to resuscitate the nuclear deal, and reopen the US consulate in East Jerusalem, as well as the PLO office in Washington, both closed by Trump.

He did neither. Rather than reviving the Middle East policy he had carried out as Obama's vice-president, he has mostly continued Trump's approach. Netanyahu's reoccupation and destruction of Gaza actually make Biden the first president to have overseen a joint Israeli–US war.[4] And the occasional tensions between the two leaders have certainly not been reflected in the staggering amount of military aid Washington has provided.[5]

"No administration has helped Israel more than I have. None. None. None. And I think Bibi should remember that", Biden repeated on 4 October. The reproach came as he speculated on a Democratic senator's suggestion that Netanyahu was blocking a ceasefire to benefit Trump.[6] The prime minister, on the other hand, lavished Biden with praise at a White House meeting while in the United States for his speech to Congress: "From a proud Israeli Zionist to a proud Irish American Zionist, I want to thank you for 50 years of public service and 50 years of support for the state of Israel."[7] This farewell to a lifelong politician who had just relinquished his party's nomination was no doubt sincere.

Biden's passing of the baton to Harris and Netanyahu's visit to Trump's Florida lair, Mar-a-Lago, both in late July, opened the war's next chapter. He needed to make the most of Biden's final months as president so that, in the best-case scenario, Trump would win and allow Israel to widen its offensive, and, at worst, Harris would inherit – and simply have to contend with – deep US involvement.

The Hamas attack has cruelly highlighted Israel's loss of credible deterrence. The country's first military defeat – analogous to the American one in Vietnam – came in 2000, when it withdrew unconditionally from Lebanon. Its 2006 conflict with Hezbollah, which had significantly improved its capabilities, turned into another quagmire. And, except for periodic attacks on Syria, Israel has been able to do nothing to stop Iran's expansion. As for Gaza, the deadly and repeated assaults launched by Israel since 2007, most often in response to rocket fire from Hamas or Islamic Jihad, have not dissuaded the two Palestinian organizations from continuing their activities.

The "Dahiya doctrine" advocates inflicting disproportionate losses on the enemy, as well as damage to its built environment – an invitation to commit war crimes, because it explicitly calls for targeting civilians.[8] It was first used in Lebanon, in Beirut's *dahiya janoubiya* (southern suburbs), a Hezbollah stronghold. The doctrine was applied twice in Gaza, in 2008–09 and in 2014. But Israel's repeated deadly campaigns since 2007, most often in retaliation for rockets fired by Hamas or Islamic Jihad, were not enough to deter the two groups.

Deterrence did work in Lebanon: Hezbollah never again carried out a cross-border offensive like that of 12 July 2006, which sparked the "Thirty-Three-Day War". Its leader, Hassan Nasrallah, publicly acknowledged a month later, on 27 August, that he would not have greenlit the operation had he known the Israeli response would be so deadly and destructive.[9] Hezbollah's resistance having proved remarkable, Tehran supplied the party with an impressive and diverse arsenal of missiles, so that it felt it had achieved a state of mutual deterrence with Israel: a relatively peaceful coexistence enforced by each adversary's capacity to seriously damage the other. This also made Hezbollah a key asset in the delicate equilibrium between Israel and Iran, which maintains a significant conventional armory aside from its regional network.

Although Israeli sources confirm that more Hamas assailants than Israelis were killed on 7 October 2023, the attack's recklessness and deadly success – which surpassed even its planners' expectations – enraged Israel, pushing it to breaking point. Netanyahu was accused of having put his country in harm's way by allowing Hamas to consolidate power in Gaza and receive money from Qatar. The goal had been to perpetuate divisions between Palestinian groups, thereby defusing any pressure to resume the so-called peace process.[10] On the morning of 7 October, Hamas exhorted "the brothers in the Islamic resistance in Lebanon, Iran, Yemen, Iraq and Syria" to join its fight.[11]

The fact that Tehran responded at all, even if only minimally and indirectly, showed just how much deterrent credibility Israel had lost. The Islamic Republic activated its network, inciting its partners – Hezbollah in Lebanon, Shia militias in Iraq, and the Houthis in Yemen – to begin a low-level war of attrition against Israel. Only Bashar al-Assad kept carefully to the sidelines, his regime continuing to block any Syria-based operation against Israeli occupation of Syria's Golan Heights. Of the three Iran auxiliaries, Hezbollah's activities bothered the Israelis most: while confined to a small area on either side of the UN-designated Blue Line (against which Israel's 2000 withdrawal was to be measured), they forced Israel to concentrate troops on its northern border and displaced tens of thousands of Israeli civilians – although even more Lebanese were forced from their homes.

Israel kept its cool in the north as long as it was heavily involved in Gaza. There, its mission had gone beyond disproportionate retaliation, mushrooming into a full reoccupation, with unprecedented destruction and massacres of genocidal proportions. "Deterrence" has been taken to the extreme against Palestinians, which explains why people in the West Bank, who largely applauded the Hamas attack, have ignored the Islamist movement's call to join its fight through all available means. Nonetheless, once Gaza had been almost completely reoccupied, the Israeli army began unleashing deadly raids on West Bank villages and towns on a scale comparable to its 2002 repression of the Second Intifada.

ISRAEL PREPARES TO ENTER LEBANON

As its focus turned to the West Bank, the Israeli army was also preparing its entry into Lebanon. Instead of repeating the bulldozer-like approach it had used in Gaza, it planned carefully. Israel pulled its punches for several months, killing hundreds of Hezbollah members in "surgical strikes" that culminated in its September assault. In Lebanon more militants than civilians perished, whereas in Gaza the violence has been indiscriminate. This was a foretaste of a long-promised offensive.

After the pager attacks (17 and 18 September) and Nasrallah's assassination (27 September), Israel quickly began sending ground troops into Lebanon. Biden's hypocrisy was visible both in the additional $8.7 billion in military aid he sent to Israel, seemingly timed to boost its efforts in Lebanon, and in his celebration of Nasrallah's death.[12]

Netanyahu was triumphant: Iran had been humiliated. Even Hezbollah members felt they had been used by their sponsor, which had neither come to the group's rescue nor stuck out its own neck. Tehran tried again on 1 October to save face, sending a second volley of missiles into Israel – an escalation, as these were ballistic missiles, harder to intercept than the drones and cruise missiles that had mostly been used in April. But the attack's scope and impact were limited, evidencing Iran's fear of being pulled into a broader conflict involving the United States and potentially even the superpower's local allies. That could invite a mass uprising against the Iranian regime, which is hated by many of its own people.

Netanyahu certainly dreams of dealing Iran a major blow that would set its nuclear program back by several years, and enshrine him as a supreme Zionist hero. He also faces pressure from allies on the extreme right as well as from the "centrist" opposition, both of whom strive to outbid him in advocating a major attack on Iran. But an attack on the country's oil infrastructure might have invited Iranian retaliation in the Gulf, triggering a worldwide economic crisis and poisoning Israel's relationships with the Arab oil monarchies.

Due to Iran's size and distance from Israel, striking the nuclear sites would have required more than the indirect US involvement seen in Gaza and Lebanon. Biden took a step toward direct participation in October when he sent a battery of high-altitude antiballistic (THAAD) interception missiles, along with around 100 soldiers trained to use them, exposing US personnel to a possible Iranian reprisal. Once again, by arming and protecting its ally, the US administration flagrantly undermined its own supposed pressure on Netanyahu to exercise restraint.

But in order to destroy Iran's subterranean nuclear installations, one-ton bombs – dozens of which were dropped to kill Nasrallah – would not be enough. Nor would the two-ton, bunker-busting GBU-28s Obama had given Israel. Nothing less than the 12-to-15-ton GBU-57s would do, each capable of penetrating sixty meters underground. Israel has neither these bombs nor the aircraft needed to use them, which is why Netanyahu opted instead for a more significant attack on Iran's defense system than the one he had ordered in April.[13] Israel's air strike on 26 October represented a further step toward direct US involvement, in that the Biden administration did not hide the fact that it was fully informed of its scope and timing.

What happens next will depend on the outcome of the 5 November presidential election. A joint US–Israeli offensive on Iran seems much more likely under Trump than under Harris. That is, unless Israel manages to drag Iran into a spiral that makes such an intervention inevitable.

NOTES

1   David E. Sanger, "US Rejected Aid for Israeli Raid on Iranian Nuclear Site", *New York Times*, 10 January 2009.
2   Eli Lake, "Obama Arms Israel", *Newsweek*, 25 September 2011.
3   See Gilbert Achcar, "Iraqis Want Both Countries Out", *Le Monde diplomatique*, *English edition*, February 2020.

4   See Chapter 11, above.

5   Jack Mirkinson, "Biden Is Mad at Netanyahu? Spare Me", *Nation*, 13 February 2024.

6   Colleen Long, "Biden Says He Doesn't Know Whether Israel Is Holding Up Peace Deal to Influence 2024 US Election", Associated Press, 4 October 2024.

7   Tovah Lazaroff, "Netanyahu to Biden: 'From One Zionist to Another, Thank You for 50 Years of Friendship'", *Jerusalem Post*, 25 July 2024.

8   See Chapter 12, above.

9   Gilbert Achcar with Michel Warschawski, *The 33-Day War: Israel's War on Hezbollah in Lebanon and Its Aftermath*, London: Saqi/Routledge, 2007, pp. 47–8.

10   Adam Raz, "A Brief History of the Netanyahu–Hamas Alliance", *Haaretz*, 20 October 2023.

11   Muhammad Deif, "We Announce the Start of the Al-Aqsa Flood" (7 October 2023), full translation, *Oasis*, 13 December 2023, at oasiscenter.eu/en.

12   "Israel Says It Has Secured $8.7 Billion US Aid Package", Reuters, 26 September 2024.

13   John Paul Rathbone, "Can Israel Destroy Iran's Nuclear Facilities By Itself?", *Financial Times*, 4 October 2024.

Epilogue

Enter Trump

THE PERIOD PRECEDING Donald Trump's inauguration and its immediate aftermath deserves a special mention in future history books as one of the most striking instances of a widespread epidemic of wishful thinking. It is also one of the most irrational, in that it fostered expectations that were in full contradiction with basic and very well-known facts. Or perhaps it was an indication of the depth of the sense of defeat that overwhelmed the vast range of opponents of Benjamin Netanyahu after the electoral victory of his political soul mate, Donald Trump. In any event, the scale of the epidemic of self-delusion about the latter's intentions was impressive indeed.

From the president who broke the long-standing bipartisan consensus in US foreign policy with regard to Israel and crossed red lines by endorsing its annexation of territory hitherto regarded as occupied by force, and hence illegally held (the Syrian Golan Heights and East Jerusalem – the latter symbolically by moving the US embassy from Tel Aviv to Jerusalem and closing the US consulate in the Arab part of the city); the president who closed the PLO office in Washington, cut off US aid to UNRWA and the PA, and treated the latter with utmost contempt, even though it owes its continued existence to Washington in the first place; the president who focused his administration's efforts on expanding the pool of Arab countries "normalizing" their relations with Israel through the Abraham Accords, signed by the United Arab Emirates and Bahrain, followed soon after by Morocco and the Sudanese military junta – from such a president, an observer endowed with normal lucidity would have expected more of the same during his second stint at the White House, four years later.

THE MYTH OF TRUMP'S ARM-TWISTING OF NETANYAHU FOR THE SAKE OF PEACE

There were also enough indications that it was primarily to please Trump that Netanyahu had withheld the implementation of the ceasefire plan negotiated by the Biden administration in the spring of 2024 – and this against pressure from a significant and increasing part of Israeli society relayed by the military and security services, represented chiefly by then-minister of "defense" Yoav Gallant. This is emphasized at the beginning of the preceding article in this book, which was written in October 2024. In July of that same year, when, after his fourth address to a joint session of the two chambers of the US Congress, Netanyahu went to Florida to meet with Trump at his Mar-a-Lago estate, in yet another gesture of support to the latter in the presidential race, there was enough evidence that he would offer him implementation of the ceasefire as a welcome gift if he won a second term. Indeed, as the Associated Press then reported, "While Netanyahu at home is increasingly accused of resisting a deal to end the 9-month-old war to stave off the potential collapse of his far-right government when it ends, he said Friday [26 July] he was 'certainly eager to have one. And we're working on it.'"[1]

This unusual "eagerness" expressed right after the meeting with Trump was obviously not fortuitous. Indeed, once the November US election was over and Trump on his way to a second inauguration on 20 January 2025, Netanyahu worked with the president-elect's envoy – Steve Witkoff, the president's old friend, former lawyer, fellow real estate speculator in cahoots with rich Arab oil states, and golfing partner – on the implementation of the ceasefire prior to the inauguration, as Trump had wished.[2] Previously,

> Mr. Witkoff, who served as a liaison for Mr. Trump to the Jewish business community during the [electoral] campaign, has praised Mr. Netanyahu and castigated Democrats who have given the prime minister a cold shoulder. He expressed disgust for the dozens of Democrats who skipped Mr. Netanyahu's address to Congress in July.[3]

And yet, despite all these indications, the sealing of the Gaza ceasefire deal on 15 January and the beginning of its implementation four days later, on the very eve of Trump's second inauguration, were widely interpreted as resulting from Trump and his envoy having twisted Netanyahu's arm. *Haaretz* conveyed the idea that Witkoff had "forced Israel to accept a plan that Netanyahu had repeatedly rejected over the past half year".[4] The same article noticed, however, that Netanyahu himself was propagating this rumor:

> His propaganda machine is pushing the no-choice narrative that it's Trump. On Monday, laments began to be heard on Channel 14 that Trump isn't what we thought. "I'm surprised all the senior officials in the US administration are saying the same thing," Yotam Zimri said on the Patriots program. "If this doesn't happen by the time Trump comes in, Hamas will understand what hell is.[5] I don't understand the Israeli interest in at least not waiting for Trump." Yinon Magal answered, "It's because Trump is pressing to do it! That's what's happening."
>
> Zimri: "So all his people have been lying – it's a big disappointment."
>
> Magal: "He talks about hell and in the meantime sends his envoy to sign a deal. It's a deal whose impact will be very difficult. That's the truth."[6]

At the other end of the political spectrum, Hamas itself cheered Trump's alleged pressure on Netanyahu. "We're prepared for a dialogue with America and achieving understandings on everything", Mousa Abu Marzouk, one of Hamas's key political leaders, enthusiastically told the *New York Times* in a phone interview from Qatar on 19 January:

> Mr. Abu Marzouk also offered high praise for Mr. Trump for his involvement in helping broker the cease-fire agreement between Israel and Hamas and called him a "serious president".
>
> "If not for President Trump, his insistence on ending the war, and his dispatching of a decisive representative, the deal wouldn't have happened", said Mr. Abu Marzouk, referring to Mr. Witkoff.[7]

The former chief of general staff of Israel's armed forces and former Zionist Laborite prime minister, Ehud Barak, contributed to accrediting the hoax as late as early February, asserting in *Haaretz*:

Following a visit to Israel by Steve Witkoff, Trump's envoy to the Middle East, who compelled Netanyahu to implement the hostage deal put together last May – from which Netanyahu bolted, costing the lives of hostages and soldiers – it appears that Trump will demand that Netanyahu allow the full deal to be completed.

The resumption of all-out war in Gaza will not be allowed ... The issue of transferring Palestinians from Gaza will evaporate rapidly ...[8]

Barak concluded: "Trump will twist Netanyahu's arm", believing even that this would help the opposition topple the prime minister, for "the responsibility for stopping the march toward a dictatorship lies with us".[9]

My pointing to this massive wave of self-delusion is not a manifestation of perspicacity in hindsight. It was perfectly possible to see through this fog for anyone not indulging in wishful thinking. I warned against that myth on 21 January in my weekly column in the London-based Arabic daily *Al-Quds al-Arabi*, before Trump's first ravings on Gaza:

Netanyahu actually used the myth of Trump's pressure on him – which the latter's representative to the Middle East, Steve Witkoff, a Zionist par excellence, was keen to substantiate – to convince his allies in the Zionist far right to accept the agreement. While the media was silent, or almost silent, about the actual pressure that was being exerted on Hamas through Egypt and Qatar, at the insistence of Trump's representative, the myth prevailed in a way that suited Netanyahu. He nevertheless promised Smotrich and Ben-Gvir that the agreement would not go beyond its first stage. Smotrich accepted the promise, while Ben-Gvir resigned from the government, saying that he would continue to support Netanyahu in the Knesset and would return to the government as soon as the war in Gaza resumed.

The commanders of the Zionist armed forces were lobbying for the agreement, in response to pressure from the Israeli public to release the hostages held in the Strip. Former Minister of Defense Yoav Gallant even resigned in protest at Netanyahu's procrastination in accepting the agreement. They all know that this agreement is nothing more than a temporary truce that will allow the release of the civilian hostages, and that the army will continue its campaign after that. Of course, Hamas's ostensible deployment of armed men, with much zeal, in trying to show that they still control the residents of the Strip, is the strongest possible incentive for the Zionist army and society to continue the war and the occupation! Anyone who believes that the current truce will morph into a final cessation of the war, accompanied by a complete withdrawal of the Zionist army from the Strip, is indulging in wishful thinking and dreaming.[10]

Once Trump had come out with his outlandish and apparently insane repeated calls to deport the Palestinian population out of Gaza, occasionally adding that they would not be allowed to return, thereby bringing tears of joy to the eyes of Netanyahu's far-right acolytes, the latter no longer needed to entertain the myth, and could therefore debunk it:

> Prime Minister Benjamin Netanyahu said reports that US Mideast envoy Steve Witkoff came in and "muscled" him to accept the Gaza cease-fire deal were "completely false".
> In an interview on Fox News, Netanyahu said he and Witkoff "had a real, not only friendly but eye-to-eye conversation", adding that it was Hamas who had continued to insist on terms "no sane Israeli government could accept. But when Trump came in, the pressure that he put was on Hamas to accept it. I didn't have to move a nanometer, but Hamas caved", Netanyahu said.[11]

Indeed, the way Trump bullied Hamas into caving in after it had decided to suspend the exchange of captives planned for Saturday 15 February in protest against Israel's lack of full implementation of its part of the ceasefire deal – he advised Israel to resume the war if "all of the hostages [not just three of them] aren't returned by Saturday 12 o'clock"[12] – was the clearest possible indication of where Trump really stands, and whose arm he is truly willing to twist.

TRUMP'S "ETHNIC CLEANSING" PLAN FOR GAZA

Taking note of this does not answer the question that has perplexed the world ever since Trump, a few days after his inauguration, declared his open advocacy of the "ethnic cleansing" of the Gaza Strip, which, he later clarified, "would be turned over to the United States by Israel at the conclusion of fighting".[13] A flurry of speculation pervaded the global media, as commentators enumerated various hypotheses as to the true intention of the US president. They boiled down to two main hypotheses: either Trump was serious about this plan (thus confirming his alleged folly in the mind of many observers), or the whole sensation was but a transactional ploy aimed at obtaining something else.

The more Trump doubled down on his plan, the more credence he gave to the first hypothesis. After all, does his utopian-dystopian vision of turning Gaza into a "Riviera of the Middle East" not fit perfectly with his instinct as a real estate magnate? Is his entire Middle East policy not largely determined by his and his family's real estate plans in the region?

The Trump Organization [a conglomerate owned by Donald Trump, with around 250 affiliates, that mainly invests in luxury real estate, such as skyscrapers, hotels and golf courses] and London-listed Dar Global [the international subsidiary of the Saudi real estate firm Dar Al Arkan] will launch two new projects in the Saudi capital of Riyadh [in 2025], as the incoming US president's family business continues to invest in the Gulf and capitalize on the region's growing real estate sector.

The real estate projects will be the fourth and fifth between the two companies... The two companies ... will also launch the Trump Tower in Jeddah, the third project between Dar Global and the Trump Organization ...

The Trump Organization has significant exposure in the Gulf and has strong ties to the region. For example, the ... Saudi Public Investment Fund-owned LIV Golf ... has hosted competitions at Trump's courses since the league began in 2022.

In July [2024], the Trump Organization announced it was working with Dar Global to build a Trump Tower in Dubai. In 2022, the two companies signed a deal to use the Trump brand for a $4 billion project in Oman, which includes a golf course, hotel and villas ... The development of a Trump International Hotel in the Omani capital Muscat is slated to be completed in December 2028.[14]

Trump himself used terms supporting the interpretation of his stated designs for Gaza as stemming from his business instincts, as in this interview aired by Fox News on 10 February:

> "There's practically no building that's livable in the whole thing, on the whole Gaza Strip. I say we go in, we knock them all down. We just create some – no more Hamas. There's no Hamas there. There's nobody there. We move them into beautiful areas of the Middle East", he explained.
>
> "... We'll build beautiful communities. Safe communities. [It] could be five, six could be two. But we'll build safe communities a little bit away from where they are, where all of this danger is. In the meantime, I would own this. *Think of it as a real estate development for the future.* It would be a beautiful piece of land."[15]

This interpretation was further corroborated by the full agreement of Trump's vision with a view expressed in February 2024 by Jared Kushner, the president's son-in-law and architect of his Middle East policy during his first term in office. Himself the scion of a New York real estate empire, Kushner, after leaving the White House, had founded Affinity Partners, an investment firm involved, in association with Emirati, Saudi, and Qatari investors, in projects worth billions of dollars across the world, and in the Middle East in particular.[16]

It was in a public interview recorded at Harvard University, his *alma mater*, on 15 February 2024, that Kushner, in reply to a question about what he would do to "end the crisis", made the following statements, provoking outrage and lots of comments:

> So, what I would do right now if I was Israel is, I would try to say, number one, you want to get as many civilians out of Rafah as possible [prior to invading it, as Israel did three months later]. I think that you want to try to clear that out. I know that with diplomacy, maybe you get them into Egypt. I know that that's been

refused. But with the right diplomacy, I think it would be possible
...

> Gaza's waterfront property, it could be very valuable too, if people would focus on building up livelihoods ... I think from Israel's perspective, I would do my best to move the people out and then clean it up.[17]

The basic ingredients of what Trump was to announce close to a year later are all there: 1. Gaza considered as a "waterfront property"; 2. The call to "move the people out" from the Strip to "clean it up" (although, in using this expression, Kushner was apparently referring to the removal of Hamas, whereas Trump would later refer to the removal of the rubble); 3. The prospect of "getting them into Egypt" – in spite of Cairo's vehemently stated rejection of this option – "with the right diplomacy". But this was just Jared Kushner's plan A. In the same Harvard interview, he described a plan B:

> But in addition to that, the thing that I would try to do if I was Israel right now is I would just bulldoze something in the Negev. I would try to move people in there. I know that won't be the popular thing to do, but I think that that's a better option to do so you can go in and finish the job ...
>
> I think Israel's gone way more out of their way than a lot of other countries would to try to protect civilians from casualties. But I do think right now, opening up the Negev, creating a secure area there, moving the civilians out and then going in and finishing the job would be the right move.[18]

THE "DEAL OF THE CENTURY"

The idea of moving Palestinians to the Negev desert is not new. It was a prominent feature of the peace plan that Kushner devised and officially released on 28 January 2020, when he was part of the first Trump administration: the famous *Peace to Prosperity* plan that Trump was so proud of that he called it the "deal of the century". On Gaza, that plan had this to say:

As a result of Hamas' terror and misrule, the people of Gaza suffer from massive unemployment, widespread poverty, drastic shortages of electricity and potable water, and other problems that threaten to precipitate a wholesale humanitarian crisis. This Vision is designed to give Palestinians in Gaza a prosperous future. *It provides for the possibility of allocating for the Palestinians Israeli territory close to Gaza (as depicted on the conceptual map) within which infrastructure may be rapidly built to address Gaza's pressing humanitarian needs, and which will eventually enable the building of thriving Palestinian cities and towns that will help the people of Gaza flourish.*

Significant improvements for the people in Gaza will not occur until there is a ceasefire with Israel, the full demilitarization of Gaza, and a governance structure that allows the international community to safely and comfortably put new money into investments that will not be destroyed by predictable future conflicts.[19]

The "Israeli territory close to Gaza (as depicted on the conceptual map)" that would be allocated to the Palestinians, according to this plan, were two enclaves in the Negev at the border with Egypt. These were meant to compensate for the territory that Israel would annex in the West Bank, thus reducing the "Future State of Palestine" there to a set of three enclaves approximately fitting the Allon Plan's early design. The whole of the Jordan Valley and areas separating the three Palestinian contiguous territories – close to one-third of the West Bank, in addition to Jerusalem – would belong to Israel, while the Palestinian enclaves themselves would be riddled with fifteen "Israeli Enclave Communities".[20] These almost insulting features of the "deal of the century", along with many others, have been abundantly criticized, even in the mainstream US media.[21] For the same reason, they were highly praised by Benjamin Netanyahu, who projected himself as an ardent supporter of the plan, followed in this by the Israeli opposition, led by Benny Gantz, prior to its entering into a coalition government with the Likud in May 2020.

Present at the White House when the plan was officially announced, Netanyahu gave one of those pompous, emphatic speeches that have become his trademark. What he said is the best indictment of the totally skewed character of the so-called peace plan and, for this, deserves to be quoted extensively:

> This is a historic day. And it recalls another historic day. We remember May 14th, 1948, because on that day, President Truman became the first world leader to recognize the State of Israel after our first Prime Minister, David Ben-Gurion, declared our independence. That day charted a brilliant future.
>
> Mr. President, I believe that down the decades – and perhaps down the centuries – we will also remember January 28th, 2020, because on this day, you became the first world leader to recognize Israel's sovereignty over areas in Judea and Samaria [Israel's Zionist name for the West Bank] that are vital to our security and central to our heritage. (Applause.) ...
>
> Too many plans tried to pressure Israel to withdraw from vital territory like the Jordan Valley. But you, Mr. President, you recognized that Israel must have sovereignty in the Jordan Valley and the other – (applause) – and other strategic areas of Judea and Samaria ...
>
> For too long – far too long – the very heart of the Land of Israel where our patriarchs prayed, our prophets preached, and our kings ruled, has been outrageously branded as illegally occupied territory. Well, today, Mr. President, you are puncturing this big lie. (Applause.)
>
> You are recognizing Israel's sovereignty over all the Jewish communities in Judea and Samaria, large and small alike. (Applause.) ...
>
> It's a great plan for Israel. It's a great plan for peace. Frankly, Mr. President, given all that you have already done for Israel, I'm not surprised. You have been the greatest friend that Israel has ever had in the White House. (Applause.) Frankly, though we've had some great, outstanding friends in these halls, it's not even close. (Applause.) ...
>
> Your peace plan advances all these goals. First, it addresses the root cause of the conflict by insisting that the Palestinians will finally have to recognize Israel as the Jewish State. (Applause.)
>
> Second, it stipulates that Israel will retain security control in the entire area west of the Jordan River, thereby giving Israel

a permanent eastern border – a permanent eastern border to defend ourselves across our longest border. This is something we've longed to have. (Applause.) We now have such a recognized boundary.

Third, your plan calls for Hamas to be disarmed and for Gaza to be demilitarized. (Applause.)

Fourth, it makes clear that the Palestinian refugee problem must be solved outside the State of Israel. (Applause.)

Fifth, it calls for our ancient capital, Jerusalem, to remain united under Israel's sovereignty. (Applause.) It, of course, ensures that religious sites remain accessible to all faiths. And it maintains the status quo on the Temple Mount.

Sixth, your plan does not uproot anyone from their homes – Israelis and Palestinians alike. Instead, it proposes innovative solutions whereby Israelis will be connected to Israel and whereby Palestinians will also be connected to one another.[22]

Unsurprisingly, the PA, and all other Palestinian groups, rejected the plan in categorical terms. While a few Arab states politely indicated that it was a proposal that could further the discussion, while emphasizing the need for any settlement to be agreed by the Palestinians, the League of Arab States added its voice to that of the PA. Worse still for Trump-Kushner, none of the countries bearing any relation to the Middle East conflict or influence in world affairs supported the plan: neither China, nor Russia, nor even the European states individually, or collectively represented by the European Union. The "deal of the century" proved indeed to be the "flop of the century".

GENUINE DESIGN OR TRANSACTIONAL PLOY?

The fiasco was so complete that it overpowered Netanyahu's desire to officially annex the territories allocated to Israel by the Kushner plan. Sensing that this would have an explosive impact in the Arab world, and even globally, the Trump administration vetoed the move. The "peace plan", so pompously heralded, was thus stillborn. The failure certainly left a bitter taste for Trump, who had so brashly promoted his great dealmaking skills. It may have been a key factor in Trump's open call for the "ethnic cleansing" of the Gaza Strip, and the deportation of its inhabitants to Egypt and Jordan. Quite plausibly, this was less a genuine design than a transactional ploy taking advantage of the new realities on the ground since Israel's reoccupation of Gaza, in order to scare the Arab regimes and the PA into accepting the 2020 plan they had rejected.

It is very difficult to believe that Donald Trump was serious about his "ethnic cleansing" grand design, and that he genuinely believed it could be implemented. He was certainly serious about the "real estate development" and US involvement in the huge business opportunity that postwar Gaza is supposed to represent, in order to clear the "demolition site" (in Trump's words) of the gigantic amount of rubble left by Israel's destructive fury, and turn the area into a construction site developing beach resorts on its waterfront.

But this latter prospect could fit perfectly into an updated version of the 2020 plan, in which the Gaza Strip would shift from the single, contiguous enclave that it had been in Kushner's "conceptual map" into a set of two or three Palestinian enclaves surrounded by land confiscated and poised to be annexed by Israel, including part of the Strip's seashore. This scenario converges with what was envisaged at the end of Chapter 12 in this book, written in May 2024. Instead of being removed in full to Egypt and Jordan, a portion of the Gazans would be removed to the Negev enclaves, as envisaged by Kushner in February 2024.

These are thus the two poles between which "the day after" oscillates under the second Trump administration, in an updated version of the polarization outlined throughout the post-7 October 2023 articles gathered in this book. At one pole, the extreme outcome of "ethnic cleansing", hitherto openly called for only by the neo-Nazis of the Israeli far right (even though a large section of Likud shared their aspiration with increasing openness), and suddenly boosted into the mainstream by Donald Trump, to the point that close to 80 per cent of Jewish Israelis supported his ravings, while only 13 per cent believed his population transfer plan to be "immoral".[23]

Unlike that unchanged extreme pole, the opposite pole did move to the right with the transition from Biden to Trump: not that there is a qualitative difference between the Biden administration's vision of the "two-state solution" and the updated version of the Trump-Kushner plan outlined above. The difference, however, is that the latter would grant more territory and other concessions to the Israeli side, while accepting the continued Israeli occupation of parts of the Gaza Strip and the relocation of part of its population (both of which were explicitly rejected by the previous administration), and put harsher conditions on the management of the "State of Palestine" – even though the new administration, like the previous one, would rely heavily on the United Arab Emirates for that part of the deal.[24]

Starting in December 2024, Mahmoud Abbas's PA strove to convince Israel and the United States of its ability to repress anti-occupation resistance in the West Bank by launching an attack on armed groups of young Palestinians, particularly in the city and refugee camp of Jenin. This effort to enhance the PA's status as a proxy for the Israeli occupation was deemed unconvincing by Israel.

The day after Trump's inauguration, on 21 January 2025, the Israeli army launched a new major military operation in the West Bank, exceeding in scale and violence all that it had done there since the operation ordered by Ariel Sharon in the spring of 2002, including the previously most violent operation of August–October 2024. At the same time, violent harassment and pogroms perpetrated by ultra-Zionist Jewish settlers in the West Bank continued to increase, facilitated by the new conditions that the far-right ministers of the Israeli cabinet had put in place. Thus, the threat of "ethnic cleansing" became almost as clear and present in the West Bank as in Gaza – especially after the extensive Gaza-like destruction committed by Israel's armed forces in the latest round, leading to the forced displacement of 40,000 West Bank Palestinians, and counting.

The Trump administration's pressure to get the support of Washington's Arab allies and protégés for an updated version of its "deal of the century" would hence be greatly facilitated by the fact that the plan they had shunned in 2020 would now appear as the "lesser evil" compared to "ethnic cleansing" pure and simple. This would pave the way for the Saudi kingdom to join the UAE, Bahrain, and Morocco, with Egypt and Jordan before them, in "normalizing" its relations with Israel, thus offering both Trump and Netanyahu an achievement of which they could both boast. Netanyahu would badly need this, lest he should appear as having been trapped by his previous high praise of the Trump-Kushner plan, reactivated after the lure of a full reenactment of the 1948 Nakba in the remaining part of the land between the river and the sea.

Netanyahu would then shift attention to Iran, partly to help assuage his far-right flank, and would endeavor to convince Trump to join him in bombing that country, along the lines summarized at the end of the previous chapter in this book. On this issue, again, much wishful thinking greeted Trump's election in the expectation that, contrary to Netanyahu's will, he would negotiate a new deal with Tehran. It is true that Trump did not exclude this option, even though he did not exclude the military option either.

However, Trump did not, in 2018, tear up the nuclear deal concluded by the Obama administration three years earlier for the sake of reinstating a similar agreement. The only new deal that Trump could regard as satisfactory would be a full capitulation by Tehran. Iran's supreme leader, Ayatollah Ali Khamenei, understood that well, which is why he declared to his armed forces two weeks into the new Trump presidency: "With such a government there should not be any negotiations as it is neither wise, nor prudent, nor dignified."[25]

The future of the Middle East thus looks very bleak indeed, fitting the ongoing impetuous unfolding of what I have called elsewhere the "age of neofascism".[26] With Trump back in the White House, bringing with him an even more execrable team, the conclusion reached at the end of the first part of this book, which I have repeatedly emphasized since the summer of 2024, has almost become a matter of common wisdom among critics of the new course. As Michelle Goldberg put it straightforwardly in the *New York Times*,

> Even before Trump took office, the "rules-based international order" was deeply decayed, in no small part because of Biden's complicity in Gaza's annihilation. Now that order is dead, along with other imperfect remnants of a less chaotic time, like the soft power America built with foreign aid and democratic ideals. Maybe Trump's menacing of Canada and Denmark and his scheme for a new colony on the Mediterranean will come to nothing. But with his renewed rhetoric of American empire, he's removed any pretense that other countries should be limited by anything except their own might.[27]

There is no room for optimism in the face of all this – only for hope that resistance to the drift among the Palestinians, the Israelis, the Arab peoples, and the entire world – and especially among young people – might eventually manage to thwart the regional and global designs of the new neofascist international. That sounds today like a very utopian wish, but history has shown that even the much more dreadful "midnight in the century" of nine decades ago – as the title of the famous 1939 novel by the Russian anti-totalitarian revolutionary Victor Serge phrased it – did not last long, and that the far-right "new order" of that epoch collapsed altogether just six years later.

16 February 2025

NOTES

1   Ellen Knickmeyer, Michelle Price, and Stephany Matat, "Netanyahu Meets with Trump at Mar-a-Lago, Offering Measured Optimism on a Gaza Cease-Fire", *Associated Press*, 27 July 2024.
2   On Steve Witkoff, see Eric Lipton, "Trump's Middle East Envoy Has Prior Ties to Oil-Rich Nations There", *New York Times*, 25 November 2024; and Ben Samuels, "Trump's Mideast Appointees Raise Ethical and Political Concerns", *Haaretz*, 31 December 2024.
3   Jonathan Weisman, "Trump's Team for Mideast Is Sure to Please Netanyahu", *New York Times*, 15 November 2024.
4   Chaim Levinson, "Trump's Mideast Envoy Forced Netanyahu to Accept a Gaza Plan He Repeatedly Rejected", *Haaretz*, 13 January 2025.
5   A reference to Trump's threat: see MJ Lee and Elise Hammond, "Trump Warns 'All Hell Will Break Out' if Gaza Hostages Aren't Released Before His Inauguration", CNN, 7 January 2025.
6   Levinson, "Trump's Mideast Envoy Forced Netanyahu".
7   Adam Rasgon, "Hamas Official Says Group Is Ready for 'Dialogue with America'", *New York Times*, 20 January 2025.
8   Ehud Barak, "Trump Will Twist Netanyahu's Arm in the Oval Office, but Israel's Fate Does Not Rest in His Hands", *Haaretz*, 4 February 2025.
9   Ibid. The day before, in the same issue of *Haaretz*, Aluf Benn had warned against such illusions, advising that "the anti-Bibi camp shouldn't get carried away fantasizing that Trump will forcibly shift Netanyahu leftward, that the president will utter the magic words that will end the war, bring back the hostages, forge peace with Saudi Arabia, eliminate the Iranian nuclear threat and bring about a change of government in Jerusalem. All that's missing here are fairies and unicorns." Aluf Benn, "Netanyahu Will Launch His Election Campaign from Trump's White House", *Haaretz*, 3 February 2025.
10   I published an English translation of that article the same day on my blog: Gilbert

Achcar, "Two Myths about the Gaza Ceasefire", at gilbert-achcar.net/gaza-ceasefire, 21 January 2025.

11 Liza Rozovsky, "Netanyahu Tells Fox News: Claims Trump Team Forced Gaza Cease-Fire on Israel Are 'Completely False'", *Haaretz*, 9 February 2025.

12 Andrew Roth, Emma Graham-Harrison, and Quique Kierszenbaum, "Trump Says Gaza Ceasefire Should Be Cancelled if All Israeli Hostages Not Freed", *Guardian*, 11 February 2025.

13 James Mackenzie and Doina Chiacu, "Trump Says Israel Would Hand Over Gaza After Fighting Is Over, No US Troops Needed", Reuters, 7 February 2025.

14 Jack Dutton, "Trump Organization to Build Luxury Housing in Saudi Capital: What We Know", *Al-Monitor*, 9 December 2024.

15 Ashley Carnahan, "Trump Says the Gaza Strip for the United States Is a 'Real Estate Development for the Future'", Fox News, 10 February 2025. My emphasis.

16 On Kushner's own business empire, see Ben Bartenstein and Heather Perlberg, "Jared Kushner's Next Bet: A Trump Hotel with Emirati Billionaire", *Bloomberg*, 16 January 2025, and Antoine Gara, James Fontanella-Khan, Marton Dunai, and David Sheppard, "What Jared Kushner Did Next", *Financial Times*, 3 February 2025.

17 Harvard's Middle East Initiative, "Middle East Dialogues: Jared Kushner in Conversation with Tarek Masoud", at youtube.com/watch?v=dtaIHr5Sots, 15 February 2024. A full transcript was posted by the *Postil Magazine* under the title "Jared Kushner's Great Game", 1 April 2024.

18 Ibid.

19 *Peace to Prosperity: A Vision to Improve the Lives of the Palestinian and Israeli People*, January 2020, p. 13. My emphasis.

20 The maps showing all this are in ibid., Appendix 1, pp. 41–2.

21 See, for example, Brent Sasley, "The White House Peace Plan Puts Israel's Concerns First – and Shortchanges Palestinians", *Washington Post*, 30 January 2020. In fact, there is hardly a page out of the 180 pages of the plan that does not include very disputable provisions. For a thorough critique of the "deal of the century", see the special issue of *The Arab World Geographer* 23: 1 (Spring 2020).

22 ToI Staff, "Full Text of Netanyahu's Speech: Today Recalls Historic Day of Israel's Founding", *Times of Israel*, 28 January 2020.

23 Jerusalem Post Staff, "Approx. 80% of Israelis Support Trump's Plan to Relocate Gazans – Survey", *Jerusalem Post*, 3 February 2025. 30 per cent of Jewish Israelis regarded the plan as "not practical, but desirable", meaning that half of the population saw it both desirable and feasible.

24 The architect of the UAE's plan for postwar Gaza is Mohammed Dahlan, the former head of the PA's security forces, who organized and directed the failed attempt to oust Hamas from power in Gaza by force in 2007, in collaboration with the George W. Bush administration. Upon later falling out with PA president Mahmoud Abbas over succession plans, Dahlan took refuge in Abu Dhabi, where he has since served as a key adviser to Mohamed bin Zayed, the former crown prince of Abu Dhabi, now ruler of the emirate and UAE president.

25 Najmeh Bozorgmehr, "Iran's Supreme Leader Rules Out Talks with Donald Trump", *Financial Times*, 7 February 2025.
26 Gilbert Achcar, "The Age of Neofascism and Its Distinctive Features", 4 February 2025, translated from my Arabic weekly column for *Al-Quds al-Arabi*, on my blog at gilbert-achcar.net/age-of-neofascism.
27 Michelle Goldberg, "Trump's Gaza Deal: War Crimes in Exchange for Beachfront Property", *New York Times*, 7 February 2025.

Appendix

Statement on Antisemitism
and the Question of Palestine

Confronted with mounting pro-Israel pressure for the adoption by Western governments and academic institutions of a definition of antisemitism assimilating any critique of Zionism and the Zionist state to a variant of antisemitism, there was a need for a statement by Arab intellectuals on this debate. It is one from which they have been largely excluded, and still are – as if they had no claim to a view on this issue, even though the state of Israel was created at the expense of the Palestinian Arabs, and subsequently enlarged at the expense of other Arab countries.

Together with my friend Raef Zreik – academic co-director of the Minerva Humanities Center at Tel Aviv University and senior research fellow at the Van Leer Jerusalem Institute – I initiated and drafted the statement below. The draft was discussed and finalized with some of the signatories before the general gathering of signatures. The statement was first published on the website of the Guardian *on 29 November 2020, under the title "Palestinian Rights and the IHRA Definition of Antisemitism".*

***

We, the undersigned, Palestinian and Arab academics, journalists, and intellectuals, are hereby stating our views regarding the definition of antisemitism by the International Holocaust Remembrance Alliance (IHRA), and the way this definition has been applied, interpreted and deployed in several countries of Europe and North America.

In recent years, the fight against antisemitism has been increasingly instrumentalized by the Israeli government and its supporters in an effort to delegitimize the Palestinian cause and silence defenders of Palestinian rights. Diverting the necessary struggle against antisemitism to serve such an agenda threatens to debase this struggle and hence to discredit and weaken it.

Antisemitism must be debunked and combated. Regardless of pretense, no expression of hatred for Jews as Jews should be tolerated anywhere in the world. Antisemitism manifests itself in sweeping generalizations and stereotypes about the Jews, regarding power and money in particular, along with conspiracy theories and Holocaust denial. We regard as legitimate and necessary the fight against such attitudes. We also believe that the lessons of the Holocaust as well as those of other genocides of modern times must be part of the education of new generations against all forms of racial prejudice and hatred.

The fight against antisemitism must, however, be approached in a principled manner, lest it defeat its purpose. Through "examples" that it provides, the IHRA definition conflates Judaism with Zionism in assuming that all Jews are Zionists, and that the State of Israel in its current reality embodies the self-determination of all Jews. We profoundly disagree with this. The fight against antisemitism should not be turned into a stratagem to delegitimize the fight against the oppression of the Palestinians, the denial of their rights, and the continued occupation of their land. We regard the following principles as crucial in that regard.

1. The fight against antisemitism must be deployed within the frame of international law and human rights. It should be part and parcel of the fight against all forms of racism and xenophobia, including Islamophobia, anti-Arab, and anti-Palestinian racism. The aim of this struggle is to guarantee freedom and emancipation for all oppressed groups. It is deeply distorted when geared toward the defense of an oppressive and predatory state.

2. There is a huge difference between a condition where Jews are singled out, oppressed and suppressed as a minority by antisemitic regimes or groups, and a condition where the self-determination of a Jewish population in Palestine/Israel has been implemented in the form of an ethnic exclusivist and territorially expansionist state. As it currently exists, the State of Israel is based on uprooting

the vast majority of the natives – what Palestinians and Arabs refer to as the Nakba – and on subjugating those natives who still live on the territory of historical Palestine as either second-class citizens or people under occupation, denying them their right to self-determination.

3. The IHRA definition of antisemitism and the related legal measures adopted in several countries have been deployed mostly against left-wing and human rights groups supporting Palestinian rights and the Boycott Divestment and Sanctions (BDS) campaign, sidelining the very real threat to Jews coming from right-wing white nationalist movements in Europe and the US. The portrayal of the BDS campaign as antisemitic is a gross distortion of what is fundamentally a legitimate non-violent means of struggle for Palestinian rights.

4. The IHRA definition's statement that an example of antisemitism is "Denying the Jewish people their right to self-determination, e.g., by claiming that the existence of *a* State of Israel is a racist endeavor" is quite odd. It does not bother to recognize that under international law the current State of Israel has been an occupying power for over half a century, as recognized by the governments of countries where the IHRA definition is being upheld. It does not bother to consider whether this right includes the right to create a Jewish majority by way of ethnic cleansing and whether it should be balanced against the rights of the Palestinian people. Furthermore, the IHRA definition potentially discards as antisemitic all non-Zionist visions of the future of the Israeli state, such as the advocacy of a binational state or a secular democratic one that represents all its citizens equally. Genuine support for the principle of a people's right to self-determination cannot exclude the Palestinian nation, nor any other.

5. We believe that no right to self-determination should include the right to uproot another people and prevent it from returning to its land, or any other means of securing a demographic majority within the state. The demand by Palestinians for their right of

return to the land from which they themselves, their parents and grandparents were expelled cannot be construed as antisemitic. The fact that such a demand creates anxieties among Israelis does not prove that it is unjust, nor that it is antisemitic. It is a right recognized by international law as represented in UNGA resolution 194 of 1948.

6. To level the charge of antisemitism against anyone who regards the existing State of Israel as racist, notwithstanding the actual institutional and constitutional discrimination upon which it is based, amounts to granting Israel absolute impunity. Israel can thus deport its Palestinian citizens, or revoke their citizenship or deny them the right to vote, and still be immune from the accusation of racism. The IHRA definition and the way it has been deployed prohibit any discussion of the Israeli state as based on ethno-religious discrimination. It thus contravenes elementary justice, and basic norms of human rights and international law.

7. We believe that justice requires full support of the Palestinians' right to self-determination, including the demand to end the internationally acknowledged occupation of their territories and the statelessness and deprivation of Palestinian refugees. The suppression of Palestinian rights in the IHRA definition betrays an attitude upholding Jewish privilege in Palestine instead of Jewish rights, and Jewish supremacy over Palestinians instead of Jewish safety. We believe that human values and rights are indivisible and that the fight against antisemitism should go hand in hand with the struggle on behalf of all oppressed peoples and groups for dignity, equality, and emancipation.

INITIAL LIST OF SIGNATORIES

(122, in alphabetical order)

Samir Abdallah
Filmmaker, Paris, France

Nadia Abu El-Haj
Ann Olin Whitney Professor of Anthropology, Columbia University,
USA

Lila Abu-Lughod
Joseph L. Buttenwieser Professor of Social Science, Columbia University,
USA

Bashir Abu-Manneh
Reader in Postcolonial Literature, University of Kent, UK

Gilbert Achcar
Professor of Development Studies, SOAS, University of London, UK

Nadia Leila Aissaoui
Sociologist and Writer on Feminist Issues, Paris, France

Mamdouh Aker
Board of Trustees, Birzeit University, Palestine

Mohamed Alyahyai
Writer and Novelist, Oman

Suad Amiry
Writer and Architect, Ramallah, Palestine

Sinan Antoon
Associate Professor, New York University, Iraq-US

Talal Asad
Emeritus Professor of Anthropology, Graduate Center, CUNY, USA

Hanan Ashrawi
Former Professor of Comparative Literature at Birzeit University,
Palestine

Aziz Al-Azmeh
University Professor Emeritus, Central European University, Vienna, Austria

Abdullah Baabood
Academic and Researcher in Gulf Studies, Oman

Nadia Al-Bagdadi
Professor of History, Central European University, Vienna, Austria

Sam Bahour
Writer, Al-Bireh/Ramallah, Palestine

Zainab Bahrani
Edith Porada Professor of Art History and Archaeology, Columbia
University, USA

Rana Barakat
Assistant Professor of History, Birzeit University, Palestine

Bashir Bashir
Associate Professor of Political Theory, Open University of Israel,
Raanana, State of Israel

Taysir Batniji
Artist-Painter, Gaza, Palestine and Paris, France

Tahar Ben Jelloun
Writer, Paris, France

Mohammed Bennis
Poet, Mohammedia, Morocco

Mohammed Berrada
Writer and Literary Critic, Rabat, Morocco

Omar Berrada
Writer and Curator, New York, USA

Amahl Bishara
Associate Professor and Chair, Department of Anthropology, Tufts
University, USA

Anouar Brahem
Musician and Composer, Tunisia

Salem Brahimi
Filmmaker, Algeria-France

Aboubakr Chraïbi
Professor, Arabic Studies Department, INALCO, Paris, France

Selma Dabbagh
Writer, London, UK

Izzat Darwazeh
Professor of Communications Engineering, University College London, UK

Marwan Darweish
Associate Professor, Coventry University, UK

Beshara Doumani
Mahmoud Darwish Professor of Palestinian Studies and of History, Brown University, USA

Haidar Eid
Associate Professor of English Literature, Al-Aqsa University, Gaza, Palestine

Ziad Elmarsafy
Professor of Comparative Literature, King's College London, UK

Noura Erakat
Assistant Professor, Africana Studies and Criminal Justice, Rutgers University, USA

Samera Esmeir
Associate Professor of Rhetoric, University of California, Berkeley, USA

Khaled Fahmy
FBA, Professor of Modern Arabic Studies, University of Cambridge, UK

Ali Fakhrou
Academic and Writer, Bahrain

Randa Farah
Associate Professor, Department of Anthropology, Western University, Canada

Leila Farsakh
Associate Professor of Political Science, University of Massachusetts Boston, USA

Khaled Furani
Associate Professor of Sociology & Anthropology, Tel-Aviv University, State of Israel

Burhan Ghalioun
Emeritus Professor of Sociology, Sorbonne 3, Paris, France

Asad Ghanem
Professor of Political Science, Haifa University, State of Israel

Honaida Ghanim
General Director of the Palestinian Forum for Israeli Studies Madar, Ramallah, Palestine

George Giacaman
Professor of Philosophy and Cultural Studies, Birzeit University, Palestine

Rita Giacaman
Professor, Institute of Community and Public Health, Birzeit University, Palestine

Amel Grami
Professor of Gender Studies, Tunisian University, Tunis

Subhi Hadidi
Literary Critic, Syria-France

Ghassan Hage
Professor of Anthropology and Social Theory, University of Melbourne, Australia

Samira Haj
Emeritus Professor of History, CSI/Graduate Center, CUNY, USA

Yassin Al-Haj Saleh
Writer, Syria

Rema Hammami
Associate Professor of Anthropology, Birzeit University, Palestine

Dyala Hamzah
Associate Professor of Arab History, Université de Montréal, Canada

Sari Hanafi
Professor of Sociology, American University of Beirut, Lebanon

Adam Hanieh
Reader in Development Studies, SOAS, University of London, UK

Kadhim Jihad Hassan
Writer and translator, Professor at INALCO-Sorbonne, Paris, France

Nadia Hijab
Author and Human Rights Activist, London, UK

Jamil Hilal
Writer, Ramallah, Palestine

Bensalim Himmich
Academic, Novelist and Writer, Morocco

Serene Hleihleh
Cultural Activist, Jordan-Palestine

Khaled Hroub
Professor in Residence of Middle Eastern Studies, Northwestern University, Qatar

Mahmoud Hussein
Writer, Paris, France

Lakhdar Ibrahimi
Paris School of International Affairs, Institut d'Etudes Politiques, France

Annemarie Jacir
Filmmaker, Palestine

Islah Jad
Associate Professor of Political Science, Birzeit University, Palestine

Lamia Joreige
Visual Artist and Filmmaker, Beirut, Lebanon

Amal Al-Jubouri
Writer, Iraq

Mudar Kassis
Associate Professor of Philosophy, Birzeit University, Palestine

Nabeel Kassis
Former Professor of Physics and Former President, Birzeit University, Palestine

Muhammad Ali Khalidi
Presidential Professor of Philosophy, CUNY Graduate Center, USA

Rashid Khalidi
Edward Said Professor of Modern Arab Studies, Columbia University, USA

Michel Khleifi
Filmmaker, Palestine-Belgium

Elias Khoury
Writer, Beirut, Lebanon

Nadim Khoury
Associate Professor of International Studies, Lillehammer University College, Norway

Rachid Koreichi
Artist-Painter, Paris, France

Adila Laïdi-Hanieh
Director General, Palestinian Museum, Palestine

Rabah Loucini
Professor of History, Oran University, Algeria

Rabab El-Mahdi
Associate Professor of Political Science, American University in Cairo, Egypt

Ziad Majed
Associate Professor of Middle East Studies and IR, American University of Paris, France

Jumana Manna
Artist, Berlin, Germany

Farouk Mardam Bey
Publisher, Paris, France

Mai Masri
Palestinian Filmmaker, Lebanon

Mazen Masri
Senior Lecturer in Law, City University of London, UK

Dina Matar
Reader in Political Communication and Arab Media, SOAS, University of London, UK

Hisham Matar
Writer, Professor at Barnard College, Columbia University, USA

Khaled Mattawa
Poet, William Wilhartz Professor of English Literature, University of Michigan, USA

Nadine Naber
Professor, Department of Gender and Women's Studies, University of Illinois at Chicago, USA

Karma Nabulsi
Professor of Politics and IR, University of Oxford, UK

Hassan Nafaa
Emeritus Professor of Political Science, Cairo University, Egypt

Issam Nassar
Professor, Illinois State University, USA

Sari Nusseibeh
Emeritus Professor of Philosophy, Al-Quds University, Palestine

Najwa Al-Qattan
Emeritus Professor of History, Loyola Marymount University, USA

Omar Al-Qattan
Filmmaker, Chair of the Palestinian Museum and the A.M. Qattan Foundation, UK

Nadim N. Rouhana
Professor of International Affairs, Fletcher School, Tufts University, USA

Ahmad Sa'adi
Professor, Haifa, State of Israel

Rasha Salti
Independent Curator, Writer, Researcher of Art and Film,
Germany-Lebanon

Elias Sanbar
Writer, Paris, France

Farès Sassine
Professor of Philosophy and Literary Critic, Beirut, Lebanon

Sherene Seikaly
Associate Professor of History, University of California, Santa Barbara,
USA

Samah Selim
Associate Professor, A, ME & SA Languages & Literatures, Rutgers
University, USA

Leila Shahid
Writer, Beirut, Lebanon

Nadera Shalhoub-Kevorkian
Lawrence D Biele Chair in Law, Hebrew University, State of Israel

Index